Criminalization of
Mental Illness Reader

Criminalization of Mental Illness Reader

Kelly Frailing

Risdon N. Slate

Carolina Academic Press

Durham, North Carolina

See catalog.loc.gov for Library of Congress Cataloging-in-Publication Data

ISBN: 978-1-5310-0430-9
eISBN: 978-1-53100-431-6

Carolina Academic Press, LLC
700 Kent Street
Durham, North Carolina 27701
Telephone (919) 489-7486
Fax (919) 493-5668
www.cap-press.com

Printed in the United States of America

I (Kelly) would like to thank my husband Jay and my daughter Matilda for their enduring love and support. You are the lights of my life. I would also like to thank Jessica Hawkins, without whom this project never would have reached completion. Finally, I would like to thank our incredible contributors for sharing their expertise with us.

I (Ris) am indebted to Kelly Frailing for her tireless leadership and work on this project, to Art Lurigio for his expert synthesis of the chapters contained within, and to each of our contributors for their focus on pertinent issues, with a cumulative aim of preventing persons with mental illnesses from ending up in the abyss of the criminal justice system.

Together, we would like to thank Carolina Academic Press for their support of this project from the beginning.

Contents

List of Tables

Author and Editor Biographies

Natalie Bonfine, Ph.D. is an assistant professor in the Department of Psychiatry at Northeast Ohio Medical University (NEOMED). Dr. Bonfine earned her doctorate in sociology from Kent State University and has been engaged in research on jail diversion for people with mental illness since 2004. Her research interests include the sociology of mental health and illness, stigma and stigma resistance, criminogenic risk and mental illness, and medical sociology.

Sarah Camille Conrey, J.D. is a graduate student in the Psychology Department at the University of California, Santa Cruz. She holds a Juris Doctorate from the University of California, Hastings College of the Law, and a bachelor's degree in psychology from the University of California, Santa Cruz.

Patrick Corrigan, Psy.D. is Distinguished Professor of Psychology at the Illinois Institute of Technology. Currently, he is principal investigator of the National Consortium for Stigma and Empowerment, a collaboration of investigators and advocates from more than a dozen institutions. He is also principal investigator of projects examining integrated primary care and behavioral health care in a health disparities framework. He has authored or edited 15 books, has written more than 350 peer-reviewed articles, is editor emeritus of the *American Journal of Psychiatric Rehabilitation*, and is editor of a new journal published by the American Psychological Association, *Stigma and Health*.

Roxy W. Davis, M.A. is a graduate student in the Psychology Department at the University of California, Santa Cruz. She holds a master's degree in psychology from the University of Nevada, Reno, and a bachelor's degree in psychology from the University of California, Santa Cruz.

Katrinna Dexter, M.S. is a former probation officer who has worked directly with both juvenile and adult individuals from a variety of diverse populations. After nearly 10 years working in the criminal justice system, Katrinna is currently the Assistant State Coordinator for the Minnesota Juvenile Detention Alternative Initiative. She holds a bachelor of science in criminal justice, a bachelor of arts in psychology, and a master of science in criminal justice.

Deborah Eckberg, Ph.D. is a professor of criminal justice at Metropolitan State University (MN). Dr. Eckberg has published research spanning a wide variety of topics in journals such as *Race and Justice, American Sociologist, The Journal of Special Populations,* and the *Journal of Marriage and Family.* She also developed an online mental health curriculum for professionals which is used by a variety of law enforcement and criminal justice agencies as part of their continuing education requirements.

Kelly Frailing, Ph.D. is an assistant professor of criminology and justice at Loyola University New Orleans. She has published on crime and disaster in the *Natural Hazards Observer, The American Journal of Economics and Sociology, The CIP Report,* and *American Behavioral Scientist.* She is also the co-editor of and author or co-author of several chapters in all three editions of the book *Crime and Criminal Justice in Disaster* and co-author of *Toward a Criminology of Disaster.* She has also published on specialty (problem solving) courts in the *International Journal of Law and Psychiatry,* the *International Journal of Forensic Mental Health, Criminal Justice Policy Review,* and *Applied Psychology and Criminal Justice.*

Katti Gray is a veteran journalist and freelancer. She shares a Pulitzer Prize with a team from *New York Newsday,* her last full-time employer, and was a 2018 Pulitzer Prize juror. She specializes in news about health and criminal justice issues, coordinates conferences and fellowships on health care in prisons and jails for the Center on Media, Crime and Justice, and is a contributing editor for *The Crime Report,* the center's national news site. She is a member of the Association of Health Care Journalists, National Association of Black Journalists, and National Writers Union, and is the program coordinator and lead instructor for New York University's Urban Journalism Workshop.

Craig Haney, Ph.D. is Distinguished Professor of Psychology and UC Presidential Chair, 2015–2018 at the University of California, Santa Cruz. He studies the psychological consequences of living and working in various prison environments.

Ken Kerle, M.A., Ph.D. worked for 23 years as a managing editor of *American Jails Magazine*, the publication of the American Jail Association. He had the opportunity to work as a jail officer in Maryland and complete police training there. He has visited 828 jails in 49 states and has published two books on the subject: *American Jails: Looking to the Future* and *Exploring Jail Operations*. He spent 10 years in academia and taught in four different states, including courses in three Maryland prisons, one of which housed offenders with mental illness.

Li-Wen Grace Lee, M.D. is a board-certified forensic psychiatrist and a clinical assistant professor at Columbia University College of Physicians and Surgeons. She previously worked as an attending psychiatrist and unit chief, providing inpatient mental health treatment and forensic evaluations for pre-trial detainees and individuals in jail custody. She is currently employed as medical director and assistant commissioner for the New York State Office of Mental Health, Division of Forensic Services. The scope of her work there includes services to restore competency to stand trial, management of insanity acquittees, correctional psychiatry, and sex offender treatment programs.

Arthur Lurigio, Ph.D. is a psychologist, Senior Associate Dean for Faculty in the College of Arts and Sciences, and a professor of criminal justice and criminology and of psychology at Loyola University Chicago. In 2003, Dr. Lurigio was named a Faculty Scholar, the highest honor bestowed on senior faculty at Loyola. In 2013, he was named a Master Researcher by the College of Arts and Sciences at Loyola in recognition of continued scholarly productivity. In praise of the overall outstanding contributions of his research to practices in the fields of psychology and criminal justice, Dr. Lurigio has earned many prestigious awards, including the University of Cincinnati Award, the Hans W. Mattick Award, the Champion for Recovery: Excellence in Research Award, the University of Illinois Distinguished Contributions to Criminal Justice Research and Practice Award, and the American Psychological Association Distinguished Career Award in 2010. He is the immediate past president of the Illinois Academy of Criminology.

Philip R. Magaletta, Ph.D. specializes in the evaluation and treatment of forensic and correctional populations and the recruitment and retention of the mental health professionals that work with them. He earned his undergraduate degree from the University of Scranton, his M.A. from Loyola College in Maryland and his Ph.D. in clinical psychology from St. Louis University. His current research interests include correctional mental health service delivery and workforce development, addictions counseling, spirituality, and telehealth.

Alix McLearen, Ph.D. is the national administrator of the Federal Bureau of Prisons' Female Offender Branch. A career law enforcement officer, she obtained her doctorate in clinical psychology and the law from the University of Alabama in 2003. Since that time, she has held positions of increasing responsibility in federal corrections including chief psychologist at the Federal Correctional Institution in Memphis, Tennessee, and National Prison Rape Elimination Act (PREA) coordinator. In her current capacity, she provides agency-wide policy and program development, training, guidance, and oversight to 122 facilities with a focus on managing women, persons with disabilities, and other vulnerable correctional populations.

Binoy B. Shah, M.A. is a doctoral student in clinical psychology at Illinois Institute of Technology. His interest in the stigma of mental illnesses initially began while interning in the psychiatry department at Nair, one of the biggest public hospitals in India. Thereafter, he went to New York to pursue further studies, and earned an M.A. in clinical psychology at Teachers College, Columbia University. During his time in New York, he worked on various projects surrounding global mental health and stigma under the mentorship of Dr. Lawrence Yang. Currently, he is working with Dr. Patrick Corrigan on research concerning mental health stigma and health disparities.

Maria "Maite" Silva is a doctoral student in clinical psychology at Loyola University Maryland. She specializes in clinical work with underserved and under-resourced communities, including racial and ethnic minorities, the LGBTQ+ community, survivors of commercial sexual exploitation, and individuals with criminal justice involvement. Currently she provides behavioral health services at Whitman-Walker Health in Washington, D.C., and develops treatment programs and policies for women and other vulnerable correctional populations for the Federal Bureau of Prisons.

Risdon Slate, Ph.D. is a professor of criminology at Florida Southern College in Lakeland, Florida. He received his Ph.D. from the Claremont Graduate School in Claremont, California. Dr. Slate has published a number of scholarly articles, and he is lead author of both editions of *The Criminalization of Mental Illness: Crisis and Opportunity for the Justice System*. He has prior criminal justice experience and has served as a trainer for law enforcement, corrections, probation, and judicial personnel on the interface of the criminal justice and mental health systems.

Karyn Sporer, Ph.D. is an assistant professor of sociology at the University of Maine. Her primary research interests are in the areas of family violence and victimization, mental illness and violence, and violent extremism and terrorism. She is the author of several articles on families of violent children with mental illness. Her interest in the intersection of the family, violence, and mental illness stems from her work with adults with mental illness. She saw firsthand how a broken mental health system negatively impacted both persons with mental illness and their families. She is hopeful that her work as an academic will inform social policy in such a way that the lives of persons with mental illness and their family caregivers are improved.

Anastasia C. Tooley is a doctoral student in the clinical psychology program at the Illinois Institute of Technology. She attended Purdue University, where she first gained research experience in child development and family physiology labs. Later, she discovered her passion for mental health stigma while developing an undergraduate research honors thesis on personality disorders. After graduating from Purdue, Tooley worked in the field as an applied behavior analysis therapist with children on the autism spectrum. Presently, she is a member of Dr. Patrick Corrigan's research team, focusing on stigma and mental health.

Introduction

Kelly Frailing & Risdon Slate

When we started to plan the *Criminalization of Mental Illness Reader*, we envisioned it as exactly that, a reader that would (indispensably) accompany the second and future editions of the *Criminalization of Mental Illness* text. We asked our contributors to start with the central concept of each chapter in the text and expand on that concept so that a thorough, multifaceted understanding of issues facing people with mental illness who are justice involved was possible. Happily, our contributors delivered in a major way and here, we briefly describe how each chapter in the text connects with that in this reader.

Chapter 1 of the text discusses what mental illness is, the prevalence of people with mental illness in the criminal justice system and the challenges this group poses to the system and vice versa, touching briefly on how cultural differences play a role. Chapter 1 in this reader, **"Cultural Factors and Mental Illness" by Deborah Eckberg and Katrinna Dexter,** does a superb job of illuminating the cultural differences in treatment and processing of racial and ethnic minorities with mental illness historically and up to the present within the mental health and criminal justice systems. Eckberg and Dexter discuss the prevalence of mental illness among culturally disparate groups, then stress the importance of both verbal and non-verbal communication cues to prevent criminal justice practitioners from misidentifying cultural norms as mental illness. They conclude by emphasizing that there is a need for cultural competence training across the criminal justice system.

Chapter 2 of the text discusses the history of criminalization of people with mental illness, with an emphasis on the factors that have fueled criminalization in the United States since the mid-twentieth century. Chapter 2 in this reader,

"Criminogenic Factors and Mental Illness" by Natalie Bonfine, adds a crucial dimension to this discussion with its coverage of criminogenic factors among people with mental illness. Bonfine identifies and elaborates on the risk-need-responsivity (RNR) model. She focuses on the challenges of and opportunities for assessing and addressing the criminogenic needs of persons with mental illnesses and calls for an integrated approach for linking justice-involved people with mental illness to appropriate supervision and treatment.

Chapter 3 in the text examines the many effects of stigma on people with mental illness, including how it can serve as an impediment to treatment seeking among this group. Chapter 3 in this reader, **"Stigma and Mental Illness" by Binoy Biren Shah, Anastasia Cherise Tooley and Patrick W. Corrigan**, augments this examination by first providing a matrix for understanding how the four types of stigma manifest for people with mental illness. They discuss the inclination to label this group as dangerous and violent and the propensity to push aberrant behavior into categories of sickness or sinfulness. They also examine the stigma that surrounds persons with substance abuse issues and compare and contrast that with the stigma experienced by people with mental illness, a particularly important addition considering the high rate of co-occurrence of mental health and substance abuse issues.

Chapter 4 of the text is focused on inpatient civil commitment, including reforms, controversies and the overhaul of the system in Virginia as a cautionary case study. Chapter 4 in this reader, **"Sexual Offending and Mental Illness" by Li-Wen Grace Lee**, covers the related and weighty issue of the relationship between sexual offending and mental illness and the civil commitment of sex offenders once their criminal sentence has been served. She discusses the laws that permit civil confinement of sex offenders, assessment tools and diagnostic considerations for this population and the sometimes grave ethical considerations of balancing treatment on the one hand and public safety on the other.

Chapter 5 in the text discusses outpatient commitment, with a focus on the controversies surrounding involuntary outpatient commitment. Typically omitted from such discussions, though, are families' experiences in getting mental health treatment for a loved one. Chapter 5 in this reader, **"Family Violence and Mental Illness" by Karyn Sporer**, tackles this essential topic. Sporer covers the research on the potential for violence against caregivers by people with mental illness. Then, relying on in-depth interviews with parents and siblings of people with mental illness, she discusses the difficult determination to seek hospitalization for a loved one and the problems with finding a hospital bed and paying for it if such a decision is made.

Chapter 6 in the text examines the law enforcement response to people with mental illness, focusing in particular on the empirically validated Crisis Intervention Team (CIT) approach. Chapter 6 in this reader, **"Discovering CIT across the CJS" by Ken Kerle,** describes his unusual introduction to criminal justice academia and his journey through the nation's jails as an auditor and magazine editor. In these capacities, he strongly advocated for jail standards that included guidelines for the recognition and treatment of people with mental illness. Utilizing his experience in Kansas, Kerle describes learning about CIT and his thoughts on its applicability to other criminal justice system elements, especially jails, while recognizing impediments to doing so.

Chapter 7 in the text focuses on the experience of people with mental illness in jails, including prevalence, screening, treatment and discharge planning. The chapter touches on training for jail officers in dealing with inmates with mental illness. Chapter 7 in this reader, **"Practicing in Corrections" by Maria "Maite" Silva, Philip Magaletta and Alix McLearen,** does an excellent job of describing the flip side of this coin, namely, what it is like to provide clinical treatment to people with mental illness in institutional corrections. They delineate five key competencies for clinicians in corrections that run the gamut from screening to interdisciplinary communication and conclude by balancing the challenges of providing clinical care to people with mental illness in institutional corrections with the personal and professional value of doing so.

Chapters 8 and 9 in the text examine laws and practices around competency to stand trial and the use of the insanity defense. These detailed discussions focus on landmark court decisions, the evaluation process, and the short and longer-term outcomes of both competency hearings and cases that involve the insanity defense. Chapter 8 in this reader, **"Media Coverage of People with Mental Illness" by Katti Gray,** uses the concepts of competency and insanity as jumping off points to investigate the way that mental illness and persons with mental illness are covered by the media. Relying on interviews with researchers, journalists and advocates, she expertly reveals the ways in which reporting on persons with mental illness who are justice involved has changed and improved. However, the concluding section clearly shows that there is still plenty of work to be done and implies that journalists can continue to chip away at the stigma against mental illness and people with mental illness through more responsible reporting.

Chapter 10 in the text begins by explaining why and how the first mental health court emerged in the U.S., then describes the development and effectiveness of mental health courts and concludes by touching on some lingering controversies. Chapter 9 in this reader, **"Mental Health Courts: Therapeutic Jurisprudence for Offenders with Mental Illness" by Arthur J. Lurigio,** takes a close and detailed look at therapeutic jurisprudence, the principle that underlies these and other specialty courts, and explains how it manifests in the structure and function of mental health courts. He deftly connects the manifestation of therapeutic jurisprudence to the generally positive outcomes observed in studies of mental health courts. However, Lurigio takes care to present thorough critiques of mental health court research and of the courts themselves that may cast something of a shadow on otherwise desirable findings.

Chapter 11 in the text examines the experience of people with mental illness in prison. It includes many of the serious challenges that people with mental illness face while incarcerated for long periods, as well as the ways prison administrators have tried to manage this group for better or worse. Chapter 10 in this reader, **"The Plight of Long-Term Prisoners with Mental Illness" by Craig Haney, Sarah Camille Conrey and Roxy Davis**, focuses largely on one such management method, solitary confinement. They convincingly describe the deleterious effects of solitary confinement on people with mental illness, including an increase in stress and psychological and emotional trauma, as well as decompensation and deterioration that can serve to worsen or even produce mental illness. The authors conclude with a call for reentry planning that includes opportunities for socialization for those who have experienced solitary confinement.

Chapter 12 in the text describes the discharge and reentry processes for people with mental illness returning to the community from incarceration, emphasizing their usually ineffective nature. Chapter 11 in this reader, **"Psychiatric Comorbidity and Reentry" by Arthur J. Lurigio**, begins by expertly connecting the criminalization of substance use to the criminalization of people with mental illness, contending that the War on Drugs is a key factor in the increase of people with mental illness going to prison. Co-occurring mental health and substance use disorders are distressingly common among the prison population, and he examines the challenges that co-occurring mental health and substance use disorders constitute for successful reentry from incarceration, including lack of the specific services required to successfully address co-occurring disorders, difficulty obtaining employment and housing, and the absence of social supports. Lurigio concludes with a call for integrated co-occurring disorder treatment while incarcerated and then in the community upon release to help stem the tide of recidivism.

Chapter 13 in the text describes the ways in which crises involving a person with mental illness drive policy toward all people with mental illness. Recognizing this post hoc policymaking as insufficient at best and dangerous at worst, the chapter and text as a whole conclude with important actions for informed policy. Chapter 12 in this reader, **"Past and Current Perspectives on Offenders with Mental Illness" by Arthur J. Lurigio**, starts by describing the causes and correlates of serious mental illness, then examines the factors responsible for the criminalization of people with mental illness, focusing on police interactions, the lack of effective mental health and related services and the War on Drugs. The chapter concludes with a stark comparison of the care that people with mental illness who are justice involved receive at each point in the criminal justice system with what this care should look like in an ideal world.

We are confident that each of the chapters in this reader are informative and thought provoking. Our hope is that they also inspire readers to take the action they can to change the status quo for people with mental illness.

Criminalization of
Mental Illness Reader

1

Cultural Factors and Mental Illness

Deborah A. Eckberg & Katrinna Dexter

Introduction

While it has been clearly established that the criminalization of mental illness is a problem that permeates throughout the criminal justice system, the issue is further complicated when we consider the cultural backgrounds of those, mentally ill or mentally healthy, with whom criminal justice professionals interact. We cannot consider issues related to culture and mental illness without first recognizing the overrepresentation of individuals of color who are arrested, charged, and incarcerated in U.S. jails and prisons. The ratio of non-whites to whites among those who have significant contact with the criminal justice system is staggering. Although the most recent Census data reports that approximately 12 percent of the U.S. population is African American (American Fact Finder, 2015), the Sourcebook of Criminal Justice Statistics (2011; 2010) documents that more than twice that, or approximately 28 percent, of arrested individuals are African American, and that African Americans comprise more than 38 percent of incarcerated individuals. Moreover, immigrants account for approximately 25 percent of the inmates in U.S. jails (Rein, 2011), even though empirical research suggests that, across the life course, the engagement of foreign-born individuals in criminal activity is remarkably low (Bersani, 2014), and that there is little to no correlation between immigration and violent crime (Spenkuch, 2014). Still, there is a perception among some policymakers and certain sectors of the general public that at least some of the crime problem can be solved by either incarcerating more racial and ethnic minorities or, in the case of immigrants, returning them to their homelands. In fact, some contend that criminal participation by immigrants is to blame for high crime rates in specific communities (see Guerette, 2016). The lines between criminality and mental illness are often blurry, and in the context of the criminalization of mental illness and immigration, this can lead to a push toward deporting the mentally ill, whether criminal or not (Murray-Tjan, 2014).

This perception of high levels of criminality by those from diverse ethnic backgrounds is due in part to a severe lack of cultural competence among the lay public. And although progress toward general cultural competence is arguably important in our increasingly diverse society, the need for cultural competence among criminal justice professionals who must, by virtue of their jobs, interact with ethnically diverse individuals, is imperative. When we consider that a proportion of those from diverse cultural backgrounds may also be exhibiting signs of mental illness, the importance of identifying what is and is not a cultural difference becomes even more critical.

The intent of this chapter is to shed light on a number of factors related to culture and mental illness, and how the two in concert intersect the criminal justice system. The chapter will address: (1) how culture relates to mental illness through theoretical frameworks, (2) racial and ethnic differences with regard to mental health service utilization, (3) misidentification of cultural norms as mental illness, and (4) the need for cultural competence among criminal justice professionals.

Culture and Mental Illness: Theoretical Frameworks

As with most issues related to race and ethnicity, we cannot explore mental illness experiences of racial minorities in a vacuum, but must instead consider them in light of the racial inequities that have characterized American history. African Americans, for example, began their American experience with slavery and hundreds of subsequent years of civil injustice (Jordan, 2002, as cited in Sue & Sue, 2013). With regard to modern medicine, African Americans were often used as "human guinea pigs" (Sue & Sue, 2013, p. 90), as in the Tuskegee experiments carried out from 1932 to 1972. Other minority groups have experienced similar, although perhaps less well-known, medical injustices. As one example, Guatemalan prisoners, soldiers, and psychiatric hospital patients were the subjects of American-run venereal disease experiments in the late 1940s (Sue & Sue, 2013). These experiences have significant implications for minority groups' attitudes toward mental illness and mental health providers who, in theory, are in business to assist them. These implications may be most pronounced for those who are foreign-born.

As strangers in a strange land, immigrants to the United States are faced with many new systems they must learn how to navigate, including systems surrounding education and employment. They must adapt to new cultural customs, and may often feel isolated in daily life (Sue & Sue, 2013). They may also have to adjust to climate differences, which can impact their levels of physical comfort, and the lack of social support networks to which they were accustomed in their countries of origin (Chung & Bemak, 2007, as cited in Sue & Sue, 2013), all of which can lead to adjustment difficulties. In addition, their countries of origin may differ vastly from the United States, in terms of gender relationships, for example, with differing approaches to spousal abuse and other acts of violence within the family. The immigrant experiencing distress may be faced with both internal and external barriers to seeking help, including barriers related to language and cultural norms.

Thus, we must understand the experience of cultural minorities in the mental health system in light of oppression and, consequently, the acculturative stress that accompanies them on their journey (Berry & Annis, 1974). This acculturative stress often prevents individuals of color, both American-born and foreign-born, from properly navigating mental health services. They may approach counseling and therapy with skepticism due to their history with institutionalized racism. This is most clearly elucidated in studies of mental health service utilization, as will be discussed in the next section.

Cultural Disparities in Mental Health Care Utilization

Mental health care utilization by racial and ethnic minorities has historically been lower than that of whites. According to the National Alliance on Mental Illness (NAMI), in the past year, about one half as many African Americans and Hispanic Americans as Caucasian Americans, and about a third as many Asian Americans, used mental health services (NAMI, 2017). In a recent study, Coleman and colleagues (2016) collected data on over 7.5 million patients who received care in 2011 from 11 different non-profit mental health care organizations included in the Mental Health Research Network. Of those 7.5 million patients, non-Hispanic whites were over 77 percent more likely to receive psychiatric medication than non-white patients. Moreover, only 34 percent of the patients with a psychiatric diagnosis received formal psychotherapy (Coleman et al., 2016). Fiscella, Franks, Doescher, and Saver (2002) corroborate these findings, reporting that after adjusting for predisposing need and enabling factors, African Americans were significantly less likely than non-Hispanic whites to have visited with a mental health professional. Among African Americans, women and more highly educated individuals are the most likely to seek treatment for mental illness (Neighbors et al., 2007). However, involuntary commitment to mental hospitals has been shown to be higher among people of color (McKenzie & Bhui, 2007), a fact that may provide empirical support for claims of institutional racism and lack of cultural sensitivity in the field of psychopathology.

Ever since Kleinman (1988) argued that the experience of illness, whether physical or mental, is culturally shaped, research into cultural psychopathology has become important to those who study psychopathology. Lopez and Guarnaccia (2000) note that there have been conceptual advances in definitions of culture as it relates to mental illness diagnosis and treatment. In fact, a specific Culture and Diagnosis Task Force was formed in preparation for the 2000 publication of the fourth edition of the American Psychiatric Association's Diagnostic and Statistical Manual (DSM-IV). This emphasis has continued during the last decades, including some researchers noting cultural differences in compliance, engagement with services, and expectations of treatment (Bhugra, 2006), and others arguing for creating culturally unique classifications for psychiatric syndromes in order to promote culturally competent mental health care (Tseng, 2006). Others in the field of psychotherapy have advocated strongly for therapists to increase their understanding of cultural differences, and ultimately to integrate this understanding into treatment models, under the umbrella term "cultural psychotherapy" (La Roche & LaRoche, 2012).

Lack of voluntary engagement with mental health services is arguably a significant problem. However, whether or not interventions are effective when cultural minorities do engage with services is also an issue. Evans, Berkman, Brown, Gaynes, and Weber (2016) examined previously published studies that evaluated effectiveness of interventions for those with serious mental illness, specifically addressing racial and ethnic disparities in mental health service utilization. They acknowledge that some interventions are promising, including collaborative care, intensive case management approaches, and therapies that have been adapted to be culturally sensitive and specific. They conclude that future research should focus on identifying interventions that can reduce disparities in health care (Evans et al., 2016). First, however, we must understand why minority utilization of mental health services is low relative to that of Caucasians.

Reasons for Minority Underutilization of Mental Health Services

There exist a variety of explanations for underutilization of mental health care in general, including concerns about stigma (Link, Yang, Phelan, & Collins, 2004) and fears of being labeled by others (Kroska, Harkness, Thomas, & Brown 2014), as well as other contextual, social, and religious factors. The barriers to mental health care utilization for ethnic minorities are substantially more pronounced, and may be related to demographics, social structure, beliefs and practices related to health and health care, and level of personal and community resources (Scheppers, van Dongen, Dekker, Geertzen, & Dekker, 2006). Recent studies suggest that ethnic minorities are less likely to utilize outpatient mental health care as compared with Caucasians (Turner, 2016), and that racial and ethnic disparities in mental health care utilization may be the result of personal and cultural beliefs, combined with concerns about access and quality of mental health care (Ault-Brutus & Alegria, 2016). Yet another study points out that racial and ethnic disparities are related to neighborhood variations in mental health care utilization, but this is due more to low rates of treatment initiation by neighborhood as opposed to access barriers (Cook, Zuvekas, Chen, Progovac, & Lincoln, 2016). Similarly, Fuller, Edwards, Procter, and Moss (2000) found that in more rural and remote communities in Australia, the fear of being stigmatized and not being self-reliant often prevented individuals from seeking necessary mental health services. The informants in this study perceived mental illness as "insanity" and were reluctant to ask for help from anyone other than a generalist. Other studies point to financial, cultural, and language barriers that prevent those who have been involved in the criminal justice system, particularly those faced with reentry after incarceration, from voluntarily taking advantage of mental health treatment (Sentell, Shuway, & Snowden, 2007; Thompson, Newell, & Carlson, 2016).

Kirmayer et al. (2011) explored the risk factors related to mental health problems specific to the stressors surrounding migration, as well as other cultural influences that impact the mental health of immigrants and refugees. The authors found that language and cultural differences in general, as well as cultural approaches to illness, family and intergenerational conflict, and issues related to assimilation into the new culture, can all be considered factors in the development of mental health problems for recent immigrants, and impediments to treatment interventions. Critically important to adequate mental health care is the ability of mental health professionals to recognize the barriers faced by ethnic minority patients. For example, while stigma may be a factor that keeps individuals of all ethnicities from seeking care, Turner, Jensen-Doss, and Heffer (2015) found that perceptions of stigma may be more pronounced for ethnic minorities, increasing obstacles toward effective utilization of care. At least one study has suggested that underutilization by both U.S.-born and African-born Blacks is related to their perceptions of discrimination from those who work in the mental health care field (Burgess, Ding, Hargreaves, van Ryn, & Phelan, 2008), a fact that may be the strongest argument yet for the need for cultural competence by mental health professionals. In short, culturally competent providers may be able to alleviate fears of discrimination which prevent individuals of color from seeking treatment in the first place, as well as provide more effective intervention once treatment is sought.

Lack of cultural competence by mental health providers, while detrimental, may still be less dangerous than lack of cultural competence by criminal justice professionals. This danger is most pronounced at the point of contact between ethnic minorities and law enforcement officers, as police are usually the first point of contact with people of diverse backgrounds who may be exhibiting symptoms of mental illness. However, it is also important for those who work in the courts, jails and prisons, and probation departments to be culturally competent and well versed in issues related to mental illness, particularly when encountering racial and ethnic minorities who may be experiencing a mental health crisis. The problems often stem from a lack of understanding of cultural norms by those who work in the system, which in turn is the impetus for more training in cultural competence for criminal justice practitioners. In the following section, we detail the ways in which cultural norms and mental illness may be conflated.

Misidentification of Cultural Norms as Mental Illness by Criminal Justice Practitioners

Before we can discuss the obstacles encountered when cultural minorities who are mentally ill come into contact with the criminal justice system, we must step back and discuss the differences in culture which may sometimes be misidentified as mental illness by those working in the system. Those trained in criminal justice are often familiar with a framework of expected behavior. Behavior that does not fit within that framework may be classified as anywhere from slightly odd to psychotic. Even mental health practitioners are often guilty of stereotyping ethnic groups and classifying behavior based on normative standards of the culture with which they are most familiar (Flaskerud, 2000). If this is true of those with graduate education and professional expertise in mental illness, consider the increased potential for misdiagnosis among criminal justice professionals without the benefit of such advanced education, or even occupation-specific training in issues of diversity and mental illness.

Misidentification can cut both ways. Certainly, criminal justice professionals encountering behavior by individuals acting according to their own cultural norms, norms which may be in conflict with the behavioral norms with which most Americans are accustomed, may classify these individuals as mentally ill. On the other hand, those from non-Western cultures who are in fact experiencing mental illness may not be identified as such because of an overreliance on cultural norms as reasons for unusual behavior. In either case, individuals from non-Western cultures are at a disadvantage.

According to Livingston, McAdoo, and Mills (2008), an appreciation of cultural and ethnic differences is necessary for human service professionals. The purpose of culture, as identified by Nobles (1986), is to provide people with guidelines for interpreting reality. In short, appreciation of cultural differences needs to go deeper than the surface understanding of differences in clothing, language, food, et cetera, and seek to understand multicultural worldviews. Kambon (1998, as cited in Livingston et al., 2008) has conceptualized cultural competence as including issues as complex as the meaning of life, the origin of the universe, and individuals' relationships with a higher power. In fact, spirituality plays an important role in how many cultures view their place in the world, including their own conceptions of psychological well-being (Sue, 2003, as cited in Livingston et al., 2008). In times of distress, for example, many Muslims reference Allah or the need to talk with God (Weatherhead & Daiches, 2010). The importance of the spiritual world for cultural and ethnic minorities must be considered when interpreting behavior that may, at first glance, appear unusual.

In essence, as individuals turn to their own cultural values and belief systems to place themselves in the world, those outside of that culture need to be culturally competent enough to respect, if not understand, their actions. Behavior which is normative for some but not others should not be misclassified as mental illness, and those who are both culturally different and mentally ill should be able to secure the help they need. In the following sections, we review the types of culturally specific behaviors most prone to misunderstanding and misidentification as mental illness by criminal justice professionals.

Verbal Communication

Verbal communication is complicated by both language and cultural differences. An assumption in the criminal justice system is that language differences can be overcome by the use of interpreters. Some have argued, however, that there is a dearth of interpreter use. It may be inconvenient for police, for example, to summon an interpreter during a response to an incident, and it may be necessary to rely on friends or family members of the victim and/or alleged perpetrator (Lewis & Ramakrishnan, 2007). This may lead to inaccurate or perhaps even dishonest communication, which can result in a misunderstanding of the situation by law enforcement. Often though, such reliance on the availability of those present may be the only option.

Many courthouses keep language interpreters on contract so that they are available for court hearings as needed; however, budget shortfalls and timing constraints may stand in the way of interpreter availability during court hearings. Not only might such a lack of interpretation affect the outcome of a trial, but it may also exacerbate the frustration of the accused, and s/he may act according to that frustration in ways deemed inappropriate or approximating the actions of someone who is mentally ill.

Even when language interpretation is available and effective, communication barriers remain. Language interpreters are required to interpret verbatim, including idiomatic expressions and non-verbal messages where possible (Morris, 2008). Idiomatic expressions specific to one culture may in fact sound psychotic to someone who is unfamiliar with that culture's language.

The difference in cultural assumptions increases misinterpretation of language (Scollon & Scollon, 2001, as cited in Liddicoat, 2009). Such misinterpretation can have important ramifications for misdiagnosis of mental illness. Alternatively, those who do not speak English will not understand the many idioms used by those in the criminal justice system, further distancing them from the process (Morris, 2008) and potentially increasing the likelihood of defendants expressing frustration.

To give just one example, Muslim individuals tend to talk with their hands and speak loudly. This is typical of communication by someone in the Somali culture, for instance, who is trying to explain a situation. Law enforcement officers arresting a Somali suspect, or court or corrections personnel interacting with someone who is Somali, may interpret such a loud voice and hand motions as physically aggressive and may assume the person is either drunk or mentally ill (Garat Ibranim, 2012, as cited in Eckberg, 2012).

Conversely, non-willingness to communicate verbally can be common among those from non-English speaking cultures, and may also be misinterpreted as mental illness. Individuals of certain Asian cultures, for example, may be more willing to communicate with others who they believe share their ethnic identity, and may be silent among those who do not (Goby, 2004). In many cultures, silence is a sign of humility toward those who are more knowledgeable or of a higher place in society, but what may be intended as deference to authorities may not be interpreted by authorities as such (Ariza, 2000). From the perspective of law enforcement or other criminal justice professionals, someone who seemingly understands questions and instructions but chooses not to respond may appear either defiant or to be experiencing some form of mental illness.

Non-Verbal Communication and Physical Behaviors

European Americans rely heavily on verbal communication, whereas some ethnic and cultural minorities employ more non-verbal cues including body language, facial expressions, eye contact, and proximity (Livingston et al., 2008). For example, "standing closer than the culturally comfortable distance can be understood as aggression or intimacy, depending on the situation. Standing farther away in some cultures may convey disinterest" (Mercer, 2008, p. 2). This may be a racial as well as a cultural difference; African Americans and Hispanics are more willing to stand close to the person with whom they are communicating, while Caucasians may interpret such behavior as an invasion of personal space. Ethnic minorities may in fact view standing outside of someone's personal space negatively, as aloofness or an assumption of superiority over the person with whom one is speaking. A criminal justice practitioner unfamiliar with this concept of proximity may view such closeness as confrontational or evidence of a disturbed mental state.

In addition to level of comfort with proximity, the level of comfort with which individuals respond to someone else touching them may also be culture-specific (Mercer, 2008). For example, many Egyptian Muslim women's relationships with their bodies, including spatial relations when interacting with others, are dictated by gender rules and men's attitudes (Toncy, 2008). It is not appropriate for a male stranger to touch a Muslim woman, even in a handshake (Garat Ibranim, 2012, as cited in Eckberg, 2012). Thus, a police officer arresting a Muslim woman may elicit an extremely disturbed response from her simply by holding her arm or attempting to handcuff her. Those of Latino descent, on the other hand, may be quite comfortable with physical contact, as it is appropriate for them to greet each other with hugs and kisses.

A Latino defendant exhibiting physical familiarity may be perceived as unusual or under the influence of drugs or alcohol.

Handshakes, while expected in American culture as a sign of greeting, are not acceptable in some other cultures (Mercer, 2008). A nod may be a more acceptable greeting for individuals of Asian descent, for example. Attorneys, probation officers, and other court staff who attempt to shake the hand of an Asian defendant may encounter what they perceive as an abnormal reaction to the simple, seemingly friendly extension of someone's hand in greeting. Other physical gestures using the hands, arms, and feet may also have culturally specific meanings; some physical gestures may be deemed impolite or aggressive and some stances deemed defiant by those of certain cultures (Mercer, 2008).

Eye contact is an important component of non-verbal communication. Individuals of Asian descent, for example, are often reluctant to make eye contact with someone who deserves respect; for those of Asian descent, it may be considered disrespectful or even confrontational to look someone who is not a close companion in the eye when communicating (Sue & Sue, 1990, as cited in Livingston et al., 2008). Such deference can easily be misinterpreted as defiance by a criminal justice practitioner who expects eye contact from someone with whom they are initiating a conversation. In many Muslim cultures, there is the additional confound of gender normative behavior, which can complicate communication. Women are not allowed to make eye contact with men who are not their husbands (Garat Ibranim, 2012, as cited in Eckberg, 2012).

In summary, cultural differences in communication style must be learned, acknowledged, and respected by criminal justice practitioners for a variety of reasons. Certainly, in a world of increasing cultural diversity, it is important for practitioners to be culturally competent simply to be more sensitive to the communities they serve and thus more efficient at their jobs. However, when considering the potential for misidentification of cultural differences as mental illness, and the even more serious risk of overlooking true signs of mental illness in racial and ethnic minorities or immigrants, the need for cultural competence becomes not only important but essential to criminal justice work. In the next section, this need for cultural competence in the criminal justice system is addressed, with particular attention paid to the intersection of culture and mental illness among those with whom the criminal justice system comes in contact.

Need for Cultural Competence in the Criminal Justice System

As we have said, misidentification of cultural norms as mental illness by criminal justice practitioners stems from a lack of cultural competence, and is detrimental to appropriate service delivery to both mentally ill and non-mentally ill offenders. This lack of cultural competence contributes to the distrust of criminal justice practitioners by racial and ethnic minorities. However, there are other underlying causes of this distrust which must also be acknowledged.

Just as the mentally ill are overrepresented in the criminal justice system, so are racial and ethnic minorities (Primm, Osher, & Gomez, 2005). Many scholars have investigated racial differences in treatment of minorities by criminal justice practitioners, as well as perceptions of unfair treatment by members of those minority groups. There exists a large body of literature on disproportionate minority confinement, due to the fact that minorities make up such a high percentage of those incarcerated in the United States (see, for example, Primm et al., 2005). Charges against non-whites tend to be harsher than those against whites, non-whites tend to be convicted more often, and sentences for minorities tend to be longer than for whites (Primm et al., 2005). Perhaps most noticeable, however, are the contacts police have with minority individuals, especially with regard to driving offenses. Research shows that African American and Hispanic drivers are significantly more likely than whites to be stopped by police and, when stopped, are more likely to be subjected to a search of their vehicles (Langan, Greenfeld, Smith, Durose, & Levin, 2001).

These facts have not gone unnoticed by those most directly impacted. Several studies have shown that racial minorities perceive unfair treatment by the criminal justice system and particularly by law enforcement. Minorities with higher levels of ethnic identity are more likely to perceive that police discriminate against them (Lee, Steinberg, & Piquero, 2010). In general, African Americans and Hispanics tend to be less satisfied with the work police are doing (Weitzer & Tuch, 2005; Lai & Zhao, 2010) and are more likely to fear police than whites, particularly if they have had negative experiences (Schuck & Rosenbaum, 2005; Schuck, Rosenbaum, & Hawkins, 2008). Many racial minorities live in disadvantaged areas where interactions with police are common, thus increasing the chance for those interactions to be negative. While community-oriented policing seeks to tip the scales to more positive police interactions, in reality, racial minorities, especially those in disadvantaged neighborhoods, are more likely to see police as their adversaries than their advocates. Furthermore, fear of the police does not seem to be explained by racial differences alone, but by police behaviors that differentially affect racial groups (Schuck et al., 2008). This speaks to the need for cultural competence among police.

Cultural Competence and Law Enforcement

In calling attention to the lack of trust many members of ethic and cultural minority groups feel toward law enforcement, we distinguish between American and foreign-born ethnic minorities, because the two groups' reasons for distrust are distinctly different. For both groups, the issues between them and law enforcement, with or without the complicating factor of mental illness, may at least in part be attributed to a lack of cultural competence among police officers.

There is ongoing debate in the criminal justice literature as to whether racial profiling of African Americans and Latinos is intentional or unintentional (Chan, 2011; Crank, 2011; Satzewich & Shaffir, 2009). However, the intent of law enforcement with regard to racial profiling may be irrelevant when we discuss issues of mental illness and perceptions of mentally ill members of racial and ethnic minority groups. If, in fact, mentally healthy African Americans and Latinos are prone to feel persecuted by law enforcement, this feeling can only be exacerbated by mental illness. A paranoid schizophrenic African American, for example, might hear from their family members and friends that police are "out to get them," which will contribute to their feeling of panic if approached by a uniformed law enforcement officer. The difficulties that untrained officers may have in interacting with the mentally ill may be exponentially greater when community members perceive a lack of cultural competence and a tendency toward racial persecution of certain groups. The distrust of police by the mentally ill may be exacerbated by the distrust of police by racial minorities, leading to a no-win situation for police, community members, offenders, or victims.

The relationship between law enforcement and the immigrant population is even more complicated. While African Americans and American-born Latinos may feel persecuted by practices that suggest racial profiling, the distrust of police by cultural immigrants may stem from more overt persecution in their countries of origin. Typically, when law enforcement interacts with American-born minorities they do not have to navigate through language barriers and deeply rooted fears of police corruption, whereas these are exactly the issues police may encounter when interacting with community members born in another part of the world. Many cultural immigrants have fled from societies where law enforcement and other criminal justice professionals are corrupt and a potential threat to the well-being of law-abiding citizens (Khashu, Busch, Latif, & Levy, 2005). This perception of police can have both negative and positive effects; Latino immigrants, for example, have been shown to view American police more favorably than American-born Latinos, due to the contrast between American police and the corrupt police in their home countries (Correia, 2010).

However, language and cultural barriers are complicating factors for police who must interact with immigrant communities (Chu & Song, 2008). Research has shown, for example, that Asian immigrants wish there were more bilingual police officers, and are frustrated with the lack of communication between police and individuals in their community (Chu, Song, & Dombrink, 2005; Chu & Song, 2008; Chu & Hung, 2010). Poor communication increases perceptions of law enforcement prejudice by immigrant community members (Chu & Song, 2008), regardless of the mental health of the immigrants in question. When mentally ill individuals are considered, we must keep in mind that the experience of involvement with the criminal justice system can be extraordinarily stressful and confusing in and of itself, and more so when language and cultural barriers are present (Parsons & Sherwood, 2016). Furthermore, when racial and ethnic minorities from other countries become victims, rather than offenders, they may be reluctant to reach out to police for help (Davis & Hendricks, 2007), which can impact the safety and protective services to which they are entitled.

It is clear that the need for cultural competence among law enforcement continues to grow, as our society continues to diversify. Traditional models of policing have been found to be lacking in interactions with both American-born and foreign-born racial and ethnic minorities. Police must be flexible and adaptable in interactions with those who do not share their ethnic background, and work toward diversifying the police force itself with more non-white individuals (Shusta, Levine, Harris, & Wong, 2002). In considering victimization issues, police must be knowledgeable now more than ever with regard to hate crimes and bias-related violence (Shusta et al., 2002).

Reforms are currently underway to encourage police to reimagine themselves as "guardians" rather than "warriors" in their interactions with the mentally ill (Wood & Watson, 2016), and officers may need further training, collaboration with mental health professionals, increased knowledge, and improved attitudes. It seems a natural extension of such training and increased knowledge to include specific law enforcement-centered education regarding mental illness challenges, and issues surrounding help seeking and mental health care utilization among the racially and ethnically diverse.[1] Those who work in the

---

1. For more on the law enforcement response to persons with mental illnesses in crises, see the chapter by the same name in *The Criminalization of Mental Illness*.

courts would also benefit from such culturally specific approaches to the mentally ill, as will be explained in the next section.

Cultural Competence and the Courts

Negative attitudes about the criminal justice system are not only limited to perceptions of law enforcement; African Americans are also less likely to perceive the court system as just, and both African Americans and Hispanics have less favorable attitudes about the court system than whites (Higgins, Wolfe, Mahoney, & Walters, 2009). The practice of legal advocacy demands that attorneys must often walk a fine line between advising clients and insisting on certain decisions, especially when advocating for clients who are struggling with mental illness. This danger of "zealous advocacy" (Perlin & Weinstein, 2016) can also be extended to situations where the defendant is an ethnic or cultural minority who does not have expertise regarding the U.S. legal system. Perlin and Weinstein (2016) argue that attorneys have an ethical obligation to adhere to their clients' wishes, even if the client is mentally ill, as long as the client is capable of autonomous decision making. These authors stress that client autonomy is critical and must be maintained in all but very few cases involving severely mentally ill clients. This argument has serious implications when considering mentally ill defendants who are also disadvantaged by language and cultural differences, and may encourage attorneys to assume a paternalistic role even more so in these situations.

Courtroom interpreters are increasingly necessary as the number of non-English speaking defendants in U.S. courtrooms continues to rise. However, as noted above, availability of interpreters, even for more common languages, is often difficult. Some jurisdictions offer telephone interpreting, which is controversial on a number of fronts (Gracia-Garcia, 2002). There have also been questions as to the training and preparation of courtroom interpreters. Because of the high demand and low supply of interpreters, many state and local jurisdictions do not require that interpreters pass an examination before being employed, often resulting in interpreters who are not entirely qualified for the job (Beitsch, 2016). When the need for qualified interpreters is considered in concert with the issues of non-English speaking mentally ill defendants, victims, or witnesses who must engage with the court process, an argument may be made for additional testing so that interpreters can be considered more well versed in mental health issues as well as the language for which they are needed.

United States criminal courts do not account for differences in culture when evaluating the guilt or innocence of criminal defendants (Davis, 2016). At times, attorneys are left with no choice but to invoke the insanity defense in order to account for differences in cultural mores which may have led to illegal behavior by their foreign-born clients (Davis, 2016). However, the forensic evaluations utilized in the determination of insanity at the time of the crime are not typically normed for multicultural populations (Ortega, 2010), which ignores the role that culture might play in determinations of mental illness (Lopez, 2000, as cited in Ortega, 2010).

One of the most promising initiatives in the last several decades has been the proliferation of criminal mental health courts,[2] which allow court professionals to work collaboratively with mental health providers and provide treatment and other services, rather than incarceration, to low-level offenders with mental illness (Ferrazzi & Krupa, 2016). The underlying concept is often referred to as "therapeutic jurisprudence" (Wesxler & Winick, 1991).[3][1] However, some have noted that the goals of such a collaborative, rehabilitative approach are more difficult to accomplish in non-urban geographic areas, and with individuals of different cultural backgrounds (Ferrazzi & Krupa, 2016). Thus, it may be that a high proportion of ethnic minorities that would benefit from mental health courts are not able to take advantage of them and are instead incarcerated in local jails. The intersection of cultural issues and mental illness permeates the corrections system as well, as we consider next.

Cultural Competence in Corrections

Approximately 15 percent of the non-white prison and jail population suffers from mental illness, and many also have a co-occurring substance abuse disorder (Primm et al., 2005). However, there is a significant lack of adequate mental health treatment options for the incarcerated, and particularly for the ethnically diverse (Primm et al., 2005). There are a number of important cultural considerations related to custodial care of the mentally ill. For an individual in custody who is both mentally ill and struggling with language and cultural differences, the fast-paced interactions in jails and prisons can add a significant level of additional stress to an already challenging situation (Parsons & Sherwood, 2016). Incarcerated individuals must learn new systems of sleeping arrangements and meals, and those with language barriers and little understanding of the U.S. corrections environment will likely have greater dif-

---

2. For more on mental health courts, see the chapter by the same name in *The Criminalization of Mental Illness*.

3. For a deeper exploration of how therapeutic jurisprudence manifests in mental health courts, see Leifman's chapter in this reader.

ficulties navigating jails and prisons than those who are American-born. In addition, many corrections programs that focus on drug treatment or talk therapy may be extremely distasteful to inmates with cultural backgrounds that prioritize privacy and family help with emotional or mental disorders. Many cultural immigrants may also prioritize religion and decline mental health services in favor of a more spiritual approach (Ortega, 2011).

Another concern has to do with the psychological assessments used in correctional facilities. These tests are used to determine a therapeutic plan while offenders are in custody. Most of these tests rely on certain assumptions regarding the individual's ability to rank stimuli and engage in self-reflection (Trimble, Lonner, & Boucher, 1983, as cited in Ortega, 2010), skills which may be exceedingly difficult for foreign-born inmates. Such difficulty might then impact diagnosis and treatment, potentially affecting release and reentry in the community for ethnic and cultural minorities with mental illness.

Some correctional institutions are implementing training programs for their staff with a focus on multicultural counseling (Ortega, 2011). One such example is a 10-hour mental health training program for correctional officers in Indiana, developed by the Indiana chapter of NAMI, the National Alliance on Mental Illness. Outcomes from this training appear encouraging, as the total number of incidents reported by staff decreased after the training (Parker, 2015). However, there is no indication from this study that any attention was paid to the cultural diversity of inmates with mental health challenges.

Conclusion

It is clear that criminal justice practitioners need more training in mental illness issues in general (Lamb, Weinberger, & Gross, 2004); what is also needed, however, is for that training to be constructed in such a way that it is culturally relevant (Thompson, Reuland, & Souweine, 2003). Criminal justice practitioners who are likely to encounter both the mentally ill and individuals of diverse cultural backgrounds must be well-trained in both mental illness awareness and cultural competence. However, this may be easier said than done, and may cause more problems if the training is not well-balanced. Overreliance on mental illness training may lead those in the field to begin seeing everything as mental illness, consequently exacerbating the potential for misidentification. By the same token, overreliance on cultural diversity or cultural competence training may subtly dissuade practitioners from "seeing" mental illness in those whose ethnic backgrounds differ from their own. In short, cultural competence and mental illness awareness must not be treated as separate silos under a training umbrella, but rather each must inform the other for the most effective outcomes. Incorporating a cultural competence component in mental illness training for criminal justice practitioners may be the simplest and wisest solution. This would assist in solving the problem of misidentification as discussed above, as well as aid criminal justice practitioners who encounter those of diverse ethnicities who are in fact suffering from mental illness.

Discussion Questions

1. Imagine you are a newly appointed chief of police. The mayor of your city has told you that he wants to implement reform within your department specific to diversity and mental health issues. What impact areas would you begin to focus on? Briefly explain how you would plan to implement change regarding the intersection of culture and mental illness in the criminal justice system.

2. If you were a community organizer with the task of increasing immigrant participation in mental health services, how would you go about completing your task?

3. What does the umbrella term "cultural psychotherapy" mean, and how would you take this concept into account when crafting policy around mental health practitioner requirements? How does cultural psychotherapy relate to the criminal justice system and the criminalization of mental illness?

4. What are some ways cultural norms and mental illness can be confused with each other? What are the ramifications of this confusion for criminal justice practitioners?

5. Identify some possible ways to improve how the criminal justice system currently understands and deals with ethnic and cultural differences and mental illness among offenders and victims.

References

American Fact Finder. (2015). Race. 2011–2015 American Community Survey 5-Year Estimates. United States Census Bureau. Retrieved from https://factfinder.census.gov/faces/tableservices/jsf/pages/productview.xhtml?pid=ACS_15_5YR_B02001&prodType=table.

American Psychiatric Association. (2000). *DSM-IV-TR: Diagnostic and statistical manual of mental disorders, text revision*. Washington, D.C.: American Psychiatric Association.

Ariza, D. M. (2000). *A socio-cultural comparative study of freshmen of Mexican descent attending Western Michigan University*. Retrieved from http://scholarworks.wmich.edu/dissertations/1433.

Ault-Brutus, A., & Alegria, M. (2016). Racial/ethnic differences in perceived need for mental health care and disparities in use of care among those with perceived need in 1990–1992 and 2001–2003. *Ethnicity & Health*. Retrieved from http://dx.doi.org/10.1080/13557858.2016.1252834.

Beitsch, R. (2016, August 17). In many courtrooms, bad interpreters can mean justice denied. The Pew Charitable Trusts. Retrieved from http://www.pewtrusts.org/en/research-and-analysis/blogs/stateline/2016/08/17/in-many-courtrooms-bad-interpreters-can-mean-justice-denied.

Berry, J. W., & Annis, R. C. (1974). Acculturative stress: The role of ecology, culture and differentiation. *Journal of Cross-Cultural Psychology, 5*(4), 382–406.

Bersani, B. E. (2014). An examination of first and second generation immigrant offending trajectories. *Justice Quarterly, 31*(2), 315–343.

Bhugra, D. (2006). Severe mental illness across cultures. *Acta Psychiatrica Scandinavica, 113*(s429), 17–23.

Burgess, D. J., Ding, Y., Hargreaves, M., van Ryn, M., & Phelan, S. (2008). The association between perceived discrimination and underutilization of needed medical and mental health care in a multi-ethnic community sample. *Journal of Health Care for the Poor and Underserved, 19*(3), 894–911.

Chan, J. (2011). Racial profiling and police subculture. *Canadian Journal of Criminology and Criminal Justice, 53*(1), 75–78.

Chu, D. C., & Hung, L. S. (2010). Chinese immigrants' attitudes toward the police in San Francisco. *Policing: An International Journal of Police Strategies & Management, 33*(4), 621–643.

Chu, D. C., & Song, J. H.-L. (2008). Chinese immigrants' perceptions of the police in Toronto, Canada. *Policing: An International Journal of Police Strategies & Management, 31*(4), 610–630.

Chu, D., Song, J. H.-L., & Dombrink, J. (2005). Chinese immigrants' perceptions of the police in New York City. *International Criminal Justice Review, 15*(2), 101–114.

Chung, R. C. Y., & Bemak, F. (2007). Immigrants and refugee populations. In M. G. Constantine (Ed.), *Clinical practice with people of color: A guide to becoming culturally competent* (pp. 125–142). New York, NY: Teachers College, Columbia University.

Chung, R. C. Y., Bemak, F., & Talleyrand, R. M. (2007). Mentoring within the field of counseling: A preliminary study of multicultural perspectives. *International Journal for the Advancement of Counselling, 29*(1), 21–32.

Coleman, K. J., Stewart, C., Waitzfelder, B. E., Zeber, J. E., Morales, L. S., Ahmed, A. T., ... & Hunkeler, E. M. (2016). Racial-ethnic differences in psychiatric diagnoses and treatment across 11 health care systems in the mental health research network. *Psychiatric Services, 67*(7), 749–757.

Cook, B. L., Zuvekas, S. H., Chen, J., Progovac, A., & Lincoln, A. K. (2016). Assessing the individual, neighborhood, and policy predictors of disparities in mental health care. *Medical Care Research and Review*. Retrieved from https://doi.org/10.1177/1077558716646898.

Correia, M. E. (2010). Determinants of attitudes toward police of Latino immigrants and non-immigrants. *Journal of Criminal Justice, 38*(1), 99–107.

Crank, J. P. (2011). Scholarly debate on racial profiling: To what end? *Canadian Journal of Criminology and Criminal Justice, 53*(1), 79–85.

Davis, A. L. (2016). In defense of cultural "insanity": Using insanity as a proxy for culture in criminal cases. *Columbia Journal of Law and Social Problems, 49*(3), 387.

Davis, R. C., & Hendricks, N. J. (2007). Immigrants and law enforcement: A comparison of native-born and foreign-born Americans' opinions of the police. *International Review of Victimology, 14*(1), 81–94.

Eckberg, D. A. (2012). *Mental illness training for law enforcement and criminal justice professionals*. Online training course created and housed by Metropolitan State University Institute for Professional Development.

Evans, T. S., Berkman, N., Brown, C., Gaynes, B., & Weber, R. P. (2016). *Disparities within serious mental illness*. Technical Brief 25, Agency for Healthcare Research and Quality. Retrieved from https://www.ncbi.nlm.nih.gov/books/NBK368427/.

Ferrazzi, P., & Krupa, T. (2016). Re: Mental health rehabilitation in therapeutic jurisprudence: Theoretical improvements. *International Journal of Law and Psychiatry, 46*, 42–49.

Fiscella, K., Franks, P., Doescher, M. P., & Saver, B. G. (2002). Disparities in health care by race, ethnicity, and language among the insured: Findings from a national sample. *Medical Care, 40*(1), 52–59.

Flaskerud, J. H. (2000). Ethnicity, culture, and neuropsychiatry. *Issues in Mental Health Nursing, 21*(1), 5–29.

Fuller, J., Edwards, J., Procter, N., & Moss, J. (2000). How definition of mental health problems can influence help seeking in rural and remote communities. *Australian Journal of Rural Health, 8*(3), 148–153.

Goby, V. (2004). If you look like me, I'll talk to you: A preliminary study of ethnic identity and inter ethnic interaction among women in Singapore. *Asian Ethnicity*, 5(2), 235–244.

Gracia-García, R. (2002). Telephone interpreting: A review of pros and cons. In S. Brennan (Ed.), *Proceedings of the 43rd Annual Conference* (pp. 195–216). Alexandria, VA: American Translators Association.

Guerette, R. T. (2016). *Migration, culture conflict, crime and terrorism*. London, UK: Routledge.

Higgins, G. E., Wolfe, S. E., Mahoney, M., & Walters, N. M. (2009). Race, ethnicity, and experience: Modeling the public's perceptions of justice, satisfaction, and attitude toward the courts. *Journal of Ethnicity in Criminal Justice*, 7(4), 293–310.

Khashu, A., Busch, R., Latif, Z., & Levy, F. (2005). *Building strong police-immigrant community relations: Lessons from a New York City project*. New York, NY: Vera Institute of Justice.

Kirmayer, L. J., Narasiah, L., Munoz, M., Rashid, M., Ryder, A. G., Guzder, J., … & Pottie, K. (2011). Common mental health problems in immigrants and refugees: General approaches in primary care. *Canadian Medical Association Journal*, 183(12), E959–E967.

Kleinman, A. (1988). *The illness narratives: Suffering, healing, and the human condition*. New York, NY: Basic Books.

Kroska, A., Harkness, S. K., Thomas, L. S., & Brown, R. P. (2014). Illness labels and social distance. *Society and Mental Health*, 4(3), 215–234.

La Roche, M. J., & La Roche, M. (2012). *Cultural psychotherapy: Theory, methods, and practice*. Thousand Oaks, CA: Sage.

Lai, Y. L., & Zhao, J. S. (2010). The impact of race/ethnicity, neighborhood context, and police/citizen interaction on residents' attitudes toward the police. *Journal of Criminal Justice*, 38(4), 685–692.

Lamb, H. R., Weinberger, L. E., & Gross, B. H. (2004). Mentally ill persons in the criminal justice system: Some perspectives. *Psychiatric Quarterly*, 75(2), 107–126.

Langan, P. A., Greenfeld, L. A., Smith, S. K., Durose, M. R., & Levin, D. J. (2001). *Contacts between police and the public: Findings from the 1999 national survey*. Bureau of Justice Statistics, National Institute of Justice.

Lee, J. M., Steinberg, L., & Piquero, A. R. (2010). Ethnic identity and attitudes toward the police among African American juvenile offenders. *Journal of Criminal Justice*, 38(4), 781–789.

Lewis, P. G., & Ramakrishnan, S. K. (2007). Police practices in immigrant-destination cities: Political control or bureaucratic professionalism? *Urban Affairs Review*, 42(6), 874–900.

Liddicoat, A. J. (2009). Communication as culturally contexted practice: A view from intercultural communication. *Australian Journal of Linguistics*, 29(1), 115–133.

Link, B. G., Yang, L. H., Phelan, J. C., & Collins, P. Y. (2004). Measuring mental illness stigma. *Schizophrenia Bulletin*, 30(3), 511–541.

Livingston, J., McAdoo, H. P., & Mills, C. J. (2008). Black studies and political ideology as predictors of self-esteem: A call for a new direction. *Journal of Black Studies*, 4(4), 726–744.

Lopez, S. R., & Guarnaccia, P. J. (2000). Cultural psychopathology: Uncovering the social world of mental illness. *Annual Review of Psychology*, 51(1), 571–598.

McKenzie, K., & Bhui, K. (2007). Institutional racism in mental health care. *British Medical Journal*, 334(7595), 649–650.

Mercer, E. (2008). Transcultural mental health in a changing world. *World Fellowship for Schizophrenia and Allied Disorders Newsletter*, Q3, 1–4. Retrieved from http://www.world-schizophrenia.org/publications/News_2008_Q3.pdf.

Morris, K. (Ed.). (2008). *Social work and multi-agency working: Making a difference*. Chicago, IL: University of Chicago Press.

Murray-Tjan, L. (2014). The tragicomedy of legitimation jurisprudence after *Watson v. Holder*. Immigration Briefings. Westlaw. Retrieved from https://papers.ssrn.com/sol3/papers.cfm?abstract_id=2640317.

National Alliance on Mental Illness (NAMI). (2017). Mental health by the numbers. Retrieved from https://www.nami.org/Learn-More/Mental-Health-By-the-Numbers.

Neighbors, H. W., Caldwell, C., Williams, D. R., Nesse, R., Taylor, R. J., Bullard, K. M., ... & Jackson, J. S. (2007). Race, ethnicity, and the use of services for mental disorders: Results from the National Survey of American Life. *Archives of General Psychiatry*, 64(4), 485–494.

Nobles, W. (1986). Ancient Egyptian thought and the renaissance of African (Black) psychology. In M. Karenga & J. Carruthers (Eds.), *Kemet and the African Worldview* (pp. 100–118). Los Angeles, CA: University of Sankore Press.

Ortega, C. N. (2010). Issues in multicultural correctional assessment and treatment. In T. J. Fagan & R. K. Ax (Eds.) *Correctional mental health: From theory to best practice* (pp. 125–143). Thousand Oaks, CA: Sage.

Parker, G. F. (2015). Impact of a mental health training course for correctional officers on a special housing unit. *Psychiatric Services*, 60(5), 640–645.

Parsons, S., & Sherwood, G. (2016). Vulnerability in custody: Perceptions and practices of police officers and criminal justice professionals in meeting the communication needs of offenders with learning disabilities and learn-ing difficulties. *Disability & Society, 31*(4), 553–572.

Perlin, M. L., & Weinstein, N. (2016). 'Said I, 'but you have no choice': Why a lawyer must ethically honor a client's decision about mental health treat-ment even if it is not what s/he would have chosen. *NYLS Legal Studies Research Paper No. 2828288*. Retrieved from https://papers.ssrn.com/sol3/papers.cfm?abstract_id=2828288.

Primm, A. B., Osher, F. C., & Gomez, M. B. (2005). Race and ethnicity, mental health services and cultural competence in the criminal justice system: Are we ready to change? *Community Mental Health Journal, 41*(5), 557–569.

Rein, L. (2011, April 22). Immigrants in U.S. jails steady at about 25 percent of inmates. *The Washington Post*. Retrieved from https://www.washingt-onpost.com/blogs/federal-eye/post/immigrants-in-us-jails-steady-at-about-25-percent-of-inmates/2011/03/23/AFRFMHPE_blog.html?utm_term=.dea0ff321041.

Satzewich, V., & Shaffir, W. (2009). Racism versus professionalism: Claims and counter-claims about racial profiling. *Canadian Journal of Criminology and Criminal Justice, 51*(2), 199–226.

Scheppers, E., van Dongen, E., Dekker, J., Geertzen, J., & Dekker, J. (2006). Potential barriers to the use of health services among ethnic minorities: A review. *Family Practice, 23*(3), 325–348.

Schuck, A. M., & Rosenbaum, D. P. (2005). Global and neighborhood attitudes toward the police: Differentiation by race, ethnicity and type of contact. *Journal of Quantitative Criminology, 21*(4), 391–418.

Schuck, A. M., Rosenbaum, D. P., & Hawkins, D. F. (2008). The influence of race/ethnicity, social class, and neighborhood context on residents' attitudes toward the police. *Police Quarterly, 11*(4), 496–519.

Sentell, T., Shumway, M., & Snowden, L. (2007). Access to mental health treat-ment by English language proficiency and race/ethnicity. *Journal of General Internal Medicine, 22*(2), 289–293.

Shusta, R. M., Levine, D. R., Harris, P. R., & Wong, H. Z. (2002). *Multicultural law enforcement: Strategies for peacekeeping in a diverse society*. Upper Saddle River, NJ: Prentice Hall.

Sourcebook of Criminal Justice Statistics. (2010). Estimated number and rate of sentenced prisoners under jurisdiction of state and federal correctional authorities. Retrieved from http://www.albany.edu/sourcebook/pdf/t6332010.pdf.

Sourcebook of Criminal Justice Statistics. (2011). Arrests by offense charged, age group, and race, United States, 2011. Retrieved from http://www.alb-any.edu/sourcebook/pdf/t4102011.pdf.

Spenkuch, J. L. (2014). Understanding the impact of immigration on crime. *American Law and Economics Review*, *16*(1), 177–219.

Sue, D. W., & Sue, D. (2013). *Counseling the culturally diverse: Theory & practice* (6th ed.). New York, NY: John Wiley.

Thompson, M. D., Reuland, M., & Souweine, D. (2003). Criminal justice/ mental health consensus: Improving responses to people with mental illness. *NCCD News*, *49*(1), 30–51.

Thompson, M., Newell, S., & Carlson, M. J. (2016). Race and access to mental health and substance abuse treatment in the criminal justice system. *Journal of Offender Rehabilitation*, *55*(2), 69–94.

Toncy, N. (2008). Behind the veil: An in depth exploration of Egyptian Muslim women's lives through dance. *International Journal of Qualitative Studies in Education*, *21*(3), 269–280.

Tseng, W. S. (2006). From peculiar psychiatric disorders through culture-bound syndromes to culture-related specific syndromes. *Transcultural Psychiatry*, *43*(4), 554–576.

Turner, E. A., Jensen-Doss, A., & Heffer, R. W. (2015). Ethnicity as a moderator of how parents' attitudes and perceived stigma influence intentions to seek child mental health services. *Cultural Diversity and Ethnic Minority Psychology*, *21*(4), 613–618.

Weatherhead, S., & Daiches, A. (2010). Muslim views on mental health and psychotherapy. *Psychology and Psychotherapy: Theory, Research and Practice*, *83*(1), 75–89.

Weitzer, R., & Tuch, S. A. (2005). Determinants of public satisfaction with the police. *Police Quarterly*, *8*(3), 279–297.

Wexler, D. B., & Winick, B. J. (1991). *Essays in therapeutic jurisprudence*. Durham, NC: Carolina Academic Press.

Wood, J. D., & Watson, A. C. (2016). Improving police interventions during mental health-related encounters: Past, present and future. *Policing and Society*, *27*(3), 289–299.

Criminogenic Factors and Mental Illness

Natalie Bonfine

Introduction

Today, approximately 14–17 percent of individuals entering jail (15 percent of men and 31 percent of women) meet criteria for serious mental illness, including schizophrenia, bipolar disorder and major depression; these prevalence rates are about three times higher than those in the general population (Osher, D'Amora, Plotkin, Jarrett, & Eggleston, 2012; Skeem, Manchak, & Peterson, 2011; Steadman, Osher, Robbins, Case, & Samuels, 2009). People with mental illness who are justice involved have a recidivism rate of about 45 percent (Bonta, Law, & Hanson, 1998; Fergeson, Ogloff, & Thomson, 2009). Justice involvement is also increased for people who use substances. Of the 17 percent of individuals entering jails meeting criteria for serious mental illness, 72 percent also have a co-occurring substance use disorder (Abram & Teplin, 1991).

Perhaps even more troubling than the prevalence of mental illness in jails is the differential effect of incarceration on these individuals. People with mental illness and substance use disorders have more difficulties while incarcerated than those without, are incarcerated for longer for the same charges and sentences, and are more likely to be viewed as noncompliant (Osher et al., 2012). People with mental illness who are likely to become incarcerated may also have a history of non-adherence to medications, lack insight into their illness, and have a history of current substance use issues, characteristics that are difficult to treat in any setting (Lamb & Weinberger, 2011). Finally, they are more likely to be victimized while incarcerated compared to the general population (Blitz, Wolff, & Shi, 2008), contributing to the increased trauma and psychological toll of incarceration.

As criminalization shifts the apparatus of social control from mental health to the criminal justice system, it may be necessary to expand efforts to help the mental health system reclaim this issue by adopting criminogenically informed services and policies (Fisher, Silver, & Wolff, 2006). Doing so would ease the burden being placed on the justice system and would be a more therapeutic environment in which to address multiple needs of people with mental illness, including those criminogenic factors that place individuals at risk for continued involvement in the justice system.

This issue has been the focus of decades of work on jail diversion programs aimed at addressing two goals: connecting people in need to mental health treatment and reducing justice involvement. The Sequential Intercept Model is a systems-level approach to jail diversion that models the progression of individuals through the justice system and identifies points where emerging and evidence-based practices can be used to intervene with individuals with serious mental illness (Munetz & Griffin, 2006).[1] Some of the most widely studied programs are law enforcement Crisis Intervention Teams (CIT), specialty mental health probation and mental health courts.[2] These programs have been shown to reduce arrests and jail days and increase treatment engagement (Burns, Hiday, & Ray, 2013; Compton, Bahora, Watson, & Oliva, 2008; Frailing, 2010; Herinckx, Swart, Ama, Dolezal, & King, 2005; Hiday & Ray, 2010; Hiday, Wales, & Ray, 2013; Lowder, Desmarais, & Baucom, 2016; McNiel & Binder, 2007; Kennealy, Skeem, Manchak, & Eno Louden, 2012; Manchak, Skeem, Kennealy, & Eno Louden, 2014; Steadman, Redlich, Callahan, Robbins, & Vesselinov, 2011; Teller, Munetz, Gil, & Ritter, 2006; Wolff et al., 2014), although there is debate about the effectiveness of these programs at meeting the needs of all clients (Bonfine, Ritter, & Munetz, 2016; Hiday et al., 2013; Honegger, 2015; Luskin & Ray, 2015).

Despite the widespread implementation and use of jail diversion programs, and their promise, there remain questions about whether or not diverting individuals to the mental health system is enough to curb justice involvement for individuals with mental illness. There is evidence that mental health treatment alone does not correlate with reducing criminogenic risk, and the provision of

---

1. For more on the Sequential Intercept Model, see the introductory and concluding chapters of in *The Criminalization of Mental Illness*.

2. For more on the law enforcement and court responses to persons with mental illnesses, see those chapters in *The Criminalization of Mental Illness*.

psychiatric services does not reliably reduce recidivism (Goodale, Callahan, & Steadman, 2013; Honegger, 2015; Skeem et al., 2011). Further, people with and without mental illness share common risk factors for criminal justice involvement, such as prior criminal history (Bonta et al., 1998; Fergeson et al., 2009; Epperson et al., 2011, 2014; Peterson, Skeem, Kennealy, Bray, & Zvonkovic, 2014; Rice & Harris, 1992). Justice-involved individuals with serious mental illness score higher on criminogenic risk assessments and have more criminogenic risk factors than offenders without serious mental illness, especially in the domains of antisocial personality patterns, pro-criminal attitudes, family/marital conflict, and education/employment under-attainment (Skeem et al., 2011; Skeem, Steadman, & Manchak, 2015).

Criminal thinking and attitudes are at least as prevalent among individuals with severe mental illness who are in jails and prisons as among those without mental illness (Morgan, Fisher, Duan, Mandracchia, & Murray, 2010; Wilson et al., 2014). Only up to 20 percent of criminal behavior committed by individuals with serious mental illness results directly from symptomatic mental illness (Junginger, Claypoole, Laygo, & Crisanti, 2006; Peterson, Skeem, Hart, Vidal, & Keith, 2010; Peterson et al., 2014). Peterson and colleagues (2014) further note that this association between psychiatric symptoms and criminal behavior is inconsistent and variable within individuals and across time.

There is growing recognition that mental health and jail diversion efforts need to recognize and address factors other than mental illness that contribute to justice involvement. It is not enough to expect that the mental health system or the criminal justice system alone can reduce justice involvement for people with mental illness. The remainder of this chapter will discuss explanations for criminal justice involvement of people with serious mental illness and approaches to identifying and addressing criminogenic risk.

Theoretical Approaches to Understanding Criminogenic Factors for People with Serious Mental Illness

There are multiple perspectives to explain why people with mental illness engage in criminal behavior. From a psychiatric perspective, it is assumed that symptoms and characteristics associated with mental disorders contribute directly to criminal behavior (Bonta et al., 1998). That is, symptoms of anxiety, depression and psychosis, including hallucinations and delusions, elicit criminal behavior. Much of the focus on addressing the needs of people with mental illness in the justice system to date has applied a psychiatric perspective to this issue by examining symptoms as direct contributors of criminal behavior; however, this appears to be the case for a minority of individuals with serious mental illness.

Other perspectives are applicable to the population of justice-involved people with serious mental illness. Sociological criminology focuses on individuals' locations within a social hierarchy and examines how social status characteristics (e.g., age, gender, race/ethnicity, socioeconomic status, and relatedly, mental illness) contribute to criminal behavior. The aim of such approaches is to draw attention to social structure and its influence on access to opportunities for crime and lawlessness, as opposed to historical explanations of criminal behavior as biologically derived phenomena (Merton, 1938). Sociological perspectives examine how gender roles and norms of feminine and masculine behavior contribute to lower rates of crime for women and higher rates for men (Newburn & Stanko, 2013; Steffensmeier & Allan, 1996), and how *de facto* racism in the post-Civil Rights era in the U.S. subjects persons of color to unequal protection of the law and increased surveillance, leading to differences in exposure to and experiences within the criminal justice system (Alexander, 2010; Heitzeg, 2015).

More specific to the population of interest, sociological criminology examines attributions about mental illness which are rooted in stereotypes around the perceived cause of illness, dangerousness, and controllability of symptoms and behaviors (Link, Phelan, Bresnahan, Stueve, & Pescosolido, 1999; Pescosolido, Monahan, Link, Stueve, & Kikuzawa, 1999), or considers the typology of crimes by people with mental illness (e.g., reactive, instrumental, disadvantaged; Hiday, 1999). Sociological perspectives also focus on community-level characteristics, such as anomie, lack of social cohesion, social isolation of impoverished communities, and persisting inequality as root causes of crime (Massey & Denton, 1993; Sampson & Wilson 1993).

A social psychological approach to criminology focuses more on individual-level, non-psychopathological factors, including criminal attitudes, cognitions and criminal associates (Andrews & Bonta, 2010). This perspective posits that criminal behavior can be understood in much the same manner as other learned behavior patterns, where the social context models and reinforces acceptable behavioral norms (Bonta et al., 1998). If the environment tolerates or encourages criminal thinking and behavior, individuals will develop attitudes and values that are supportive of crime (Bonta et al., 1998).

The social psychological perspective is becoming the preeminent approach to understanding people with mental illness in the criminal justice system. Focus is shifting towards identifying how stakeholders and community agencies serving people with mental illness in the criminal justice system can best identify and address clients' needs across multiple domains, including clinical needs, criminogenic risk, substance use and violence risk (Campbell et al., 2015; Munetz & Bonfine, 2015; Osher et al., 2012). This perspective incorporates treatment principles from criminal justice and mental health approaches, which emphasize the need to identify and prioritize individual criminogenic and clinical mental health and substance abuse treatment needs within a system of care that is capable of addressing such needs (Andrews & Bonta, 2010).

The Risk-Need-Responsivity Model

The Risk-Need-Responsivity (RNR) model is a leading social psychological framework for understanding criminogenic factors for justice-involved people with mental illness. The RNR model addresses criminal factors and informs treatment and supervision designed to reduce recidivism (Osher et al., 2012). The RNR model is closely allied with social learning theory, whereby criminal behavior is the outcome of an interaction between certain situational and personal factors (criminogenic needs) which increase the likelihood (risk) of crime (Hollin & Palmer, 2006). Each of the principles in the model, risk, need and responsivity, is described below.

The risk principle acknowledges that criminal behavior is predictable, and to effectively enact change in behavior and reduce recidivism, the level of supervision and treatment services must be matched to the level of criminogenic risk (Andrews & Bonta, 2010). Individuals who have higher levels of criminogenic risk should receive more intensive and extensive services than those with low or no criminogenic risk. This principle also suggests that individuals with low criminogenic risk should not be combined with others with high criminogenic risk who could encourage antisocial or pro-criminal behavior (Lowenkamp, Latessa, & Holsinger, 2006). If intensive services are provided to individuals with low levels of criminogenic risk, an iatrogenic or harmful effect is possible, with a greater likelihood of having sanctions or violations due to close supervision, and there is the potential that taking part in intensive supervision services may interrupt positive activities that are likely to reduce recidivism, for example, employment and family relationships (Osher et al., 2012). Offenders with lower levels of criminogenic risk do better with no or minimal, targeted criminogenic intervention (Osher et al., 2012).

The need principle relates to the goal of correctional rehabilitation targeting dynamic criminogenic needs, meaning those factors which can be changed and that contribute to the likelihood of reoffending (Andrews & Bonta, 2010).

Table 2.1 Central Eight Risk/Need Factors Associated with Criminal Behavior

Risk/Need Factor	Description
Big Four	
1. Presence of antisocial behavior	Early and continuing involvement in antisocial activities (in a variety of settings)
2. Antisocial personality pattern	Tendencies for impulsive behavior, adventurous/pleasure seeking, aggression and or callous disregard for others
3. Antisocial cognition	Attitudes, beliefs, values and rationalizations that are favorable to crime
4. Antisocial associates	Includes both association with pro-criminal others and isolation from anti-criminal others
Moderate Four	
5. Family/marital circumstances	Poor interpersonal relationships, with little evidence of mutual caring, respect or nurturing; low expectations from family members about avoiding criminal behavior
6. School/work	Low level of performance in school or work domains, coupled with low satisfaction and poor interpersonal relationships
7. Leisure/recreation	Low level of involvement and satisfaction in anti-criminal leisure pursuits
8. Substance abuse	Abuse of alcohol and/or other drugs (excluding tobacco)

Sources: Adapted from Andrews and Bonta (2010) and Osher et al. (2012).

When discussing dynamic criminogenic needs, we typically refer to the Central Eight risk/need factors. As seen in Table 2.1, the "Big Four," antisocial behavior, personality, criminal associates and criminal thinking, are the primary causal factors for criminal behavior (Andrews & Bonta, 2010).

Criminogenic needs, particularly the "Big Four," are the strongest predictors of recidivism among adults, regardless of offender type (Andrews & Bonta, 2010; Gendreau, Little, & Goggin, 1996). Substance abuse is a criminogenic need and a clinical issue for the majority of justice-involved people with mental illness. For this group, addressing substance use alone may significantly lower the risk of recidivism (Fergeson et al., 2009). Program administrators may reduce recidivism by addressing one need, but benefits may be enhanced if multiple needs are addressed simultaneously (Osher et al., 2012).

It should be noted that criminogenic needs are different from other factors that must also be addressed, such as healthcare needs, self-esteem, anxiety, and the like. However, these non-criminogenic needs are likely unrelated to recidivism and should not be the focus of correctional treatment or supervision at the expense of addressing criminogenic needs (Skeem et al., 2015). Instead, it is likely that program administrators will need to address both criminogenic and non-criminogenic needs to ensure that the goals of reducing recidivism and enhancing treatment engagement are both achieved.

The responsivity principle suggests that correctional treatment programs should be delivered in a manner that is consistent with the ability and learning style of the offender. Responsivity factors influence the delivery of services and the interactions between individuals and treatment/supervision environment (Holsinger, Lowenkamp, & Latessa, 2006). General responsivity refers to the approach and ability of interventions to meet their goal of addressing dynamic criminogenic risk/need factors. The most effective strategies for addressing criminogenic factors are cognitive-behavioral and cognitive social learning strategies (Osher et al., 2012). Specific responsivity refers to the need for correctional treatment to address the distinct, personal needs of individuals to enhance their response and receptivity to the treatment or intervention (Andrews & Bonta, 2010; Bonta, 1995; Osher et al., 2012). Specific responsivity issues may include addressing clinical mental health needs, physical health needs, housing and safety concerns, the individuals' level of motivation, personality, and culture, as well as race/ethnicity, age, and gender.

The RNR model was developed in criminology to address justice involvement among the general population. However, this framework is gaining ground when focusing on people with mental illness who are involved in the criminal justice system. Recent applications of the RNR model show improved recidivism outcomes among participants of a mental health court (Campbell et al., 2015), as well as positive outcomes for specialized probation that adheres to RNR principles (Manchak et al., 2014; Wolff et al., 2014).

Emphasizing the principles of the RNR model when considering justice-involved persons with mental illness advances the field in two ways. First, it challenges prior notions that criminal justice involvement can be reduced by providing psychiatric treatment or reducing symptoms. As discussed, this assumption is overwhelmed by research that shows that mental illness is a contributing factor for criminal justice involvement for some people only some of the time (Peterson et al., 2014). Incorporating RNR principles means a consideration of multiple risk/need factors so that appropriate interventions tailored along the dimensions of clinical impairment, substance use and criminogenic risk can be applied (Osher et al., 2012; Prins & Draper, 2006). Second, the RNR model acknowledges that there are general risk factors for criminal behavior across offender groups, and that individuals with mental illness share the same common risk factors as those without mental illness (Bonta, Blais, & Wilson, 2014). As seen above, these factors include antisocial behavior, personality, thoughts and associates, substance abuse, family or marital conflict, low levels of education, unemployment, and a lack of appropriate recreational activities (Andrews & Bonta, 2010; Gendreau et al., 1996; Rice & Harris, 1992).

Ultimately, the RNR model guides correctional assessment and treatment by identifying *who* to treat, *what* to treat and *how* to best treat people at risk of justice involvement (Andrews, 2012; Andrews & Bonta, 2010). That is, the risk principle seeks to identify those at high risk of recidivating, the need principle aims to identify the variable risk factors for criminal justice involvement, and the responsivity principle aims to identify the factors that affect reception of treatment to maximize the effect of treatment and treatment engagement (Andrews, 2012). Central to this framework are valid and reliable assessment tools and practices for identifying criminogenic risk and using such information to inform and guide the treatment response.

Assessing and Addressing Criminogenic Needs of People with Mental Illness

There is a considerable literature on assessment tools and practices to address criminogenic risk for the general adult population and for people with mental illness in the justice system. The current generation of screening and assessment approaches combines the assessment of dynamic criminogenic risk with guidelines for service plans and delivery (Andrews Bonta, & Wormith, 2006). For instance, the Level of Service/Case Management Inventory (LS/CMI) and Correctional Offender Management Profiling for Alternative Sanctions (COM-PAS) are frequently used assessment instruments that instruct practitioners on appropriate services to meet the individuals' needs (Andrews et al., 2006; Skeem et al., 2015). A comprehensive and recent discussion of screening and assessment tools for co-occurring substance use and mental health disorders may be found in a Substance Abuse and Mental Health Services Administration (2016) report entitled *Screening and Assessment of Co-Occurring Disorders in the Justice System.*

Systematic assessment may be challenging to do with fidelity in practice, yet it is necessary to identify and address the needs of justice-involved people with mental illness. At a minimum, there should be regular and consistent assessment of mental and substance use disorders, criminogenic risk, violence and suicide risk, motivation to change and trauma. Assessment can be a resource-intensive endeavor for agencies, and it is tempting to use a brief screening tool alone, without following up with more rigorous assessment. However, in-depth assessments identify clients' needs so that program administrators can ensure availability and application of services to meet those needs, or to ensure that programs are structured to those needs, such as offering multiple tracks with different requirements over different lengths of time (Gustaferro, 2012; Luskin & Ray, 2015). It is also important to offer adequate and frequent staff training and conduct quality control checks of the assessment process to ensure assessments are being done validly and reliably.

Jail diversion programs that have focused on people with mental illness in the criminal justice system have traditionally attempted to reduce criminal justice involvement by focusing on addressing only clinical factors (Skeem et al., 2011). This is effective for the minority of cases (around 10 percent) where psychiatric symptoms cause criminal behavior (Lamb & Weinberger, 2013; Peterson et al., 2014). This approach also makes sense from a humanity perspective—if someone is experiencing psychiatric symptoms and distress, regardless of the connection to criminal behavior, it is important to intervene to alleviate symptoms, increase functioning and improve quality of life. Focusing too much on addressing criminogenic needs, at the expense of addressing clinical mental health and substance abuse needs, will not achieve the goals of treatment engagement and recovery (Skeem et al., 2015). Finally, even for those individuals whose criminal behavior is not a direct result of psychiatric symptoms, there may be an indirect association between untreated mental illness and criminal behavior due to psychological factors, such as lack of control, impulsivity, impaired judgment and paranoia, or due to social conditions, including homelessness, poverty, or unemployment (Hiday, 1999; Lamb & Weinberger, 2013).

However, according to the need principle of the RNR model, addressing only non-criminogenic factors will not effectively reduce criminogenic risk (Andrews & Bonta, 2010) and will limit the ability of treatments to reduce criminal justice involvement and link individuals to mental health treatment. For effective criminogenic programming, then, there is a necessary shift in focus from addressing only clinical variables to one that also addresses externalizing criminogenic factors, such as antisocial behavior, anger management, impulse control, and substance use (Hiday, 1999; Peterson et al., 2014; Skeem et al., 2015). There is commonality in the treatment approaches to addressing clinical need and criminogenic risk, including in the type of approach, such as cognitive behavioral therapy, and in the goal, such as stabilization and regulation of emotions (Skeem et al., 2015). Thus, there is potential to engage people with mental illness in the criminal justice system in treatments that can address clinical *and* criminogenic issues in a way that is familiar and effective.

Cognitive-based therapies have been shown to be most efficacious at addressing criminogenic factors, yielding significant reductions in pro-criminal attitudes and recidivism (Cullen et al., 2012; Rees-Jones, Gudjonsson, & Young, 2012; Morgan, Kroner, Mills, Bauer, & Serna, 2014). However, few programs have been validated for people with mental illness in the criminal justice system (Edgely, 2014; Skeem et al., 2015). Reasoning and Rehabilitation (R&R) is one program that has been modified for this population (Young & Ross, 2007). Another advancement is a targeted service delivery approach that can be applied to existing interventions to increase effectiveness of these programs across multiple settings (Wilson, Farkas, Bonfine, & Duda-Banwar, 2017; Wilson, Bonfine, Farkas, & Duda-Banwar, 2017). The targeted service delivery approach is designed to make existing interventions accessible to the needs of justice-involved people with mental illness by modifying delivery strategies, including amplification, active coaching, low-demand practice, and maximizing participation (Wilson, Farkas et al., 2017). While such developments show promise in improving access and responsivity to existing programs, additional research is needed to examine outcomes of these approaches. Developing and promulgating accessible criminogenic interventions for the population of justice-involved people with mental illness is certainly an area of future program development.

Challenges and Opportunities for Addressing Criminogenic Factors

Efforts to identify and address criminogenic factors for mental illness have pointed to the need for an integrated and comprehensive approach. There are two key issues facing policy and program development that must be better understood to improve our approach to addressing criminogenic factors.

The first issue is improving programming to address criminogenic needs of justice-involved people with mental illness. This is a responsivity issue. Beyond the efforts to develop programming and delivery approaches to address criminogenic factors for people with mental illness in the justice system as discussed above, we also need to examine how mental illness, substance use and criminogenic needs relate to one another, shaping an individual's ability to respond to interventions (Skeem et al., 2015). Clinical mental health factors appear to aggravate the impact of criminogenic risk on justice involvement, even though mental illness is not a strong independent predictor of criminal behavior. Substance use disorders further complicate the distinction between risk/need factor and responsivity factor, as substance use is both a criminogenic need and a condition that may affect responsivity to supervision or treatment. This is especially true given the high prevalence of co-occurring substance use disorders among justice-involved individuals with mental illness (Chiles, Cleve, Jemelka, & Trupin, 1990; Lurigio et al., 2003; Peters, Kremling, Bekman, & Caudy, 2012). Program administrators must be aware of the interaction of substance abuse, mental illness and criminogenic risk and how it affects responsivity to interventions.

The second issue affecting our ability to address criminogenic factors is clarifying the most appropriate setting for delivering criminogenic-based programming for justice-involved people with mental illness and determining who is best suited to deliver these interventions. This is a question of ownership. Mental health clinicians are well-versed and trained to deliver cognitive behavioral therapy, but primarily focus on mental health outcomes. Criminal justice personnel and probation officers also provide cognitive behavioral therapy, but typically within a criminal justice setting, focusing on achieving desired criminal justice outcomes. Studies are needed that compare how mental health practitioners and criminal justice personnel address criminogenic factors within case management and supervision sessions (Eno Louden, Skeem, Camp, Vidal, & Peterson, 2012).

Because many justice-involved people with serious mental illness receive clinical services in a community mental health setting, these agencies could provide criminogenic interventions along with mental health services (Wilson, Bonfine et al., 2017). If the goal of jail diversion programming is to limit justice involvement and treat people with mental illness in a therapeutic environment, then it may make sense to empower mental health professionals to provide criminogenic risk treatment within the community.

Criminogenic factors should be addressed across multiple settings by professionals who are cross-trained to recognize clinical and criminogenic needs. Such integration is challenging in part because disciplines define and describe needs differently. There are different literatures with no clear language. For example, depending on the context or professional perspective, risk may refer to criminogenic risk, violence risk, suicide risk, risk of relapse or risk of hospitalization (Munetz & Bonfine, 2015). Cross-system training on RNR principles, as well as developing a shared language across systems, are important steps toward integrating perspectives to address the risks and needs of people with mental illness in the criminal justice system (Munetz & Bonfine, 2015; Wolff et al., 2013).

It is a comfort to know that we need not start from scratch; the bodies of knowledge in criminal justice and mental health can be applied to develop targeted solutions tailored to the specific needs of individuals. Our challenge moving forward is to create an integrated approach to link justice-involved people with mental illness to appropriate supervision and clinical services that best meet their needs so that they are able to recover *and* end criminal justice involvement. This requires appropriate treatment to be available and offered by staff who have been cross-trained and who work within systems willing to share resources, programming and services.

Discussion Questions

1. What factors contribute to the overrepresentation of people with mental illness in the justice system?

2. Describe each of the principles of the Risk-Need-Responsivity Model.

3. What are the strongest predictors of criminal behavior for justice-involved people with mental illness?

4. Why is responsivity an issue for justice-involved people with mental illness?

5. Devise a cross-systems approach to addressing the risks and meeting the needs of justice-involved people with mental illness.

6. Identify factors that might inhibit the development of an effective cross-systems approach to addressing the risks and meeting the needs of justice-involved people with mental illness.

References

Abram, K. M., & Teplin, L. A. (1991). Co-occurring disorders among mentally ill jail detainees: Implications for public policy. *American Psychologist*, 46(10), 1036–1045.

Alexander, M. (2012). *The new Jim Crow: Mass incarceration in the age of colorblindness*. The New York, NY: The New Press.

Andrews, D. A. (2012). The risk-need-responsivity (RNR) model of correctional assessment and treatment. In J. A. Dvoskin, J. L. Skeem, R. W. Novaco, & K. S. Douglas (Eds.), *Using social science to reduce violent offending* (pp. 127–156). New York, NY: Oxford University Press.

Andrews, D. A., & Bonta, J. (2010). *The psychology of criminal conduct*. London, UK: Routledge.

Andrews, D. A., Bonta, J., & Wormith, J. S. (2006). The recent past and near future of risk and/or need assessment. *Crime & Delinquency*, 52(1), 7–27.

Blitz, C. L., Wolff, N., & Shi, J. (2008). Physical victimization in prison: The role of mental illness. *International Journal of Law and Psychiatry, 31*(5), 385–393.

Bonfine, N., Ritter, C., & Munetz, M. R. (2016). Exploring the relationship between criminogenic risk assessment and mental health court program completion. *International Journal of Law and Psychiatry, 45,* 9–16.

Bonta, J. (1995, September). The responsivity principle and offender rehabilitation. *Forum on Corrections Research, 7*(3), 34–37.

Bonta, J., Blais, J., & Wilson, H. A. (2014). A theoretically informed meta-analysis of the risk for general and violent recidivism for mentally disordered offenders. *Aggression and Violent Behavior, 19*(3), 278–287.

Bonta, J., Law, M., & Hanson, K. (1998). The prediction of criminal and violent recidivism among mentally disordered offenders: A meta-analysis. *Psychological Bulletin, 123*(2), 123–142.

Burns, P. J., Hiday, V. A., & Ray, B. (2013). Effectiveness 2 years postexit of a recently established mental health court. *American Behavioral Scientist, 57*(2), 189–208.

Campbell, M. A., Canales, D. D., Wei, R., Totten, A. E., Macaulay, W. A. C., & Wershler, J. L. (2015). Multidimensional evaluation of a mental health court: Adherence to the risk-need-responsivity model. *Law and Human Behavior, 39*(5), 489–502.

Chiles, J. A., Cleve, E. V., Jemelka, R. P., & Trupin, E. W. (1990). Substance abuse and psychiatric disorders in prison inmates. *Psychiatric Services, 41*(10), 1132–1134.

Compton, M. T., Bahora, M., Watson, A. C., & Oliva, J. R. (2008). A comprehensive review of extant research on crisis intervention team (CIT) programs. *Journal of the American Academy of Psychiatry and the Law, 36*(1), 47–55.

Cullen, A. E., Clarke, A. Y., Kuipers, E., Hodgins, S., Dean, K., & Fahy, T. (2012). A multi-site randomized controlled trial of a cognitive skills programme for male mentally disordered offenders: Social-cognitive outcomes. *Psychological Medicine, 42*(03), 557–569.

Edgely, M. (2014). Why do mental health courts work? A confluence of treatment, support and adroit judicial supervision. *International Journal of Law and Psychiatry, 37*(6), 572–580.

Eno Louden, J., Skeem, J. L., Camp, J., Vidal, S., & Peterson, J. (2012). Supervision practices in specialty mental health probation: What happens in officer-probationer meetings? *Law and Human Behavior, 36*(2), 109–119.

Epperson, M. W., Wolff, N., Morgan, R. D., Fisher, W. H., Frueh, B. C., & Huening, J. (2011). *The next generation of behavioral health and criminal justice interventions: Improving outcomes by improving interventions.* Center for Behavioral Health Services and Criminal Justice Research. New Brunswick, NJ: Rutgers University.

Epperson, M. W., Wolff, N., Morgan, R. D., Fisher, W. H., Frueh, B. C., & Huening, J. (2014). Envisioning the next generation of behavioral health and criminal justice interventions. *International Journal of Law and Psychiatry, 37*(5), 427–438.

Fergeson, A. M., Ogloff, J. R., & Thomson, L. (2009). Predicting recidivism by mentally disordered offenders using the LSI-R: SV. *Criminal Justice and Behavior, 36*(1), 5–20.

Fisher, W. H., Silver, E., & Wolff, N. (2006). Beyond criminalization: Toward a criminologically informed framework for mental health policy and services research. *Administration and Policy in Mental Health and Mental Health Services Research, 33*(5), 544–557.

Frailing, K. (2010). How mental health courts function: Outcomes and observations. *International Journal of Law and Psychiatry, 33*(4), 207–213.

Gendreau, P., Little, T., & Goggin, C. (1996). A meta analysis of the predictors of adult offender recidivism: What works! *Criminology, 34*(4), 575–608.

Goodale, G., Callahan, L., & Steadman, H. J. (2013). Law & psychiatry: What can we say about mental health courts today? *Psychiatric Services, 64*(4), 298–300.

Guastaferro, W. P. (2012). Using the level of service inventory-revised to improve assessment and treatment in drug court. *International Journal of Offender Therapy and Comparative Criminology, 56*(5), 769–789.

Heitzeg, N. A. (2015). "Whiteness," criminality, and the double standards of deviance/social control. *Contemporary Justice Review, 18*(2), 197–214.

Herinckx, H. A., Swart, S. C., Ama, S. M., Dolezal, C. D., & King, S. (2005). Rearrest and linkage to mental health services among clients of the Clark County mental health court program. *Psychiatric Services, 56*(7), 853–857.

Hiday V. A. (1999). Mental illness and the criminal justice system. In A. V. Horwitz & T. L. Scheid (Eds.), *A handbook for the study of mental health* (pp. 508–525). New York, NY: Cambridge University Press.

Hiday, V. A., & Ray, B. (2010). Arrests two years after exiting a well-established mental health court. *Psychiatric Services, 61*(5), 463–468.

Hiday, V. A., Wales, H. W., & Ray, B. (2013). Effectiveness of a short-term mental health court: Criminal recidivism one year postexit. *Law and Human Behavior, 37*(6), 401–411.

Hollin, C. R., & Palmer, E. J. (2006). Criminogenic need and women offenders: A critique of the literature. *Legal and Criminological Psychology, 11*(2), 179–195.

Holsinger, A. M., Lowenkamp, C. T., & Latessa, E. J. (2006). Exploring the validity of the Level of Service Inventory-Revised with Native American offenders. *Journal of Criminal Justice, 34*(3), 331–337.

Honegger, L. N. (2015). Does the evidence support the case for mental health courts? A review of the literature. *Law and Human Behavior, 39*(5), 478–488.

Junginger, J., Claypoole, K., Laygo, R., & Crisanti, A. (2006). Effects of serious mental illness and substance abuse on criminal offenses. *Psychiatric Services, 57*(6), 879–882.

Kennealy, P. J., Skeem, J. L., Manchak, S. M., & Eno Louden, J. (2012). Firm, fair, and caring officer-offender relationships protect against supervision failure. *Law and Human Behavior, 36*(6), 496–505.

Lamb, H. R., & Weinberger, L. E. (2013). Some perspectives on criminalization. *Journal of the American Academy of Psychiatry and the Law, 41*(2), 287–293.

Link, B. G., Phelan, J. C., Bresnahan, M., Stueve, A., & Pescosolido, B. A. (1999). Public conceptions of mental illness: Labels, causes, dangerousness, and social distance. *American Journal of Public Health, 89*(9), 1328–1333.

Lowder, E. M., Desmarais, S. L., & Baucom, D. J. (2016). Recidivism following mental health court exit: Between and within-group comparisons. *Law and Human Behavior, 40*(2), 118–127.

Lowenkamp, C. T., Latessa, E. J., & Holsinger, A. M. (2006). The risk principle in action: What have we learned from 13,676 offenders and 97 correctional programs? *Crime & Delinquency, 52*(1), 77–93.

Lurigio, A. J., Cho, Y. I., Swartz, J. A., Graf, I., Johnson, T. P., & Pickup, L. (2003). Standardized assessment of substance-related, other psychiatric, and comorbid disorders among probationers. *International Journal of Offender Therapy and Comparative Criminology, 47*(6), 630–652.

Luskin, M. L., & Ray, B. (2015). Selection into mental health court: Distinguishing among eligible defendants. *Criminal Justice and Behavior, 42*(11), 1145–1158.

Manchak, S. M., Skeem, J. L., Kennealy, P. J., & Eno Louden, J. (2014). High-fidelity specialty mental health probation improves officer practices, treatment access, and rule compliance. *Law and Human Behavior, 38*(5), 450–461.

Massey, D. S., & Denton, N. A. (1993). *American apartheid: Segregation and the making of the underclass.* Cambridge, MA: Harvard University Press.

McNiel, D. E., & Binder, R. L. (2007). Effectiveness of a mental health court in reducing criminal recidivism and violence. *American Journal of Psychiatry, 164*(9), 1395–1403.

Merton, R. K. (1938). Social structure and anomie. *American Sociological Review*, *3*(5), 672–682.

Morgan, R. D., Fisher, W. H., Duan, N., Mandracchia, J. T., & Murray, D. (2010). Prevalence of criminal thinking among state prison inmates with serious mental illness. *Law and Human Behavior*, *34*(4), 324–336.

Morgan, R. D., Kroner, D. G., Mills, J. F., Bauer, R. L., & Serna, C. (2014). Treating justice involved persons with mental illness: Preliminary evaluation of a comprehensive treatment program. *Criminal Justice and Behavior*, *41*(7), 902–916.

Munetz, M. R., & Bonfine, N. (2015). From boundary spanning to deep partnerships. *Psychiatric Services*, *66*(9), 901.

Munetz, M. R., & Griffin, P. A. (2006). Use of the sequential intercept model as an approach to decriminalization of people with serious mental illness. *Psychiatric Services*, *57*(4), 544–549.

Newburn, T., & Stanko, E. A. (2013). *Just boys doing business? Men, masculinities and crime*. London, UK: Routledge.

Osher, F., D'Amora, D. A., Plotkin, M., Jarrett, N., & Eggleston, A. (2012). *Adults with behavioral health needs under correctional supervision: A shared framework for reducing recidivism and promoting recovery*. New York, NY: Council of State Governments Justice Center.

Pescosolido, B. A., Monahan, J., Link, B. G., Stueve, A., & Kikuzawa, S. (1999). The public's view of the competence, dangerousness, and need for legal coercion of persons with mental health problems. *American Journal of Public Health*, *89*(9), 1339–1345.

Peters, R. H., Kremling, J., Bekman, N. M., & Caudy, M. S. (2012). Co-occurring disorders in treatment based courts: Results of a national survey. *Behavioral Sciences & the Law*, *30*(6), 800–820.

Peterson, J., Skeem, J. L., Hart, E., Vidal, S., & Keith, F. (2010). Analyzing offense patterns as a function of mental illness to test the criminalization hypothesis. *Psychiatric Services*, *61*(12), 1217–1222.

Peterson, J. K., Skeem, J., Kennealy, P., Bray, B., & Zvonkovic, A. (2014). How often and how consistently do symptoms directly precede criminal behavior among offenders with mental illness? *Law and Human Behavior*, *38*(5), 439–449.

Prins, S. J., & Draper, L. (2009). *Improving outcomes for people with mental illnesses under community corrections supervision: A guide to research-informed policy and practice*. New York, NY: Council of State Governments Justice Center.

Rees-Jones, A., Gudjonsson, G., & Young, S. (2012). A multi-site controlled trial of a cognitive skills program for mentally disordered offenders. *BMC Psychiatry*, *12*(1), 44.

Rice, M. E., & Harris, G. T. (1992). A comparison of criminal recidivism among schizophrenic and nonschizophrenic offenders. *International Journal of Law and Psychiatry*, *15*(4), 397–408.

Sampson, R. J., & Wilson, W. J. (1995). Toward a theory of race, crime, and urban inequality. In J. Hagan & R. D. Peterson (Eds.), *Crime and inequality* (pp. 37–56). Stanford, CA: Stanford University Press.

Skeem, J. L., Manchak, S., & Peterson, J. K. (2011). Correctional policy for offenders with mental illness: Creating a new paradigm for recidivism reduction. *Law and Human Behavior*, *35*(2), 110–126.

Skeem, J. L., Steadman, H. J., & Manchak, S. M. (2015). Applicability of the Risk-Need-Responsivity model to persons with mental illness involved in the criminal justice system. *Psychiatric Services*, *66*(9), 916–922.

Steadman, H. J., Osher, F. C., Robbins, P. C., Case, B., & Samuels, S. (2009). Prevalence of serious mental illness among jail inmates. *Psychiatric Services*, *60*(6), 761–765.

Steadman, H. J., Redlich, A., Callahan, L., Robbins, P. C., & Vesselinov, R. (2011). Effect of mental health courts on arrests and jail days: A multisite study. *Archives of General Psychiatry*, *68*(2), 167–172.

Steffensmeier, D., & Allan, E. (1996). Gender and crime: Toward a gendered theory of female offending. *Annual Review of Sociology*, *22*(1), 459–487.

Substance Abuse and Mental Health Services Administration. (2016). *Screening and assessment of co-occurring disorders in the justice system*. HHS Publication No. (SMA)-15-4930. Rockville, MD: Substance Abuse and Mental Health Services Administration.

Teller, J. L., Munetz, M. R., Gil, K. M., & Ritter, C. (2006). Crisis intervention team training for police officers responding to mental disturbance calls. *Psychiatric Services*, *57*(2), 232–237.

Wilson, A. B., Bonfine, N., Farkas, K. J., & Duda-Banwar, J. (2017). Translating interventions that target criminogenic risk factors for use in community based mental health settings. *Community Mental Health Journal*. Retrieved from doi:10.1007/s10597-017-0119-6.

Wilson, A. B., Farkas, K., Bonfine, N., & Duda-Banwar, J. (2017). Interventions that target criminogenic needs for justice-involved persons with serious mental illnesses: A targeted service delivery approach. *International Journal of Offender Therapy and Comparative Criminology*. Retrieved from https://doi.org/10.1177/0306624X17695588.

Wilson, A. B., Farkas, K., Ishler, K. J., Gearhart, M., Morgan, R., & Ashe, M. (2014). Criminal thinking styles among people with serious mental illness in jail. *Law and Human Behavior*, *38*(6), 592–601.

Wolff, N., Epperson, M., Shi, J., Huening, J., Schumann, B. E., & Sullivan, I. R. (2014). Mental health specialized probation caseloads: Are they effective? *International Journal of Law and Psychiatry*, *37*(5), 464–472.

Wolff, N., Frueh, B. C., Huening, J., Shi, J., Epperson, M. W., Morgan, R., & Fisher, W. (2013). Practice informs the next generation of behavioral health and criminal justice interventions. *International Journal of Law and Psychiatry*, *36*(1), 1–10.

Young, S. J., & Ross, R. R. (2007). *R&R2 for youths and adults with mental health problems: A prosocial competence training program*. Ottawa, Ontario: Cognitive Centre of Canada.

Stigma and Mental Illness

Binoy Biren Shah, Anastasia Cherise Tooley &
Patrick W. Corrigan

Introduction

Many of the challenges that beset people with mental illness happen because of stigma, the prejudice and discrimination that occur when the public believe stereotypes about people with mental illness involved with the criminal justice system. This chapter begins by describing stigma and its impact. We discuss prevalent stereotypes about people with mental illness, including those related to causal attributions of crime, via sin or sickness. We then examine interactions between people with mental illness and law enforcement officials, where the prejudicial and behavioral manifestations of stigma are especially prevalent. We conclude with the stigma of substance abuse disorders and its implications for the criminalization of mental illness.

Overview of Stigma

As seen in Table 3.1, stigma can be understood in terms of a matrix of structures by types. We illustrate each cell in the matrix with an example relevant to people with mental illness. The three structures of stigma are: *stereotypes*, *prejudice*, and *discrimination*. *Stereotypes*, defined as shared beliefs about individuals belonging to a social group, are cognitive in nature (Krueger, 1996). There is a difference between acknowledging and endorsing a stereotype (Jussim, Nelson, Manis, & Soffin, 1995). When endorsed stereotypic beliefs

Table 3.1 A Matrix for Understanding Stigma

	Public Stigma	Self-Stigma	Label Avoidance	Structural Stigma
Stereotype	Ex-offenders are dangerous.	Criminal offenders can't be good employees.	People with mental illness are "psycho."	People with mental illness are dangerous.
Prejudice	Landlords feel scared of me because I am an ex-offender.	As an ex-offender, I do not deserve a job. Who would want to employ someone like me?	I have a mental illness and am ashamed to be seen as a "psycho."	The public is afraid to work alongside people with mental illness.
Discrimination	Landlords won't rent me an apartment.	I think "why try" and stop looking for employment.	I don't seek treatment for my condition because of my shame.	New legislation restricting entry of people with mental illness into the workforce.

combine with a negative emotional reaction, *prejudice* occurs (Crocker, Major, & Steele, 1998). *Discrimination* is the behavioral result, which arises when prejudice towards a minority group is acted upon.

There are four types of stigma: public stigma, self-stigma, label avoidance, and structural stigma. *Public stigma* is the result of members of society endorsing negative stereotypes regarding a specific group of individuals, and the discrimination that follows. Public stigma causes obstacles to healthcare (Clement et al., 2015; Hatzenbuehler, Phelan, & Link, 2013), and employment (Corrigan, Powell, & Rusch, 2012; Draper, Reid, & McMahon, 2011). These barriers can create a negative loop and further exacerbate stigma. For example, stereotyping ex-offenders serves as a barrier to obtaining employment (Varghese, Hardin, Bauer, & Morgan, 2010), which can result in failed reintegration and higher recidivism (Visher, Debus-Sherrill, & Yahner, 2011). Ex-offenders become recurrent offenders and the negative stereotypes are reinforced. Stigmatized individuals learn to anticipate and internalize the nearly constant flow of negative societal reactions they encounter (Link, Cullen, Struening, Shrout, & Dohrenwend, 1989).

Self-stigma occurs when individuals with mental health issues (1) become *aware* of negative public stereotypes regarding mental illnesses, (2) *agree* with these negative stereotypes, and (3) *apply* the stereotypes to themselves (Corrigan, Watson, & Barr, 2006). Consider this experience in people with serious mental illness involved in the criminal health system (Moore, Tangney, & Stuewig, 2016). Attributes such as "drug addicts" and "violent" are frequently associated with offenders. The more offenders are aware of these, the more likely they are to agree with them, and in turn, start seeing themselves as violent drug addicts. Self-stigma negatively impacts the individual's self-concept and leads to self-discrimination (Corrigan & Rao, 2012). Consequences range from social withdrawal and diminished self-esteem (Drapalski et al., 2013; Livingston & Boyd, 2010), to underutilization of treatment services (Clement et al., 2015; Earnshaw & Quinn 2012), and even suicide (Oexle et al., 2017; Sharaf, Ossman, & Lachine, 2012). The end result of self-stigma is the "why try" effect (Corrigan, Bink, Schmidt, Jones, & Rusch, 2016; Corrigan, Larson, & Rusch, 2009). One example, "Why try to get a job? Someone like me is unworthy of it," is seen in Table 3.1.

Label avoidance are efforts to avoid stigmatizing labels or diagnoses in order to avoid the harmful effects of public and/or self-stigma. For example, ex-offenders might avoid situations where their prior status as a criminal might be flagged, from travelling overseas to applying for jobs. Individuals with mental illnesses avoid and/or disengage from treatment services in attempts to avoid the label (Clement et al., 2015; Pietrzak, Johnson, Goldstein, Malley, & Southwick, 2009). In turn, this exacerbates mental health issues (Penttilä, Jääskeläinen, Hirvonen, Isohanni, & Miettunen, 2014; Shaw et al., 2012), which may result in re-incarceration (Hawthorne et al., 2012). *Structural stigma* refers to private and public organizational norms, regulations, rules, and behaviors that lead to marginalization of stigmatized individuals (Corrigan, Markowitz, & Watson, 2004; Hatzenbuehler & Link, 2014; Kelly, 2006). It can be intentional or unintentional. For example, the use of physical restraints in treating psychiatric hospital patients (Cleary & Prescott, 2015) may be *intentional* structural stigma. Conversely, incarcerated individuals with mental illnesses might find it hard to navigate the criminal justice system (Pugh, Hatzenbuehler, & Link, 2015), which is an example of *unintentional* structural stigma. Structural stigma can negatively impact outcomes without deliberately attempting to do so.

Dangerous and Violent

There are several beliefs that illustrate stereotypes of mental illness and/or criminal involvement. Members of the public commonly stereotype individuals with mental illness and ex-offenders as "dangerous." A 2013 survey estimated that 46 percent of Americans view people with mental illness as significantly more dangerous than the general public (Barry, McGinty, Vernick, & Webster, 2013); this perception seems to have increased over the past 50 years (Phelan, Link, Stueve, & Pescosolido, 2000).

There are general versus specific effects of mental illness stigma that require distinction. The public tends to *generally* stigmatize all persons with mental illness as different and with disdain, and *specifically* stigmatize those individuals with more serious mental illnesses, such as psychoses, beyond the baseline label (Corrigan et al., 1999). For example, the public generally views all people with mental illness negatively regardless of diagnosis. An individual with any mental illness is looked down upon, more so than someone without. However, within mental illness, some diagnoses are seen as "worse" than others. For example, persons with a diagnosis of schizophrenia are specifically stigmatized as lower or less than individuals with depression. Members of the public will avoid employing and living near people with a mental illness, but particularly those with serious disorders like schizophrenia (Corrigan & Penn, 1999).

Why might certain diagnoses carry different public stigma? Swanson and colleagues (2006) examined specific symptoms of schizophrenia and found that individuals with positive symptoms like delusions were more strongly associated with violence than those with negative symptoms like social withdrawal. Additionally, victimization and history of childhood conduct problems were identified as important factors influencing violence among those with mental illness (Swanson et al., 2006). The data suggest that making broad statements about serious mental illness or even specific diagnostic labels is not a helpful approach. Rather, in order to make any inference about the relationship between mental illness and violence, one must first consider specific symptoms, as well as multiple demographic factors.

The Treatment Advocacy Center (TAC) asserts that people with mental illnesses have an inordinate propensity for violence. Citing multiple studies that appear to support the idea that mental illness and violence are strongly tied, the TAC estimated that people with serious mental illness are responsible for about 10 percent of homicides in the United States (TAC, 2016). However, more careful epidemiological research has sought to explain the putative link between violence and mental illness. Swanson, Holzer, Ganju, and Jono (1990) analyzed data from the Epidemiological Catchment Area survey, seeking to make sense of it vis-à-vis base rate information from the U.S. Census. Their analyses suggested that age and gender are better predictors of dangerousness than mental illness diagnosis. Additionally, they found a huge false positive rate, with more than 100,000 individuals with mental illness being potentially labeled violent when they were not (Swanson et al., 1990). Other studies have found similar links between mental disorders and violence, further supporting Swanson et al.'s (1990) assertions that gender, for example, is a better predictor of dangerousness than mental illness diagnosis alone (Fazel, Singh, Doll, & Grann, 2012; Wallace et al., 1998). Recent data from the National Epidemiologic Survey on Alcohol and Related Conditions (NESARC), suggest that while the rates of violence are higher for people with serious mental illness, this relationship is significant only for those with co-occurring substance use issues. More importantly, serious mental illness does not predict future violent behavior independent of other historical, dispositional and environmental stressors (Elbogen & Johnson, 2009).

Why might stereotypes of mental illness and violence thrive? Members of the public rely on the media, including newspapers, television, radio and the Internet, as sources of information regarding mental illnesses. Content analysis of the media reveals that descriptions of mental illness are distorted by inaccuracies, exaggerations, and misinformation (Klin & Lemish, 2008). Dangerousness and violence are some of the most commonly depicted themes, and such themes repeatedly arise due to selective attention on violent subgroups (Corrigan et al., 2005; Klin & Lemish, 2008). Such depictions impair self-esteem, help-seeking behaviors, treatment adherence and overall recovery (Corrigan, Powell, & Michaels, 2013; Stuart, 2006). While external forces like media can account for the diffusion of stigma, we might have to look internally to better understand cause.

Inherent cognitive biases or heuristics may explain why the media is so successful in fanning the flames of stigma. The availability heuristic, for example, relies on immediate associations to explain social judgments, which are especially influenced by salient and memorable events (Tversky & Kahneman, 1974). The media feeds this vulnerability by selectively providing us with "juicy" stories of violence in "mental patients." As a result, wrongful associations become even more vivid and accessible. The out-group heuristic also contributes to perceptions of dangerousness (Boldry, Gaertner, & Quinn, 2007). Stereotypes about salient individuals in a group may be generalized to the entire group.

Senseless Crimes: Sin or Sickness?

On December 14, 2012, a shooter stormed into Sandy Hook Elementary School in Newtown, Connecticut, and killed 26 people, including 20 children under the age of seven. It was a horrific year; in the preceding 12 months, 12 were killed at a theatre in Aurora, Colorado, seven at Oikos University in Oakland, and two at a mall in Clackamas County, Oregon. Heinous crimes like these beg for answers and demand action. Why might people do these inexplicable horrors and how can they be stopped in the future? The stigma of mental illness worsens in the absence of suitable answers. In earlier times, such events were attributed to moral sin and "evil," but in a more scientifically enlightened age, we focus on psychiatric sickness, leading to calls for action to better treat mental illness in order to stop future horrors. Focusing on mental health issues offers an incomplete picture that distorts our understanding of these tragedies. This kind of misunderstanding then generates flawed policy responses that further chip away at the rights of citizens labeled mentally ill. We admit the idea of sin is a strange and strained bedfellow, but believe a conceptual unpacking where sin meets sickness helps us to better understand these crimes and lessen stigma.

Social psychologists theorize that humans have an intrinsic need to understand events, especially those involving life and death. Attribution theory, for example, attempts to make sense of a killer's actions by framing them in terms of perceived control (Weiner, 2006). People committing heinous crimes cannot possibly be responsible for this kind of behavior and hence must be mentally ill. Conversely, attribution theory implies if shooters are in control of their behavior, then they are sinners with significant moral flaws. Psychology's focus on attributions of control parallels legal questions on *mens rea* and criminal intent. According to the law, a crime is senseless, and hence based on mental illness, when its intent either fails to reflect normative motivators of crime or lacks legal justification; these motivators include greed, retribution, economic need, peer group pressure, passion, and protection from prosecution (Hannon & DeFronzo, 1998). Normal motives are not obviously present at the Sandy Hook tragedy, so mental illness is presumed. However, American jurisprudence recognizes not all instances of inexplicable crime represent mental illness. We adopted a test from English common law, the M'Naghten Rule, which courts use to determine whether mental illness is a significant mitigating factor in a crime.[1] But when we are unable to (or unwilling to) make a judgment about

---

1. The M'Naghten Rule states that a person is not responsible for a criminal act if at the time of the act, he was "laboring under such a defect of reason, from disease of the mind, as not to know the nature and quality of the act he was doing or if he did know it, that he did not know he was doing what was wrong" (Biggs, 1955) and is at the root of the insanity defense in the United States. For more on the insanity defense, see that chapter in *The Criminalization of Mental Illness*.

someone's mental state when a terrible crime is committed, we may be tempted to look to moral failure, in other words, to sin, as the reason.

Sin as an explanation of behavior is mostly absent from modern psychiatry and psychology research, rejected by proponents of psychological determinism such as Sigmund Freud and B. F. Skinner, and those of the human potential movement such as Carl Rogers (Mowrer, 1960). Mowrer (1960) believed this kind of distancing robbed psychiatry of any authority in matters related to values. Sinners became an illegitimate concern of mental health services. Unfortunately, stripping out the moral deprives us from considering alternative explanations. Consider the issue from a statistical viewpoint. Proxies of mental illness and general human behavior are associated with aggression, but only modestly at best (Fazel et al., 2012). These kind of small effect sizes make phenomenological sense to mental health providers and researchers who know that the vast majority of people with mental illnesses are unlikely to be violent. Might not some proxy of sin help to explain the behavior of these vicious killers? Perhaps some indicator of moral failing could add significantly to the prediction of violence?

Of course, here's the rub. How does behavioral science divorced from moral thought develop a meaningful measure of sin? We do not propose a method to do so here. Nor do we postulate a conceptual *rapprochement* between sin and sickness, some translational bridge that might be used to answer questions about these tragedies. We lack the skills and credentials to do so and many of these questions are outside our purview. In order to be able to one day answer them, at least in part, it is necessary to partner with those who might complement the mental health answer, including social ethicists, legal scholars, or theologians; it is no accident that these groups are assuming greater prominence in the practice of modern medicine. This is by no means a facile partnership thrown together in the hectic hours and days after a tragedy. It requires extensive discussion and research with counterpart experts in ethics, an authority that the vast majority of mental health providers lack. Mental health providers are generally not competent to publicly comment on these issues, though they may feel pressure to do so in the hours and days after a tragedy such as Sandy Hook.

Some might question the harm of a mental health focus on violent crime, contending that this is an opportunity to advance resources for mental health (e.g., Torrey, 2002). This "ends justify the means" approach is plausibly unethical, because it further harms not only people labeled mentally ill, but the community violated by this crime. First, research shows public education programs stressing the connection between violence and mental illness fail to improve public endorsement of greater funds for mental health (Corrigan, Watson, Warpinski, & Garcia, 2004). On the contrary, media messages that link violence and mental illness significantly increases discriminatory calls for social avoidance, institutional segregation, and coercive treatment. Second, any predictive tool of violence yields massive false positives, leading to possibly egregious civil rights violations against many (Fazel et al., 2012). Third, research shows that the resulting fears of being labeled violent are likely to drive people away from needed services rather than drawing them in. Lastly, even if these threats to civil rights are somehow justified, the police burden that results would be untenable. The number of people that would need to be monitored to avoid another Sandy Hook would easily overload any combined mental health/police effort, likely taking away significant resources from both institutions for other responsibilities.

So let us be clear about what to do the next time a tragic crime like Sandy Hook occurs and the news reporter or legislator comes with queries. Almost all of us are unable to answer such questions. Instead, let us direct them to the handful of researchers who have tried to span the sin and sickness chasm. And, let us support scholarship attempting to make sense of this split.

Stigma and Police

Law enforcement plays a critical role in understanding stigma here. Though it might seem that individuals with mental illness are engaged in crime at greater rates, these claims are not scientifically supported (Watson, Corrigan, & Ottati, 2004; Heslop, Hartford, Rona, Stitt, & Schrecker, 2002). However, police do handle a greater proportion of mental health crises. Research has sought to make sense of this problem by examining biases of both the police and those who are arrested with mental illness. When individuals with mental illness were asked about their personal experiences, 17 percent of those with schizophrenia and 6 percent with a major depressive disorder reported feeling discriminated against by the police (Thornicroft et al., 2009). Other studies showed from 10 to 20 percent of people with mental illness reported feeling discriminated against by police (Corker et al., 2013; Svensson, Stjernswärd, & Hansson, 2013).

What about police attitudes? One study found that a large percent of the police viewed those with mental illness as dangerous, requiring hospitalization, and unable to recover (Psarra et al., 2008). Vignette studies have found that police officers see individuals with schizophrenia as less responsible, more dangerous, more worthy of help, and far less likely to take action for victims and witnesses who have a mental illness (Watson, Corrigan, & Ottati, 2003, 2004).

Stigma and Substance Use Disorders

Problems with criminal behavior and mental illness are often intertwined with that of substance use and addiction, which engenders a unique set of prejudices and discrimination. The stigma of addiction is in some ways socially, politically, and/or legally sanctioned in most places around the world. As a result, what seems to be an easy mantra of the stigma movement for mental health — erase its effects to promote recovery — is muddied for addiction, and we describe reasons for this below.

Discrimination against People with Addictions Is Legal

Unlike mental illness, many of the discriminations against those with addictions are legally sanctioned. Although the justice system is often concerned about the role of mental illness in criminal guilt and fitness to stand trial, it mostly protects the civil rights of people with serious mental illness (Callard et al., 2012). It is much less concerned for people with substance use disorders (SUDs). Use of controlled substances, including cocaine, heroin, marijuana, and some medications such as amphetamines, opioids and barbiturates without a prescription, is illegal in most of the U.S. Penalties for illicit use can vary from monetary fines to extended prison terms. Even more benign substances such as alcohol and tobacco are legally controlled in most places; for example, people under age 18 to 21, depending on jurisdiction, are not permitted to purchase or use these substances. Supervisors can reprimand employees found to be under the influence of alcohol or other psychoactive substances while at work.

This kind of stigma is likely worsened by criminalization where drug use is conflated with felonious behavior. In the Western world, pairing criminal behavior with addiction got a significant boost with the launch of the War on Drugs by the Nixon administration. The war's effects were significant; one in every 136 adults was incarcerated for drug possession in 2005 (Peterson, 2005). Although public sentiment about criminalizing drugs has waned, research shows people who endorse criminal penalties for drug use still endorse the stigma of people labeled with SUD (West, Yanos, & Mulay, 2014).

Addiction stigma also impacts interpretations of civil law. Consider, for example, reasonable accommodation requirements in the Americans with Disabilities Act (ADA). Reasonable accommodations are guaranteed under the law to help people with disabilities, for example, people in wheelchairs, or those with serious mental illness, successfully complete work-related duties so they can accomplish vocational goals. ADA protections for addictions are comparatively limited. Individuals with addictions do qualify for ADA protections if they have been successfully treated and are no longer engaged in the illegal use of drugs or are currently engaged in a treatment program and not using illegal drugs. Relapse leads to trouble, however. Employers are not violating these acts when disciplining employees, including by denying promotions and termination, who are currently engaged in the illegal use of drugs. The ADA and reasonable adjustments do not falter for the person with mental illness experiencing recurring symptoms.

Stigma Is Used to Promote Prevention

Stigma may be purposefully incorporated into health communication strategies to promote substance use prevention in two ways (Schomerus et al., 2011). The first way is by stressing the criminal-addiction connection. For example, health campaigns have paired drug use with illegal or unethical activity. The United Nations established the Office for Drug Control and Crime Prevention (ODCCP) to emphasize this connection. Similarly, Mothers Against Drunk Driving (MADD) builds much of its public awareness campaign by pairing alcohol and drug use with horrific scenes of car accidents and death. An ad that aired during the 2002 Super Bowl compared drug use to terrorism by connecting illegal drug buys to the extremists who operate the narco-market beneath them.

The second way is through the use of public service announcements (PSAs), which seek to promote prevention by tying drug use to poor health (Guttman & Salmon, 2004), an especially popular approach for youth programs. The ODCCP released a 30-second PSA in 2010 that followed four young people whose health deteriorates as they use drugs. The 2014 Worlds AIDS campaign targeted 15- to 24-year-olds by tying drug use to contracting HIV.

Some Interventions Worsen Self-Stigma

Twelve step and some other programs address SUDs by encouraging members to recognize their absence of power vis-à-vis addictions, admit character defects that result from this powerlessness, and make amends to those they have wronged. This partly corresponds with disease models that frame people as unable to control substance use because of biological predispositions (Acker, 1993) and may unintentionally promote self-stigma. In mental illness research, self-stigma is often found as an unintended effect of presenting disease models, often diminishing feelings of self-worth among people. Recovery models have offset these effects with two models of recovery emerging: outcome and process

(Ralph & Corrigan, 2005). Outcome models describe recovery as a state where symptoms are remitted, disabilities overcome, and goals achieved. Process models view recovery as a journey underscored by hope where people pursue personally defined goals regardless of symptoms and disabilities. Recovery reintroduced hope and optimism into discussion of serious mental illnesses, in the process becoming a fundamental tool in tearing down the stigma of mental illness.

Definitions of recovery from addictions are a bit more complex (White, 2010). Recovery is a continuum for mental illness, but it is often presented as a clear end state, namely, abstinence, for disease models of addiction. Failure to abstain may promote self-stigma. Beliefs about achieving goals may vary depending on whether someone assumes abstinence must be accomplished first. Although recovery from mental illness is grounded in hope, recovery from addiction sometimes begins with hopelessness and hitting bottom for many programs adopting a disease model. Recovery from addiction, according to this perspective, may only occur when people recognize their powerlessness in the face of substances.

This sense of powerlessness suggests different perspectives on self-determination between the mental health and addiction communities. Fundamental to mental health are systems that empower people to define life goals for themselves and then select interventions that help them achieve those goals. Self-determination may be tempered by twelve step and other addiction programs with concerns about impulsivity, where people are warned not to be fooled by aspirations in the face of their past failures (Stevens et al., 2014).

The Goal of Erasing Stigma Is Less Clear

Social injustices such as stigma rally progressives with a clarion call to erase them. And while the end is difficult to achieve and decades in the making, the goal is easy to understand. Stop the stigma. Stop the stereotypes, prejudices and discrimination against people with mental illness. Rarely are mental health and policy advocates derailed by misunderstanding the goal.

Not so for addictions. Because some stigmas are legally or socially sanctioned, changing them becomes a much more complex task. In mental health, advocates just say no to stigma. In addictions, stopping it is not so easy. Nor are there easy changes to right the ship of anti-stigma efforts for addictions. Criminalizing addiction might be stigmatizing, but no easy consensus will be found in decreasing stigma by breaking the connection between SUDs and crime. Using stigma to promote prevention might seem contrary to public health intentions, but we doubt activists will agree this tool should be eliminated. Unlike mental health, the stigma of addiction does not target an irrefutable goal for social advocates. Might the status quo of addiction stigma serve some positive function? As advocates of social change, this is an exquisitely complex question and one that advocates, providers, and people with lived experience need to consider in conjunction with the benefit of empirical research.

Conclusion

Stigma, the combination of stereotypes, prejudices, and discrimination, exists in many forms including public stigma, self-stigma, label avoidance, and structural stigma. There are several ways in which stigma uniquely harms the opportunities of people with serious mental illness involved in the criminal justice system. One of the most prominent stereotypes of individuals with mental illness is the idea that they are inherently dangerous or violent, even though epidemiological investigation reveals that such claims are exaggerated. In order reduce stigma and by extension, its deleterious effects, anti-stigma programs need to become an important element of service systems as they seek to improve interventions and opportunities for people with mental illness.

Discussion Questions

1. In what ways can service systems better incorporate anti-stigma perspectives?

2. What possible positive functions does the status quo of addiction stigma serve, if any?

3. How can we use what we know about stigma to help reduce the incidence of future senseless crimes?

4. What important issues should be considered for future researchers working towards the development of a meaningful measure of sin?

References

Acker, C. J. (1993). Stigma or legitimation? A historical examination of the social potentials of addiction disease models. *Journal of Psychoactive Drugs*, *25*, 193–205.

Barry, C. L., McGinty, E. E., Vernick, J. S., & Webster, D. W. (2013). After Newtown: Public opinion on gun policy and mental illness. *New England Journal of Medicine*, *368*, 1077–1081.

Biggs. J. (1955). *The guilty mind: Psychiatry and the law of homicide*. Baltimore, MD: Johns Hopkins University Press.

Boldry, J. G., Gaertner, L., & Quinn, J. (2007). Measuring the measures: A meta-analytic investigation of the measures of outgroup homogeneity. *Group Processes & Intergroup Relations*, *10*, 157–178.

Callard, F., Sartorius, N., Arboleda-Flórez, J., Bartlett, P., Helmchen, H., Stuart, H., … & Thornicroft, G. (2012). *Mental illness, discrimination and the law: Fighting for social justice*. Hoboken, NJ: Wiley Blackwell.

Cleary, K. K., & Prescott, K. (2015). The use of physical restraints in acute and long-term care: An updated review of the evidence, regulations, ethics, and legality. *The Journal of Acute Care Physical Therapy*, *6*, 8–15.

Clement, S., Schauman, O., Graham, T., Maggioni, F., Evans-Lacko, S., Bezborodovs, N., … & Thornicroft, G. (2015). What is the impact of mental health-related stigma on help-seeking? A systematic review of quantitative and qualitative studies. *Psychological Medicine*, *45*, 11–27.

Corker, E., Hamilton, S., Henderson, C., Weeks, C., Pinfold, V., Rose, D., … & Thornicroft, G. (2013). Experiences of discrimination among people using mental health services in England 2008–2011. *The British Journal of Psychiatry*, *202*, 58–63.

Corrigan, P. W., Bink, A. B., Schmidt, A., Jones, N., & Rusch, N. (2016). What is the impact of self-stigma? Loss of self-respect and the "why try" effect. *Journal of Mental Health*, *25*, 10–15.

Corrigan, P. W., Larson, J. E., & Rusch, N. (2009). Self-stigma and the "why try" effect: Impact on life goals and evidence-based practices. *World Psychiatry*, *8*, 75–81.

Corrigan, P. W., Markowitz, F. E., & Watson, A. C. (2004). Structural levels of mental illness stigma and discrimination. *Schizophrenia Bulletin*, *30*, 481–491.

Corrigan, P. W., & Penn, D. L. (1999). Lessons from social psychology on discrediting psychiatric stigma. *American Psychologist*, *54*, 765–776.

Corrigan, P. W., Powell, K. J., & Michaels, P. J. (2013). The effects of news stories on the stigma of mental illness. *The Journal of Nervous and Mental Disease*, *201*, 179–182.

Corrigan, P. W., Powell, K. J., & Rusch, N. (2012). How does stigma affect work in people with serious mental illnesses? *Psychiatric Rehabilitation Journal*, *35*, 381–384.

Corrigan, P. W., & Rao, D. (2012). On the self-stigma of mental illness: Stages, disclosure, and strategies for change. *The Canadian Journal of Psychiatry*, *57*, 464–469.

Corrigan, P. W., River, L. P., Lundin, R. K., Wasowski, K. U., Campion, J., Mathisen, J., ... & Kubiak, A. (1999). Predictors of participation in campaigns against mental illness stigma. *Journal of Nervous and Mental Disease*, *187*, 378–380.

Corrigan, P. W., Watson, A. C., & Barr, L. (2006). The self-stigma of mental illness: Implications for self-esteem and self-efficacy. *Journal of Social and Clinical Psychology*, *25*, 875–884.

Corrigan, P. W., Watson, A. C., Gracia, G., Slopen, N., Rasinski, K., & Hall, L. L. (2005). Newspaper stories as measures of structural stigma. *Psychiatric Services*, *56*, 551–556.

Corrigan, P. W., Watson, A. C., Warpinski, A. C., & Garcia, G. (2004). Implications of educating the public on mental illness, violence, and stigma. *Psychiatric Services*, *55*, 577–580.

Crocker, J., Major, B., & Steele, C. (1998). Social stigma. In D. T. Gilbert, S. T. Fiske, & G. Lindzey (Eds.), *The handbook of social psychology* (4th ed., Vol. II, pp. 504–553). Boston: McGraw Hill.

Drapalski, A. L., Lucksted, A., Perrin, P. B., Aakre, J. M., Brown, C. H., DeForge, B. R., & Boyd, J. E. (2013). A model of internalized stigma and its effects on people with mental illness. *Psychiatric Services*, *64*, 264–269.

Draper, W. R., Reid, C. A., & McMahon, B. T. (2011). Workplace discrimination and the perception of disability. *Rehabilitation Counseling Bulletin*, *55*, 29–37.

Earnshaw, V. A., & Quinn, D. M. (2012). The impact of stigma in healthcare on people living with chronic illnesses. *Journal of Health Psychology*, *17*, 157–168.

Elbogen, E. B., & Johnson, S. C. (2009). The intricate link between violence and mental disorder: Results from the National Epidemiologic Survey on Alcohol and Related Conditions. *Archives of General Psychiatry*, *66*, 152–161.

Fazel, S., Singh, J. P., Doll, H., & Grann, M. (2012). Use of risk assessment instruments to predict violence and antisocial behaviour in 73 samples involving 24,827 people: Systematic review and meta-analysis. *BMJ: British Medical Journal, 345*, 1–12.

Guttman, N., & Salmon, C. T. (2004). Guilt, fear, stigma and knowledge gaps: Ethical issues in public health communication interventions. *Bioethics, 18*, 531–552.

Hannon, L., & DeFronzo, J. (1998). The truly disadvantaged, public assistance, and crime. *Social Problems, 45*, 383–392.

Hatzenbuehler, M. L., & Link, B. G. (2014). Introduction to the special issue on structural stigma and health. *Social Science & Medicine, 103*, 1–6.

Hatzenbuehler, M. L., Phelan, J. C., & Link, B. G. (2013). Stigma as a fundamental cause of population health inequalities. *American Journal of Public Health, 103*, 813–821.

Hawthorne, W. B., Folsom, D. P., Sommerfeld, D. H., Lanouette, N. M., Lewis, M., Aarons, G. A., … & Jeste, D. V. (2012). Incarceration among adults who are in the public mental health system: Rates, risk factors, and short-term outcomes. *Psychiatric Services, 63*, 26–32.

Heslop, L., Hartford, K., Rona, H., Stitt, L., & Schrecker, T. (2002). Trends in police contacts with persons with serious mental illness in London, Ontario. Paper presented at the First Annual Conference on Police/Mental Health Liaison, Montreal, Canada.

Jussim, L., Nelson, T. E., Manis, M., & Soffin, S. (1995). Prejudice, stereotypes, and labeling effects: Sources of bias in person perception. *Journal of Personality and Social Psychology, 68*, 228–246.

Kelly, B. D. (2006). The power gap: Freedom, power and mental illness. *Social Science & Medicine, 63*, 2118–2128.

Klin, A., & Lemish, D. (2008). Mental disorders stigma in the media: Review of studies on production, content, and influences. *Journal of Health Communication, 13*, 434–449.

Krueger, J. (1996). Personal beliefs and cultural stereotypes about racial characteristics. *Journal of Personality and Social Psychology, 71*, 536–548.

Link, B., Cullen, F., Struening, E., Shrout, P., & Dohrenwend, B. (1989). A modified labeling theory approach to mental disorders: An empirical assessment. *American Sociological Review, 54*, 400–423.

Livingston, J. D., & Boyd, J. E. (2010). Correlates and consequences of internalized stigma for people living with mental illness: A systematic review and meta-analysis. *Social Science & Medicine, 71*, 2150–2161.

Moore, K. E., Tangney, J. P., & Stuewig, J. B. (2016). The self-stigma process in criminal offenders. *Stigma and Health, 1,* 206–214.

Mowrer, O. H. (1960). "Sin": The lesser of two evils. *American Psychologist, 15,* 301–304.

Oexle, N., Rüsch, N., Viering, S., Wyss, C., Seifritz, E., Xu, Z., & Kawohl, W. (2017). Self-stigma and suicidality: A longitudinal study. *European Archives of Psychiatry and Clinical Neuroscience, 267,* 359–361.

Penttilä, M., Jääskeläinen, E., Hirvonen, N., Isohanni, M., & Miettunen, J. (2014). Duration of untreated psychosis as predictor of long-term outcome in schizophrenia: Systematic review and meta-analysis. *The British Journal of Psychiatry, 205,* 88–94.

Peterson, K. (2005, January 14). National Reforms Needed to Help Inmates Return Home. The Pew Charitable Trusts. Retrieved from http://www.pewtrusts.org/en/research-andanalysis/blogs/stateline/2005/01/14/national-reforms-needed-to-help-inmates-return-home.

Phelan, J. C., Link, B. G., Stueve, A., & Pescosolido, B. A. (2000). Public conceptions of mental illness in 1950 and 1996: What is mental illness and is it to be feared? *Journal of Health and Social Behavior, 41,* 188–207.

Pietrzak, R. H., Johnson, D. C., Goldstein, M. B., Malley, J. C., & Southwick, S. M. (2009). Perceived stigma and barriers to mental health care utilization among OEF-OIF veterans. *Psychiatric Services, 60,* 1118–1122.

Psarra, V., Sestrini, M., Santa, Z., Petsas, D., Gerontas, A., Garnetas, C., & Kontis, K. (2008). Greek police officers' attitudes towards the mentally ill. *International Journal of Law and Psychiatry, 31,* 77–85.

Pugh, T., Hatzenbuehler, M., & Link, B. (2015, August). Structural stigma and mental illness. Commissioned Paper for Committee on the Science of Changing Behavioral Health Social Norms. Retrieved from http://sites.nationalacademies.org/cs/groups/dbassesite/documents/webpage/dbasse_170045.pdf.

Ralph, R. O., & Corrigan, P. W. (2005). *Recovery in mental illness: Broadening our understanding of wellness.* Washington, D.C.: American Psychological Association.

Schomerus, G., Lucht, M., Holzinger, A., Matschinger, H., Carta, M. G., & Angermeyer, M. C. (2011). The stigma of alcohol dependence compared with other mental disorders: A review of population studies. *Alcohol and Alcoholism, 46,* 105–112.

Sharaf, A. Y., Ossman, L. H., & Lachine, O. A. (2012). A cross-sectional study of the relationships between illness insight, internalized stigma, and suicide risk in individuals with schizophrenia. *International Journal of Nursing Studies, 49,* 1512–1520.

Shaw, M., Hodgkins, P., Caci, H., Young, S., Kahle, J., Woods, A. G., & Arnold, L. E. (2012). A systematic review and analysis of long-term outcomes in attention deficit hyperactivity disorder: Effects of treatment and non-treatment. *BMC Medicine, 10,* 99–112.

Stevens, L., Verdejo-García, A., Goudriaan, A. E., Roeyers, H., Dom, G., & Vanderplasschen, W. (2014). Impulsivity as a vulnerability factor for poor addiction treatment outcomes: A review of neurocognitive findings among individuals with substance use disorders. *Journal of Substance Abuse Treatment, 47,* 58–72.

Stuart, H. (2006). Media portrayal of mental illness and its treatments. *CNS Drugs, 20,* 99–106.

Svensson, B., Stjernswärd, S., & Hansson, L. (2013). Training in mental health first aid: An effect study in two counties. (Translated from Swedish). Lund: CEPI.

Swanson, J. W., Holzer, C. E., Ganju, V. K., & Jono, R. T. (1990). Violence and psychiatric disorder in the community: Evidence from the Epidemiologic Catchment Area surveys. *Psychiatric Services, 41,* 761–770.

Swanson, J. W., Swartz, M. S., Van Dorn, R. A., Elbogen, E. B., Wagner, H. R., Rosenhack, R. A., … Liberman, J. A. (2006). A national study of violent behavior in persons with schizophrenia. *Archives of General Psychiatry, 63,* 490–499.

Thornicroft, G., Brohan, E., Rose, D., Sartorius, N., Leese, M., & INDIGO Study Group. (2009). Global pattern of experienced and anticipated discrimination against people with schizophrenia: A cross-sectional survey. *The Lancet, 373,* 408–415.

Torrey, E. F. (2002). Stigma and violence. *Psychiatric Services, 53,* 1179.

Treatment Advocacy Center. (2016). Serious mental illness and homicide. Retrieved from http://www.treatmentadvocacycenter.org/storage/documents/backgrounders/smi-and-homicide.pdf.

Tversky, A., & Kahneman, D. (1974). Judgment under uncertainty: Heuristics and biases. *Science, 185,* 1124–1131.

Varghese, F. P., Hardin, E. E., Bauer, R. L., & Morgan, R. D. (2010). Attitudes toward hiring offenders: The roles of criminal history, job qualifications, and race. *International Journal of Offender Therapy and Comparative Criminology, 54,* 769–782.

Visher, C. A., Debus-Sherrill, S. A., & Yahner, J. (2011). Employment after prison: A longitudinal study of former prisoners. *Justice Quarterly, 28,* 698–718.

Wallace, C., Mullen, P., Burgess, P., Palmer, S., Ruschena, D., & Browne, C. (1998). Serious criminal offending and mental disorder: Case linkage study. *The British Journal of Psychiatry, 172*, 477–484.

Watson, A. C., Corrigan, P. W., & Ottati, V. (2003). Police responses to persons with mental illness: Does the label matter? *The Journal of the American Academy of Psychiatry and the Law, 32*, 378–385.

Watson, A. C., Corrigan, P. W., & Ottati, V. (2004). Police officers' attitudes toward and decisions about persons with mental illness. *Psychiatric Services, 55*, 49–53.

Weiner, B. (2006). *Social motivation, justice, and the moral emotions: An attributional approach.* Mahwah, NJ: Erlbaum.

West, M. L., Yanos, P. T., & Mulay, A. L. (2014). Triple stigma of forensic psychiatric patients: Mental illness, race, and criminal history. *International Journal of Forensic Mental Health, 13*, 75–90.

White, W. L. (2010). Nonclinical addiction recovery support services: History, rationale, models, potentials, and pitfalls. *Alcoholism Treatment Quarterly, 28*, 256–272.

4

Sexual Offending and Mental Illness

Li-Wen Grace Lee

Introduction

The topic of sexual offenses inspires intense reactions and conflicting points of view, veering from attitudes that blame victims to those that vilify offenders. For example, a 2016 study reviewed over 4,000 comments posted to 52 rape-related articles published in four large newspapers and determined that over 25 percent of the comments either blamed the victim or supported the alleged perpetrator (Zaleski, Gunderson, Baes, Estupinian, & Vergara, 2016). In contrast, others focus on the underreporting of sexual offenses and stigmatization of victims (National Research Council, 2014). Concurrent with these perspectives is the stigma faced by sexual offenders. In correctional settings, sexual offenders are more likely to be stigmatized by correctional officers and their inmate peers alike than any other type of offender (Ricciardelli, 2013). After incarceration, sex offenders may have registry mandates and residency restrictions in the community, among other requirements that other offenders do not experience (Tewksbury, 2005). Additionally, almost half of the states and the federal government have sexually violent predator (SVP) laws that allow for ongoing civil commitment of sexual offenders after incarceration.

The evolution of SVP laws is based on the premise that some sexual offenders are mentally disordered and can benefit from treatment and that treatment is necessary for public safety. The legislatively mandated role of state mental health systems in the provision of sexual offender treatment has led to attention to the issues and controversies surrounding the topic of mental illness and sexual offending. This chapter explores the relationship between mental illness and sexual offending and how civil commitment under sexually violent predator statutes is implemented.

Relationship between Mental Illness and Sexual Offending

Mental illness and violence have a complex relationship. Public perception has long been that mental illness and violence are closely connected, while the mental health profession has viewed the two as frequently unrelated. Research has shown that serious mental illness contributes to only 3–5 percent of violence in the general population (Friedman, 2006), and that persons diagnosed with mental illness are more likely to be victims of violent acts rather than the perpetrators (Choe, 2008). As summarized by Monahan (1992), even if most violence is not attributable to individuals with mental illness, the reality of the relationship between mental illness and violence is nuanced—with a modest, but consistent, elevation in the risk for violence associated with mental illness. That relationship is further exaggerated when substance use is also present.

Sexual offending, as a form of violence, also has a complex association with mental illness. As with other forms of violence, sexual offenses have not been generally attributed to individuals with serious mental illness (Harris, Veysey, Ragusa, & Lurigio, 2010). Consistent with research about non-sexual violence, individuals with severe mental illness have been found to be at substantially increased risk for becoming victims, rather than the perpetrators, of sexual violence (Khalifeh et al., 2015). The connection between mental illness and sexual offending can be divided into two categories. On the one hand, there is the problem of individuals diagnosed with disorders categorized as traditional mental illnesses and who also commit sexual offenses. These illnesses are those diagnoses for which the mental health system has traditionally provided treatment, including schizophrenia, major depression, and bipolar disorder. The other category concerns the question of whether individuals, who may not suffer from traditional mental illness but who pose an increased risk of committing sexual offenses for a variety of other reasons, might still be considered as suffering from some form of mental disorder. The use of the term disorder rather than illness in SVP statutes is significant. SVP statutes allow for consideration of a more expanded list of conditions than are typically eligible for traditional civil commitment.

In the literature, sexual offending is described as resulting from the interplay of sexual interests, distorted attitudes and beliefs, problems with socio-affective management, and difficulty with self-management (Thornton, 2002). Research on the rate of traditional mental illness among sexual offenders has yielded variable findings. Some articles cite figures indicating that most sexual offenders do not suffer from mental illness. For example, a meta-analysis of 82 recidivism studies found that deviant sexual preferences and antisocial orientation were the major predictors of sexual recidivism, rather than mental illness (Hanson & Morton-Bourgon, 2005). Another meta-analysis reviewed several studies about the prevalence of mental illness among incarcerated sexual offenders and concluded that a relatively low percentage of sex offenders meet criteria for serious mental illness, but also noted there were relatively high rates of dysthymia, anxiety disorders, and depression (Harris et al., 2010).

Kingston, Olver, Harris, Wong, and Bradford (2015) reviewed 401 incarcerated sexual offenders receiving sex offender treatment and 586 outpatient sexual offenders. They found that mental health diagnoses were not predictive of recidivism, but substance use disorders and some personality disorders showed some predictive validity. Alden, Brennan, Hodgins, and Mednick (2007) examined a Danish birth cohort of over 350,000 individuals and found that men with hospitalization for a psychotic disorder were three times more likely to have been arrested for a non-physically aggressive sex offense, when compared with men who had never been psychiatrically hospitalized. There was associated increase in risk for physically aggressive sex offenses. However, there was a six-fold increase in risk for physically aggressive sexual offenses when psychotic disorder was co-morbid with substance use disorder or personality disorder.

Despite the lack of clarity around the exact rate of traditional mental illness among sexual offenders and around the correlation between the presence of traditional mental illness and recidivism, the presence of serious mental illness is still an important clinical factor to consider in the treatment and management of sexual offenders. When mental illness has been diagnosed, the connection between the mental illness and sexual offending, specific to the individual, must be explored. Here, the construct used in considering lack of criminal responsibility due to mental illness for non-sexual offenses also applies. To understand this, the nature of mental illness must be considered.

The Nature of Mental Illness and Sexual Offending

The experience of mental illness, even among persons who meet criteria for the same diagnosis, is extremely variable and dependent on individual characteristics. Consider, for example, the diagnosis of schizophrenia. The fifth edition of the *Diagnostic and Statistical Manual of Mental Disorders*, the *DSM-5*, lists criteria that must be met for schizophrenia to be diagnosed (American Psychiatric Association, 2013). Among those criteria is a requirement that at least one of the following three be present: delusions, hallucinations, or disorganized speech. As a result of these distinctions within a given diagnostic label, among individuals diagnosed with schizophrenia, some, but not all, will experience hallucinations. Others may experience delusions but not hallucinations, or both. Yet others may not have prominent delusions or hallucinations but, rather, experience significant disorganization in their thought process. Some individuals diagnosed with schizophrenia may experience all three symptoms. The practical significance of this is that the presence of a mental health diagnosis is not enough to draw specific conclusions about how that diagnosis affects a particular person.

Additional variables are the degree of severity and the manner in which symptoms manifest. Some individuals may internally experience relatively minor and un-intrusive symptoms and thus be able to manage those symptoms without any outward manifestations. A person who hears voices, for example, may be able to attribute auditory hallucinations to their illness and ignore those voices. Another person who hears voices may feel compelled to speak back to them or even follow instructions from those voices. Symptom frequency and chronicity can also vary, as can responsiveness to treatment. Some persons with mental illness experience symptoms rarely, or only occasionally, or only under certain circumstances. They may be highly functioning members of society. Others may experience symptoms frequently. Some individuals respond well to conventional treatment; others struggle with symptoms of mental illness that persist despite treatment.

Another area for consideration are external stressors that contribute to symptom exacerbation. Stressors such as significant personal loss, difficulty meeting basic needs, employment challenges, physical health problems, and a variety of other problems can result in loss of mental health stability or exacerbated symptoms. Co-morbid conditions such as substance use or personality disorder can confound the symptom presentation and make accurate diagnosis difficult.

With criminal responsibility in sexual offenses, all these factors come into play. The mere determination of a diagnosable mental illness does not necessarily mean that the mental illness is causal to all subsequent behavior. When a sexual offender has a diagnosed mental illness, the analysis includes inquiry into the symptoms that were present around the time of the offense, and whether the symptoms are causal, indirectly contributory, or only coincidental to the offense. Serious mental illness, primary sexual deviance, and underlying character pathology are three areas to be considered for their contributions to sexual offending behavior (Rotter, 2007).

Examples of mental illness directly causing or contributing to sexual offending behavior include sex offenses committed as a response to psychotic symptoms, such as auditory hallucinations commanding the individual to perform particular actions, or a delusional belief requiring a specific behavior. Another possibility is hypersexuality associated with bipolar disorder. Also, during a manic phase, an individual with bipolar disorder might suffer from psychotic symptoms such as hallucinations or delusions. Symptoms of mental illness might be indirectly contributory by impairing judgment or self-control, thereby leading to the individual acting upon impulses they would otherwise have controlled. In other instances, a sexual offender who has a serious mental illness might have been without active symptoms of illness at the time of offense, in which case the mental illness would not be considered as having a role in the sexual offending behavior. It is also possible that the individual experienced symptoms of mental illness around the time of the offense, but those symptoms had no relationship with the offense itself.

Regardless of whether symptoms of mental illness played any role in the commission of a sexual offense, it is possible that the presence of mental illness may interfere with sexual offender treatment. Psychotic symptoms may impede rational understanding and participation in treatment. Depressive or anxiety symptoms may interfere with motivation. As a result, detection of mental illness and accurate diagnosis is critical to sexual offender treatment. Additionally, the presence of serious mental illness does not rule out co-morbid personality disorder, substance use disorder, or paraphilia, or any of the other risk factors that contribute to sexual offending among individuals who do not have a mental illness.

Civil Commitment of Sexually Dangerous Persons

All states have civil commitment laws for the psychiatric hospitalization of persons with serious mental illness. Asylums for persons with mental illness began appearing in the United States in the early part of the 1800s (Testa,

2010). By the 1960s, asylums were being criticized as ineffective and run-down, and new medications were emerging with the potential to treat the symptoms of mental illness more effectively than ever before. These factors led to the emergence of the concept of deinstitutionalization, or the relocation of patients for appropriate care in the community under more humane circumstances.[1] One side effect of deinstitutionalization was the movement from a need-for-treatment model for inpatient care to a model where both the presence of mental illness and dangerousness due to that mental illness had to be determined to justify civil commitment (Testa, 2010).

While most states have required an element of dangerousness for involuntary civil commitment, sexual offenders without traditional mental illnesses have not typically been considered as qualifying for commitment under standard civil commitment laws. Sexual offender commitment laws, also called civil commitment of sexually dangerous persons or sexually violent predators, have a different standard for commitment. These laws are, in fact, an acknowledgement that individuals with such predispositions do not fit traditional inpatient settings, hence the concept of creating specific inpatient settings that can address sex offender treatment-specific needs.

These laws originated in the 1930s, but for various reasons, states that passed such statutes, for the most part, either eventually removed them or did not use them to a significant degree. This changed in 1990, when Washington State passed what is considered the first of a second generation of sexual offender commitment laws. Twenty states and the District of Columbia have passed sexual offender commitment laws. These laws allow for indefinite civil commitment that begins after completion of a sentence for the conviction of a sexual offense. Besides conviction, there must also be a "mental disorder" or "mental condition" that predisposes the individual to re-offend, and a high likelihood of re-offense due to serious difficulty controlling behavior (Jumper, Babula, & Casbon, 2012).

Concerns about sexual offender commitment statutes included the interpretation of these statutes as ultimately seeking to extend punishment of sexual offenders and protect society, an issue thought to be better addressed by changing sentencing practices. Additionally, there was concern about the potential to misuse psychiatric diagnoses. The American Psychiatric Association argued that "sexual predator status is based on a vague and circular determination that an offender has a 'mental abnormality'" (Zonana et al., 1999, p. 174). The cost

---

1. For more on deinstitutionalization and other aspects of historical treatment of persons with mental illness, see that chapter in *The Criminalization of Mental Illness*.

of indefinite confinement for a potentially expanding population was also cited as a significant problem.

Despite concerns, these laws have withstood legal challenge over the years. *In re Young and Cunningham*, in 1993, affirmed that sexually violent predator (SVP) commitment laws qualify as civil, and not criminal, proceedings because the stated goal is treatment rather than punishment. Andre Brigham Young was incarcerated after conviction for rape and had a history of committing other rapes. One day prior to release, the state filed for commitment under the Washington sexually violent predator statute. Vance Russell Cunningham was convicted of an unrelated rape, and he also had a history of committing prior sexual offenses. In Cunningham's case, the state filed for commitment several months after he had been released from prison. Young and Cunningham argued that the statute violated the double jeopardy clause and the prohibition against ex post facto laws. The Washington Supreme Court concluded that the statute is civil rather than criminal and that double jeopardy and ex post facto prohibitions did not apply, noting that commitment requires a mental disorder leading to the commission of violent sexual offenses. The Court further noted that committed persons are treated in a psychiatric facility and released as soon as they are no longer dangerous.

Kansas v. Hendricks, a Supreme Court ruling in 1997, reaffirmed that SVP laws are civil and can be used to segregate those who are dangerous to the public and cannot control themselves. Leroy Hendricks was convicted of taking indecent liberties with two 13-year-old boys and incarcerated. Shortly before release, the state sought to civilly confine Hendricks as a sexually violent predator under the Kansas SVP Act. During his trial to determine whether he qualified as a sexually violent predator, Hendricks testified about his lengthy history of sexual offenses against children. He further admitted to abusing children whenever not confined, and while he expressed the hope to not offend against children again, he stated that the only guarantee was "to die." He agreed with the diagnosis of pedophilia, acknowledged that he was not cured, and further opined that the treatment was ineffective. He was found to be a sexually violent predator and to have a mental abnormality qualifying him for confinement under the act. Hendricks claimed that the act violated the due process, double jeopardy, and ex-post facto clauses of the Constitution.

The Supreme Court did not agree, instead ruling that the definition of mental abnormality in the act satisfied substantive due process requirements, in that the act required a pre-commitment finding of dangerousness linked to a mental abnormality. By using the term "mental abnormality," the Kansas statute did not rely on risk of dangerousness alone but instead, "narrows the class of persons eligible for confinement to those who are unable to control their dangerousness" (*Kansas v. Hendricks*, 1997). The Court did not require the specific term "mental illness." The Court further found that lack of effective treatment did not make the act unconstitutional. Double jeopardy and ex-post facto prohibitions were not violated, as the act was again affirmed to be civil in nature, with therapeutic rather than punitive goals.

The Supreme Court returned to the Kansas SVP Act in a 2002 case, *Kansas v. Crane*. Michael Crane was convicted of a sexual offense, and the state pursued civil commitment hearings under the Kansas SVP Act. He was diagnosed with exhibitionism and antisocial personality disorder by a psychiatric witness for the state, and the trial court ordered his commitment without a finding regarding whether he could control his dangerous behavior. Crane's commitment was overturned on appeal, and Kansas subsequently argued that the interpretation of the Kansas Supreme Court that *Hendricks* always requires proof that a dangerous individual is completely unable to control his behavior is too rigid an interpretation.

The Supreme Court determined that complete lack of control was not necessary, but to distinguish offenders subject to civil commitment from those appropriately addressed exclusively through criminal proceedings, the presence of a serious mental disorder and a serious lack of ability to control behavior are necessary. Because lack of control is not demonstrable with "mathematical precision," the Court noted that serious difficulty controlling behavior was adequate. The Court recognized that there is not a clear distinction between purely "emotional" and "volitional" mental abnormality and further recognized that there may be overlap. The case was remanded to the lower court for review (*Kansas v. Crane*, 2002). *U.S. v. Comstock* (2010) addressed the federal statute. The question was whether the federal government has the authority to commit sexually dangerous persons and the Supreme Court determined that the federal government did have this authority.

Although the Supreme Court has confirmed the constitutionality of SVP statutes, in recent years, some state programs in Minnesota (*Karsjens v. Minnesota*, 2012) and Missouri (*Van Orden v Schafer*, 2015) have faced additional legal challenges. The Minnesota program was established by legislative action in 1994. In a 2011 report issued by Minnesota's Office of the Legislative Auditor, concerns were raised by the state about the Minnesota Sexual Offender Program (MSOP) (Nobles et al., 2011). The report noted that the number of committed sex offenders had quadrupled in the last decade and was expected to almost double in the next decade, and that of the 20 states with civil commitment statutes, Minnesota had the highest number of civilly committed sex offenders per capita. These numbers were attributed partly to the observation that MSOP had not discharged any individuals since its inception. Criticisms included lack of alternatives to high-security commitment and difficulties in maintaining a therapeutic environment. The report commented that, "Without releases, Minnesota is susceptible to lawsuits challenging the adequacy of the treatment program" (Nobles et al., 2011, p. ix).

As foreseen by the report from the Office of the Legislative Auditor, lawsuits did in fact follow, culminating in the decision in *Karsjens v. Jesson* (2015). In this decision, the federal court determined that MSOP did not reassess risk and did not provide a mechanism for committed individuals meeting discharge criteria to petition for release. Additionally, the court criticized MSOP for using a "no longer dangerous standard" rather than "no longer highly likely to reoffend" standard for release determinations, making the standard for release higher than that for commitment. The lack of discharges, in the court's opinion, indicated a lack of "meaningful relationship between treatment and custody." However, in January 2017, the United States Court of Appeals for the Eighth Circuit reversed the Minnesota decision and found no constitutional violation. At the time of this writing, the case was remanded to the district court (*Karsjens v. Johnson Piper*, 2017).

In the *Van Orden* decision, Missouri Sex Offender Rehabilitation and Treatment Services (SORTS) was found to violate due process by failing to provide risk assessments and release procedures (McCullough, 2015). In Missouri, similar to Minnesota, no committed sexual offenders had been released. In the courts' analyses in both *Karsjens* and *Van Orden*, this resulted in the programs becoming punitive lifetime detention, rather than civil commitment for treatment (McCullough, 2015).

Diagnostic Considerations

A criticism levied at SVP statutes is that the use of civil commitment to detain sexual offenders expands the traditional understanding of mental illnesses for which inpatient mental health care is appropriate. In *Hendricks*, the Court commented that "the term 'mental illness' is devoid of any talismanic significance. Not only do 'psychiatrists disagree widely and frequently on what constitutes mental illness, *Ake v. Oklahoma*, 470 U.S. 68, 81 (1985),' but the Court itself has used a variety of expressions to describe the mental condition of those properly subject to civil confinement" (*Kansas v. Hendricks*, 1997). The Court went on to say, "we have never required state legislatures to adopt any particular nomenclature in drafting civil commitment statutes" and noted that the definitions used by the states, in such statutes as those concerning criminal responsibility and competency, "do not fit precisely with the definitions employed by the medical community." In *Hendricks*, the Court sanctioned this difference in definition, saying, "Legal definitions, however, which must 'take into account such issues as individual responsibility ... and competency,' need not mirror those advanced by the medical profession."

The *DSM*, published by the American Psychiatric Association, establishes standard criteria for the classification of mental disorders and is an accepted standard among clinicians, regulatory agencies, health insurance companies, and the legal system. The fifth edition of the *DSM* (*DSM-5*) is the most recent revision of the *DSM* and was released in 2013. *DSM-5* contains a "Cautionary Statement for Forensic Use of *DSM-5*," stating, "it is important to note that the definition of mental disorder included in *DSM-5* was developed to meet the needs of clinicians, public health professionals, and research investigators rather than all of the technical needs of the courts and legal professionals" (APA, 2013).

Regardless of the distinctions between legal and medical definitions, the diagnostic opinions of mental health experts have been critical in the execution of sexual offender commitment statutes (First, 2008). As sexual offender commitment statutes seek to close a perceived loophole in standard civil commitment laws, it logically follows that those individuals who are committed under these statutes have a different diagnostic profile than those in traditional mental health settings. For example, Jumper et al. (2012) reviewed the diagnostic profiles of civilly committed sexual offenders in Illinois and compared the results with seven other states. The authors found significant variation in the rates of various diagnoses across states, but a consistent finding was that of high rates of paraphilic diagnoses, substance use disorders, and personality disorders, with low rates of psychotic disorders. A 2012 Sex Offender Civil Commitment Programs Network (SOCCPN) annual survey of states with civil commitment statutes found similar results. Seventeen states responded to the survey and indicated that high frequency diagnoses included pedophilia, paraphilia, antisocial personality disorder, personality disorder not otherwise specified, unspecified mood disorder, and substance use disorders. Additional diagnoses encountered in civil commitment programs, but occurring with relatively lower frequency, included sexual sadism, exhibitionism, borderline personality disorder, anxiety disorders, psychotic disorders, and intellectual disorders. Correlating with the high rates of pedophilic disorder diagnoses was data in the SOCCPN survey showing that, for those states responding to the survey, 59 percent of committed offenders had offended only against children, 29 percent offended against both children and adults, and only 17 percent offended against only adults (D'Orazio, 2012).

One criticism of the *DSM* is the "value judgment" historically associated with sexual disorders. Homosexuality was officially classified as a mental disorder in *DSM I*, published in 1952. It was not removed from the *DSM* until

1973. The timeline of homosexuality in relationship to *DSM* is seen as reflective of evolving cultural views and social tolerance, rather than a result of an advance in scientific knowledge. This example has been cited as casting doubt on other sexual disorders in the *DSM* and whether those conditions represent disorders at all. Regarding paraphilic disorders specifically, a critique has been that the not otherwise specified category offers a catch-all option that is overly expansive and vulnerable to abuse (Sreenivasan, 2003). Another criticism has been that not all individuals with a paraphilic disorder act on the paraphilia or necessarily cause harm to others, opening the possibility of over-pathologizing. And an additional criticism is that the paraphilic diagnoses allow for behavioral indicators and do not require knowledge of what the individual's motivations might be (Federoff, Di Gioacchino, & Murphy, 2013). A further challenge is diagnostic reliability. A study of diagnoses in SVP commitment in New Jersey found questionable agreement across various diagnoses, but fair agreement for diagnoses of pedophilia (Perillo, Spada, Calkins, & Jeglic, 2014).

Along with the cautionary statement in the *DSM-5* regarding the limitations of using *DSM* classification in legal proceedings, the revisions to paraphilic disorder from *DSM-IV-TR* to *DSM-5* carefully considered the forensic impact of any changes (First, 2014), as paraphilic disorder diagnoses are primarily seen in forensic settings. The presence of such a diagnosis may impact sentencing, categorization under community notification statutes, assignment to sexual offender treatment during incarceration, and confinement under sexual offender commitment statutes.

The *DSM-5* lists the diagnostic criteria for pedophilic disorder as follows:

A. Over a period of at least 6 months, recurrent, intense sexually arousing fantasies, sexual urges, or behavior involving sexual activity with a prepubescent child or children (generally age 13 years or younger).
B. The individual has acted on these sexual urges, or the sexual urges or fantasies cause marked distress or interpersonal difficulty.
C. The individual is at least age 16 years and at least 5 years older than the child or children in Criterion A.

There is a further notation that the criteria are not meant to include "an individual in late adolescence involved in an ongoing sexual relationship with a 12- or 13-year-old."

The *DSM-5* also provides criteria for Other Specified Paraphilic Disorder. In this disorder, "symptoms characteristic of a paraphilic disorder that cause clinically significant distress or impairment in social, occupational, or other important areas of functioning predominate but do not meet the full criteria for any of the disorders in the paraphilic disorders diagnostic class." Paraphilic disorder in the *DSM-5* was revised from the *DSM-IV-TR* criteria for paraphilia. The change in terminology reflects an attempt to differentiate between the mere presence of an atypical sexual arousal pattern and actual psychopathology. For a paraphilic disorder diagnosis to be made, criteria must be met for categories A, B, and C. By meeting these categories, a paraphilic disorder can only be diagnosed if the atypical sexual arousal pattern is persistent and intense and accompanied by clinically significant distress or impairment.

As noted, civil commitment under SVP statutes does not simply hinge upon a diagnosable sexual disorder alone. For example, not all individuals diagnosed with pedophilia qualify for civil commitment. Instead, there must be evidence of dangerousness and an inability to control their behavior, drawn in part from evidence of past sexual offenses.

In the contentious environment of civil commitment proceedings, individuals being evaluated under SVP statutes would not necessarily be expected to be forthcoming about their sexual thoughts and fantasies. In some ways, this is not entirely unique from traditional civil commitment assessments. There are individuals with traditional mental illness, such as schizophrenia, who experience delusional thinking or hallucinations, yet will not admit to these experiences due to an awareness that such an admission may be seen by others as evidence of illness. In these instances, outward behaviors resulting from these internally experienced symptoms might become the basis for establishing the presence of mental illness. By requiring a pattern of behavior rather than the single occurrence of one sexual offending behavior, and by examining that pattern of behavior for potential indicators of deviant sexual interests, it may be possible to argue that the diagnosis of a paraphilia is reasonable despite the lack of an admission of such from the person under evaluation, but the practice is debated among experts.

Also as noted, besides sexual disorders, personality disorders are commonly diagnosed in civilly committed sexual offenders. Personality disorders are described in the *DSM-5* as "enduring and inflexible pattern[s] of long duration that lead to significant distress or impairment." Under this definition, personality disorder is manifested across a range of settings and can affect cognition, emotional response, interpersonal functioning, and impulse control. Antisocial personality disorder is one such commonly diagnosed personality disorder among forensic populations. As with paraphilic disorders, a criticism has been that personality disorders is an expansive category without specific connection to sexual offending. It has been counter-argued that for some individuals, with an established history of repeated sexual offending, repeated offenses may be evidence of the personality disorder manifesting in a specific, idiosyncratic way for that individual.

According to the *DSM-5*, antisocial personality disorder "is a pervasive pattern of disregard for, and violation of, the rights of others that begins in childhood or early adolescence and continues into adulthood." For a diagnosis of antisocial personality disorder to be made, the *DSM-5* specifies that three or more of the following seven factors be present:

1. Failure to conform to social norms with respect to lawful behaviors, as indicated by repeatedly performing acts that are grounds for arrest.
2. Deceitfulness, as indicated by repeated lying, use of aliases, or conning others for personal profit or pleasure.
3. Impulsivity or failure to plan ahead.
4. Irritability and aggressiveness, as indicated by repeated physical fights or assaults.
5. Reckless disregard for safety of self or others.
6. Consistent irresponsibility, as indicated by repeated failure to sustain consistent work behavior or honor financial obligations.
7. Lack of remorse, as indicated by being indifferent to or rationalizing having hurt, mistreated, or stolen from another.

There are additional criteria that require that the individual be over the age of 18 at the time the diagnosis is made, that there is evidence of conduct disorder prior to age 15, and that the antisocial behavior does not occur only during the course of schizophrenia or bipolar disorder.

Borderline personality disorder is another personality disorder found in the civil commitment population. Whereas antisocial personality disorder criteria revolve around traits that lend themselves to criminal or dangerous behavior, borderline personality disorder is characterized by unstable interpersonal relationships, unstable sense of self, and unstable emotions. Like antisocial personality disorder, borderline personality disorder can also be associated with violent behavior, though the root causes and emotional states associated with that behavior are different. While antisocial personality disorder is not typically considered grounds for standard civil commitment for treatment of traditional mental illness, symptoms associated with borderline personality disorder may lead to acute crises necessitating relatively brief periods of inpatient treatment. In the civil commitment of sexual offenders with borderline personality disorder, however, commitment is not typically brief.

Whereas the connection between the paraphilic disorders to sexual offending behavior is direct, that between the personality disorders, impulse control disorders, and substance use disorders is not necessarily so clearly drawn. An indirect connection is that the emotional dysregulation, impulsivity, and disinhibition related to these diagnoses are the problems that render the individual to become more likely to act on inappropriate sexual impulses. While the overwhelming majority of individuals diagnosed with these classes of disorders do not sexually offend, for certain individuals, the symptoms may contribute to a pattern of sexual offenses. As noted, behavior may be motivated by a confluence of factors. For sexual offending, with or without the presence of a paraphilic disorder, the addition of one or more disorders that contributes to further emotional instability, impulsivity, or antisocial orientation may increase the likelihood of offending behaviors.

Treatment in Sexual Offender Commitment Programs

When sexual offending is directly and solely related to a traditional mental illness, adequate treatment of the underlying illness may be the primary therapy, with all the typical challenges associated with mental health treatment. Individuals suffering from mental illness who have committed some form of sexual offense are present across various mental health treatment settings. This category of sexual offender, however, is a small fraction of the larger sexual offender population.

For those other categories of sexual offenders found to have some form of mental abnormality, other forms of treatment to address sexual deviance may be necessary. Cognitive behavioral therapy (CBT) is a commonly used model in the delivery of therapy to sexual offenders (Gordon & Grubin, 2003). The goal is to help sexual offenders take responsibility for their behaviors and to develop the cognitive and behavioral skills to avoid the situations and patterns that lead to their offending behaviors. Most CBT in sexual offender treatment is delivered in group therapy where various aspects of sexual offending are discussed and examined in depth. Aversion therapy, also called arousal reconditioning, is a form of CBT used to reduce deviant sexual arousal. Aversion therapy may utilize noxious olfactory or gustatory stimuli to associate deviant arousal with negative sensations. Covert sensitization is another CBT tool intended to reduce deviant arousal. These various therapies may be delivered within a particular philosophy of treatment. One such example is the Risk-Need-Responsivity (RNR) model.[2] The RNR model employs three principles. The first, risk, emphasizes the importance of matching the level of service to the level of risk of reoffending. The second, need, concerns the assessment of

---

2. For more on the RNR model, see Chapter 2 in this reader.

criminogenic needs to be targeted in treatment. Finally, the third, responsivity, requires treatment to be tailored to the abilities of the offender (Andrews, 2007). Sex offender treatment programs may supplement RNR with the Good Lives Model (GLM) (Jackson, 2016). GLM is based on the idea that there are 11 primary human needs, or goods, and that offenders have developed maladaptive means of meeting those needs. By helping them meet those needs in more appropriate ways, offending is theoretically less likely.

When traditional mental illness is present but not the direct or sole cause of sexual offending, the symptoms must still be treated, either as a partial contributor to offending behaviors or as a potential destabilizer that may increase the possibility that an offender acts on deviant sexual interests (Kafka, 2012). Even in the absence of a traditional mental illness, however, psychotropic medication may be used for some individuals. Selective serotonin reuptake inhibitors (SSRIs) have been known to cause sexual dysfunction and have been used to reduce libido in sex offenders. SSRIs may also have a role in reducing the obsessive-compulsive aspects of sexual behaviors, as well as improving mood problems and impulsivity associated with offending. Degree of benefit is varied, and it is recommended that SSRI use, if indicated, should still be combined with psychotherapy (Briken, 2007; Garcia, Delavenne, Assumpcao, & Thibaut, 2013).

References to surgical castration can be found in literature regarding treatment of sexual behaviors. For example, Weinberger, Sreenivasan, Garrick, and Osran (2005) discussed the complexities involved with surgical castration. Psychological interventions were noted to have moderate effect in reducing recidivism, but not complete recidivism reduction. Surgical castration, by eliminating testosterone, has been shown to reduce sexual recidivism, but castration also does not eliminate the possibility of a sexual re-offense. Male human sexuality is not driven solely by testosterone, and some degree of sexual functioning may be retained after castration. Even so, due to the permanent nature of castration and the association with punishment, there are ethical concerns about the use of surgical castration. Castration without attendant psychological change might be insufficient to manage risk of recidivism in the community; moreover, internalized changes from psychotherapy alone are difficult to measure (Weinberger et al., 2005)

Hormonal treatment offers a reversible alternative to surgical castration. Since the 1940s, estrogen was used to reduce libido in sexual offenders. The side effects, which ranged from uncomfortable to medically serious, were problematic (Gordon & Grubin, 2003). Alternative hormonal treatments now in use include cyproterone acetate (not available in the United States), medroxyprogestrone, and long-acting gonadotrophin-releasing hormone agonists, such as leuprolide acetate. These medications vary in their pharmacologic mechanism of action, but the end result is the reduction of testosterone. The newer hormonal treatments are safer than estrogen, but side effects, including weight gain, lethargy, nightmares, hypertension, and bone density loss, remain an issue. As mentioned above, reduction of testosterone does not eliminate the possibility of sexual offending, and as a result, psychotherapy is still considered an important component of sexual offender treatment, even when hormonal treatment is utilized (Briken, 2007).

A challenge for all forms of sex offender treatment is the limited ability to determine the efficacy of treatment. In treatment of other disorders, the gold standard of research is the double-blinded, randomized trial compared against a control group. In sex offender treatment, the risk to the public in deliberately choosing not to provide treatment for research purposes is obviously problematic (Gordon & Grubin, 2003).

Assessment Tools

With the limitations to self-report inherent in sexual offender evaluations, the need for a means of objective assessment becomes evident. Actuarial instruments such as the STATIC-2002 or Sex Offender Risk Appraisal Guide (SORAG) may be useful in estimating potential risk based on historical factors (Langton et al., 2007), but they do not predict treatment response. Polygraph, typically associated with criminal investigations, has been utilized in some settings and may be useful in monitoring outpatient sexual offenders (Gordon & Grubin, 2003). The problem of potential exposure to new criminal sanctions for offenses discovered through polygraph, juxtaposed with an emphasis on full disclosure in treatment, is one issue raised by the use of such techniques in treatment settings.

Penile plethysmograph (PPG) is another instrument used in sexual offender evaluations. PPG attempts to determine the degree of sexual arousal to various visual or auditory stimuli by measuring changes in penile volume or circumference (Murphy et al., 2015). The use of PPG has been criticized as an intrusive test. A weakness of PPG includes the possibility that some individuals are able to fake non-arousal. Another complication is the possibility of finding deviant arousal on PPG that has unclear significance in relationship to the individual's known offending history. In some treatment settings, PPG is also used to demonstrate an offender's ability to utilize skills learned in treatment to manage deviant arousal. Given the limitations, both polygraph and PPG are recommended for use as aids to treatment and should not be used to determine guilt or predict future behavior (Gordon & Grubin, 2003).

Ethical Concerns

Civil commitment of sexual offenders raises concerns that the mental health system is diverted in favor of preventive detention. The degree to which this concern is true depends in part on the way in which civil commitment is utilized, in terms of who is committed, how treatment is delivered, who is released, and their outcomes in the community. There are also concerns that an involuntarily committed individual cannot give true voluntary consent to treatment, with voluntary consent as a traditional mainstay of medical treatment. This aspect might be considered similar to other involuntary status patients, such as patients with psychosis who agree to antipsychotic medication despite the involuntary nature of the hospitalization. Levenson and D'Amora (2005) articulated a rationale for ethical care in SVP treatment. Sex offender treatment can promote autonomy by empowering long-term change. Treatment can be provided with fairness and respect and by targeting interventions to the nature and seriousness of needs. Additionally, because recidivism has negative consequences for the offender as well as the victim and community, treatment to reduce recidivism may also benefit the recipient of treatment.

Conclusion

Controversy is inherent in the civil commitment of sexual offenders, including civil liberties concerns and diagnostic and treatment challenges. Sexual offenders comprise a heterogeneous population, with varied reasons for commission of sexual offenses. Accordingly, their treatment needs vary as well. Successful treatment depends on thoughtful assessment and individualized treatment targeting identified areas of need. A challenge for treatment providers is the dual responsibility of treatment of the individual and concern for public safety. Given the complex nature of sexual offenses and sexual offending, the difficulty of treating the population, and the challenges of managing risk in the community, the management and treatment of sexual offenders are certain to continue to evolve over time.

Discussion Questions

1. What factors are thought to contribute to sexual offending? Are any of these factors surprising to you? Why or why not?

2. In what ways are these factors relevant when serious mental illness is present? Do you think sexual offending should be considered a mental illness in and of itself? Why or why not?

3. What are the common elements of sexually violent predator laws? Do you think civil confinement after a criminal sentence is served should be allowed? If so, in what circumstances? If not, why not?

4. How are sexual offenders assessed? What tools are available to assist evaluation? Do you think future behavior can be reliably predicted? Why or why not?

5. What treatment options exist for sexual offender treatment? Should treatment be mandatory for sexual offenders? Why or why not?

References

Alden, A., Brennan, P., Hodgins, S., & Mednick, S. (2007). Psychotic disorders and sex offending in a Danish birth cohort. *Archives of General Psychiatry*, *64*, 1251–1258.

American Psychiatric Association. (2013). *Diagnostic and statistical manual of mental disorders*, (5th ed.). Arlington, VA: American Psychiatric Association.

Andrews, D. A., & Dowden, C. (2007). The Risk-Need-Responsibility model of assessment and human service in prevention and corrections: Crime-prevention jurisprudence. *Canadian Journal of Criminology and Criminal Justice*, *49*, 439–464.

Briken, P., & Kafka, M. P. (2007). Pharmacological treatments for paraphilic patients and sex offenders. *Current Opinions in Psychiatry*, *20*, 609–613.

Choe, J., Teplin, L., & Abram, K. (2008). Perpetration of violence, violent victimization, and severe mental illness: Balancing public health concerns. *Psychiatric Services*, *59*, 153–164.

D'Orazio, D., Jackson, R., & Schneider J. (2012). SOCCPN annual survey of sexual offender commitment programs 2012. Paper presented at the Sexual Offender Civil Commitment Programs Network conference in Denver, CO.

Federoff, P., Di Gioacchino, L., & Murphy, L. (2013). Problems with paraphilias in the *DSM-5*. *Current Psychiatry Reports, 15,* 363.

First, M. B. (2014). *DSM-5* and paraphilic disorders. *Journal of the American Academy of Psychiatry and the Law, 42,* 191–201.

First, M. B., & Halon, R. L. (2008). Use of *DSM* paraphilia diagnoses in sexually violent predator commitment cases. *Journal of the American Academy of Psychiatry and the Law, 36,* 443–454.

Friedman, R. (2006). Violence and mental illness—How strong is the link? *New England Journal of Medicine, 355,* 2064–2066.

Garcia, F. D., Delavenne, H. G., Assumpcao, A. F., & Thibaut, F. (2013). Pharmacologic treatment of sex offenders with paraphilic disorder. *Current Psychiatry Reports, 15,* 356.

Gordon, H., & Grubin, D. (2003). Psychiatric aspects of the assessment of treatment of sex offenders. *Advances in Psychiatric Treatment, 10,* 73–80.

Hanson, R. K., & Morton-Bourgon, K. (2005). Predicting relapse: A meta-analysis of sexual offender recidivism studies. *Journal of Consulting and Clinical Psychology, 66,* 348–362.

Harris, A., Veysey, B., Ragusa, L., & Lurigio, A. (2010). Sex offending and serious mental illness: Directions for policy and research. *Criminal Justice and Behavior, 37,* 520–536.

In re Young & Cunningham, 857 P.2d. 989 (1993).

Jackson, R. (2016). Treatment during civil commitment for sexual offending behaviors. *Current Psychiatry Reports, 18,* 69.

John Van Orden et al. v. Schafer et al. (2015).

Jumper, S., Babula, M., & Casbon, T. (2012). Diagnostic profiles of civilly committed sexual offenders in Illinois and other reporting jurisdictions: What we know so far. *International Journal of Offender Therapy and Comparative Criminology, 56,* 838–855.

Kafka, M. (2012). Axis I psychiatric disorders, paraphilic sexual offending and implications for pharmacological treatment. *Israel Journal of Psychiatry and Related Sciences, 49,* 255–261.

Kansas v. Crane, 543 U.S. 407 (2002).

Kansas v. Hendricks, 521 U.S. 346 (1997).

Karsjens et al. v. Minnesota Department of Human Services et al. (2012).

Karsjens v. Jesson, No. 11-3659, 2015 WL 3755870 (D. Minn. 2015).

Karsjens v. Johnson Piper, No. 15-3485 (8th Cir. 2017).

Khalifeh, H., Moran, P., Borschmann, R., Dean, K., Hart, C., Hogg, J., … Howard L. M. (2015). Domestic and sexual violence against patients with severe mental illness. *Psychological Medicine, 45,* 875–886.

Kingston D. A., Olver M. E., Harris, M., Wong, S. C. P., & Bradford, J. M. (2015). The relationship between mental disorder and recidivism in sexual offenders. *International Journal of Forensic Mental Health, 14,* 10–22.

Langton, C. M., Barbaree, H. E., Seto, M. C., Peacock, E. J., Harkins, L., & Hansen, K. T. (2007). Actuarial assessment of risk for reoffense among adult sex offenders. *Criminal Justice and Behavior, 34,* 37–59.

Levenson, J., & D'Amora, D. (2005). An ethical paradigm for sex offender treatment: Response to Glaser. *Western Criminology Review, 6,* 145–153.

McCullough, A. (2015). No end in sight: Failed treatment in civil commitment of sex offenders. *American Criminal Law Review.* Retrieved from http://www.americancriminallawreview.com/aclr-online/no-end-sight-failed-treatment-civil-commitment-sex-offenders.

Monahan, J. (1992). Mental disorder and violent behavior: Perceptions and evidence. *American Psychologist, 47,* 511–521.

Murphy, L., Ranger, R., Federoff, J. P., Stewart, H., Dwyer, R. G., & Burke, W. (2015). Standardization of penile plethysmography testing in assessment of problematic sexual interests. *The Journal of Sexual Medicine, 12,* 1853–1861.

National Research Council. (2014). *Estimating the incidence of rape and sexual assault.* Washington, D.C.: The National Academies Press. Retrieved from https://www.ncbi.nlm.nih.gov/books/NBK202264/.

Nobles, J., Alter, J., Bennett, E., Bombach, V., Hauer, J., Kirchner, D., … Yunker, J. (2011). *Evaluation report: Civil commitment of sex offenders.* St Paul, MN: Office of the Legislative Auditor, State of Minnesota, Program Evaluation Division. Retrieved from http://www.auditor.leg.state.mn.us/ped/pedrep/ccso.pdf.

Perillo, A., Spada, A., Calkins, C., & Jeglic, E. (2014). Examining the scope of questionable diagnostic reliability in sexually violent predator (SVP) evaluations. *International Journal of Law and Psychiatry, 37,* 190–197.

Ricciardelli, R., & Moir, M. (2013). Stigmatized among the stigmatized: Sex offenders in Canadian penitentiaries. *Canadian Journal of Criminology and Criminal Justice, 55,* 353–385.

Rotter, M. (2007). Sexual offenders with mental illness: Special considerations for a special population. *Psychiatric Times, 24.* Retrieved from http://www.psychiatrictimes.com/articles/sexual-offenders-mental-illness-special-considerations-special-population.

Sreenivasan, S., Weinberger L. E., & Garrick, T. (2003). Expert testimony in sexually violent predator commitments: Conceptualizing legal standards of "mental disorder" and "likely to reoffend." *Journal of the American Academy of Psychiatry and the Law, 31,* 471–485.

Testa, M., & West, S. (2010). Civil commitment in the United States. *Psychiatry*, *7*, 30–40.

Tewksbury, R. (2005). Collateral consequences of offender registration. *Journal of Contemporary Criminal Justice*, *21*, 67–81.

Thornton, D. (2002). Constructing and testing a framework for dynamic risk assessment. *Sexual Abuse: A Journal of Research and Treatment*, *14*, 139–153.

U.S. v. Comstock, 560 U.S. 126 (2010).

Weinberger, L., Sreenivasan, S., Garrick, T., & Osran, H. (2005). The impact of surgical castration on sexual recidivism risk among sexually violent predatory offenders. *Journal of the American Academy of Psychiatry and Law*, *33*, 16–36.

Zaleski, K., Gunderson, K., Baes, J., Estupinian, E., & Vergara, A. (2016). Exploring rape culture in social media forums. *Computers in Human Behavior*, *63*, 922–927.

Zonana, H., Abel, G., Bradford, J., Hoge, S. K., Metzner, J., Becker, J., … Fitch, L. (1999). *Dangerous sex offenders: A task force report of the American Psychiatric Association*. Washington, D.C.: American Psychiatric Association.

5

Family Violence and
Mental Illness

Karyn Sporer

Introduction

For decades, family violence—especially intimate partner violence, child abuse, and elder abuse—has been at the forefront of empirical investigation. There is extensive documentation of the negative outcomes associated with these types of violence, yet research on family violence in which the perpetrator is a child with mental illness is often neglected. This chapter focuses on a kind of family violence that is usually hidden behind closed doors: parents and siblings of violent persons with mental illness. In particular, I focus on how family caregivers struggle both to care for their child with mental illness and to navigate a complex mental health system, all while living within a destructive and violent household.

I begin this chapter with a discussion of the stressors and burdens associated with providing care for a loved one with mental illness. In the second half of the chapter, I focus on my own research with families of violent persons with mental illness. I use my participants' narratives to describe the day-to-day lives and the many struggles caregivers face when trying to support a child or sibling with mental illness, other family members (i.e., spouse, healthy children or siblings, and parents), and themselves. I end the chapter by discussing barriers to reliable and affordable treatment and services, and the difficulties associated with commitment. I hope that by illuminating this social problem, readers will better understand how to support families coping with a violent child or sibling with mental illness.

Mental Illness and Family Caregivers

Mental illness is a unique stressor situation for family members. It seems that mental illness, as a chronic condition, appears neither randomly nor for a short amount of time. In fact, there is often a history of bizarre behaviors and other warning signs. Eventually, however, the family will witness a dangerous or violent event that pushes them to pursue formal assistance, such as the criminal justice system or the mental health system (Johnson, 2000). The negative effects of caregiving for a person with mental illness will permeate virtually every aspect of the caregiver's life. Inpatient hospitalizations, interactions with the criminal justice system, symptomatic behavior, disruptions at home, and symptoms of the mental illness each provide unique stressor situations in which families must continue to function (Slate, Buffington-Vollum, & Johnson, 2013; Maurin & Boyd, 1990; Solomon & Draine, 1994; Thompson & Doll, 1982). It is not surprising then that caregivers are at a greater risk of psychiatric morbidity and stress-related illness than the general population (Stengard, Honkonen, Koivisto, & Salokangas, 2000; Yee & Schultz, 2000).

Each element in the treatment and caregiving of a family member with mental illness, from first hospitalization to discharge, can be stressful. Clarke and Winsor (2010) interviewed 10 parents of children recently admitted to their first inpatient psychiatric hospitalization. The participants reported various and conflicting emotions, including relief, disbelief, loneliness, stigmatization, and grief. Although parents were relieved that their child was safe and receiving professional support, they were also shaken by the reality that their child was in a locked psychiatric facility. Unfortunately, poor relationships and interactions with mental health staff exacerbated the stress and tension. Parents reported a lack of support from inpatient staff and were excluded from treatment team and discharge meetings. As a result, parents were ill-prepared for their child's return home (Clarke & Winsor, 2010). These findings are consistent with prior research (Doornbos, 2002; Ferriter & Huband, 2003; Johnson, 2000; Kinsella, Anderson, & Anderson, 1996; Solomon & Marcenko, 1992). Indeed, Johnson (2000) found parents often felt dismissed or disregarded by hospital staff, especially when parents tried to inform the staff of their child's warning signs or stages of decompensation. Solomon and Marcenko (1992) also conducted research on parents of children with mental illness. They found hospital and mental health staff did not provide parents with information or guidance that would help to ease the transition from hospital to home. In particular, parents were not trained on crisis intervention techniques, medication management, or various means of emotional support. Moreover, parents were neither educated on how to cope with having a mentally ill child nor on how to motivate their child to engage with treatment providers.

Stress and tension do not disappear after a family member's discharge from an inpatient psychiatric facility. Because mental illness is not "cured" during hospitalization, family members are often tasked with sole caretaking responsibility. For example, family members need to monitor mental health symptoms and make sure their loved one adheres to treatment recommendations (e.g., medication management) and attends psychiatry or therapy appointments. At the same time, however, caregivers also manage the rest of the household and try to provide a safe and healthy environment for all other family members. These responsibilities add confusion to family members' identities and role expectations. Pearlin (1983), for example, identified six types of stress that are related to such role strains: excessive demands of certain roles, inequities of rewards, the failure of reciprocity in roles, role conflict, role captivity, and role restructuring. Such stressors add to the complexity and difficulty of caregiving.

Because of the chronic nature of mental illness, these role strains are unlikely to dissipate in time; rather, the role strains will more likely become a daily stressor for parents and siblings of those with mental illness. Research has consistently shown that parents struggle to balance their caregiving responsibilities with roles associated with being a spouse and a parent of a healthy child (Bernheim & Leham, 1985; Safer, 2002; Seligman & Darling, 1997). These parents report higher levels of emotional burden, feelings of confusion, guilt, loss, grief, anxiety, shame, sadness, stigma, anger, and a sense of loss for themselves (e.g., setting aside one's own life goals while caring for family member) and their children (Bernheim & Leham, 1985; Harper & Hoopes, 1990). Spouses also report moderate to severe levels of hardship and conflict in their marriages due to the stress of having a chronically ill child (Bernheim & Leham, 1985; Safer, 2002; Seligman & Darling, 1997). These feelings are compounded when one parent perceives a lack of spousal support, such as help with caregiving and other household tasks (Atkin & Ahmad, 2009).

Mental illness also affects siblings both psychologically and socially. Koocher and O'Malley (1981) found healthy siblings tend to feel excluded by their parents, and jealous and resentful of their sibling with mental illness. They are also at an increased risk of maladjustment and behavioral problems, including difficulty in school settings, decreased self-esteem, and social isolation, as well as developmental delays, low IQ scores, and impulsive and aggressive behavior (Williams, 1997). Moreover, adolescents with a sibling with mental illness tend to participate in fewer school-related activities (Brett, 1988; Cox, Marhall, Mandleco, & Olson, 2003; Tritt & Esses, 1988; Williams, Lorenzo, & Borja, 1993). Healthy children often report feeling abandoned, invisible, or forgotten by their parents; these feelings are compounded when children perceive their parents to be focused primarily on their sibling with mental illness (Lukens, Thorning, & Lohrer, 2004; Marsh & Dickens, 1997).

Like parents, additional caretaking and household responsibilities increase perceived role strain among siblings; however, their personal loss perceptions tend to be more severe than those experienced by parents (Leith & Stein, 2012). The increase in household-related responsibilities, referred to as "parentification" (Akhtar & Kramer, 1999), often leads to confusion, embarrassment, resentment of the sibling with mental illness (Bernheim & Leham, 1985; Rosenblatt, 1994), and insecure attachments with family and friends (Nathiel, 2007). Siblings also reject their sibling or distance themselves when they perceive their sibling with mental illness to be stubborn, lazy, or manipulative (Johnson, 2000). These negative attributions were common among siblings who had increased household and caregiving responsibilities.[1]

---

1. Despite the extensive list of negative effects, research has also found positive outcomes for families with mental illness. For example, Johnson (2000) interviewed 180 family members of persons with severe mental illness. Despite the frequent disruptions and time-consuming nature of caregiving, family members reported fondness and concerns for the wellbeing of their child or sibling with mental illness. Family members reported these positive feelings and a desire to help in any capacity even if there were restraining orders in place. Siblings of persons with mental illness have also reported a greater sense of purpose, greater empathy, and greater closeness with their families (Aschbrenner, Greenberg, Allen, & Seltzer, 2010; Greenberg, Seltzer, & Judge, 2000; Koocher & O'Malley, 1981; Marsh, Lefley, Evans-Rhodes, Ansell, & Doerzbacher, 1996). For example, Kinsella and colleagues (1996) found siblings and children of persons with mental illness reported increased feelings of empathy and compassion for others, resiliency in the face of adverse conditions, and overall assertiveness. Furthermore, the researchers found these family members often became advocates for their family member with mental illness, particularly in seeking out mental health services, changing outsiders' views of mental illness, and increasing public awareness. They also reported a heightened gratitude for their own lives and an eagerness to live fully (Kinsella et al., 1996). Similarly, siblings tend to be more protective of their brothers and sisters, have increased empathy for others, and are less self-centered (Faux, 1993). Teachers also report these children to be more cooperative and assertive in the classroom, and to have higher levels of self-control than their peers (Mandleco, Olsen, Robinson, Marshall, & McNeilly-Choque, 1998).

Violence and Mental Illness

The relationship between mental illness and violence has been empirically investigated for decades and findings on the prevalence and risk of violence among persons with mental illness are conflicted. Some studies suggest most persons with mental illness will almost never commit a violent act (Brekke, Prindle, Bae, & Long, 2001; Slate et al., 2013; U.S. Department of Health and Human Services, 1999), with estimates ranging from one percent (McCampbell, 2001) to seven percent (Swanson, Holzer, Ganju, & Jono, 1990) of persons with mental illness who will exhibit violent behavior in their lifetime. In fact, an individual is more likely to be killed by a lightning strike (Szmukler, 2000) or to die of influenza (Dobson, 1998) than to be murdered by a stranger with mental illness. Other researchers, however, have found mental illness and psychopathy to be highly related to violent behaviors and violent crime (Nordström & Kullgren, 2003). Indeed, researchers have found substance abuse to be an important predictor of increased violence by persons with mental illness. Elbogen and Johnson (2009), for example, found serious mental illness and violence in the community to be related when there were co-occurring substance abuse or dependence issues, a finding confirmed by other researchers with varying methodologies.[2]

Caregiving-related behaviors are also risk factors for aggression by persons with mental illness. These risk factors include over-involvement by family members (Bebbington & Kuipers, 1994), financial dependence of the family member with mental illness on a family caregiver (Estroff, Swanson, Lachicotte, Swartz, & Bolduc, 1998; Solomon, Cavanaugh, & Gelles, 2005), attempts to bring a person with mental illness to a treatment facility, admission or involuntary commitment (Binder & McNeil, 1986), and persuasive or coercive limit setting (Straznickas, McNiel, & Binder, 1993). Because families assume the majority of caretaking responsibilities, it is unsurprising that persons with mental illness often direct their aggression toward family members and caregivers (Binder & McNeil, 1986; Gondolf, Mulvey, & Lidz, 1990; Straznikas, McNeil, & Binder, 1993; Torrey, 2006; Vaddadi, Soosai, Gilleard, & Adlard, 1997). Family members are also more likely to fall victim to the more severe and violent outbursts, including serious and fatal injuries (Nordström & Kullgren, 2003). Vaddadi and colleagues (1997) found that, among those with a

---

2. For a discussion on methodological differences across studies that examined at the relationship between violence, mental illness, and substance abuse, see Slate et al. (2013) and Torrey (2008).

family member with mental illness, 40 percent felt threatened by violence at some point, 22 percent were threatened in the last year, 40 percent were hit or struck at some point, and 17 percent had sustained a substantial injury. Gondolf and colleagues (1990) investigated emergency room patients awaiting a psychiatric evaluation and found that 36 percent had assaulted a family member prior to their hospitalization. Similarly, Phillips, Bowie, Wan, and Yukevich (2016) examined violence among inpatient children (ages 5–12) with mental illness. They identified 76 percent of the children as perpetrators of sibling violence. These children also had a history of directing harm towards themselves and others, particularly their peers, mothers, and teachers. Labrum and Solomon (2015) examined rates of victimization among 573 adults whose adult relative had a psychiatric disorder or disorders. Almost half of their sample (47 percent) reported falling victim to their relative's violent outbursts, and 22 percent of these family members were victimized in the prior six months.

In the next section, I describe the experiences of persons who live with a relative with mental illness who has exhibited violence. The data used are drawn from my larger study on individual- and family-level coping strategies among parents and siblings of a family member with mental illness who has been violent (see Sporer, 2016a, 2016b). I conducted ethnographic interviews with 42 family members between May 2013 and March 2015; the participants represented 29 distinct families from 17 states. The sample included 26 mothers, six fathers, eight sisters, and two brothers. Their ages ranged from 16 to 83, and the median age was 45. While many themes emerged during data analysis, this chapter will focus on themes of violence and victimization, and the difficulty of commitment. First, I describe the difficult decision to commit a family member with mental illness and the various issues posed by unsupportive informal and formal social supports. Second, I describe the larger systemic problems inherent in the American mental health system as perceived by family members.

Deciding to Hospitalize:
A Not-So-Easy Process

The decision to hospitalize typically came after an escalation of violence or concerning behavior and/or professional recommendation. Parents, in particular, struggled with this decision because they felt obligated to care for their child with mental illness (CMI), the other children in the home, and themselves. The parents balanced the unmanageability of the violence and the disorganization on one hand with the need for refuge and safety on the other.

In the following example, Sarah described how she and her husband, John, decided to seek professional help, which eventually led to her son's first psychiatric hospitalization. In the weeks leading up to this decision, their son, Jack, dropped out of college and returned home to live with his parents and younger brother.

> When he came home that's when all hell broke loose here and when we finally sought help … it was exactly like a Stephen King novel here. It was awful. He was breaking furniture.… He was taking pool cues and poking them through the ceiling.… Even though he hadn't gotten help yet, I was afraid of him. I didn't want him sleeping upstairs. The basement is finished. He had a room down there. I went to put laundry away and he had carved in his dresser, it was a three-drawer-dresser, it was "fuck this shit" in huge letters. It had taken a really long time. I called for help immediately. I knew it, we just knew it, we just kept putting it off. That person, that was Gina Garbo [a case manager], she was great.… So she met with us, the two of us and Jack, and then us separately, and Jack separately. When we all left she said to us, "This is very serious and I'm thinking hospitalization." I thought she was crazy. As bad as it was, I thought she was crazy. I thought, "Hospital-ization?" That was so foreign to us, the thought of somebody being in a mental hospital. That was the beginning. (10/14/13)

Sarah and John admitted to being in denial for years. They described certain behaviors as bizarre—like his intense gaze and stare or various hand gestures—but they did not think they were signs of mental illness. The accumulation of those behaviors and the later addition of aggressive behavior prompted them to seek professional help. Even after that realization, however, the need for hospitalization seemed drastic and hard to accept.

In contrast to Sarah and John, Janna and Don looked for help before their daughter, Meredith, turned eight. Janna explained how she and her husband sought consultation after her daughter became homicidal towards their other children. Prior to their daughter's hospitalization, Janna and her husband first relied on medication and outpatient services, including therapy, to manage Meredith's conduct problems. By her eighth birthday, Meredith's behavior es-calated to a point that Janna and Don knew they needed more support. Janna described how she and her husband communicated with professionals on how to move forward, which led to their decision to hospitalize.

> We ended up going, had a couple more consultations with that same psychiatrist, tried several medications, and ended up the first week of December that year with our first week of inpatient psychiatric hos-

pitalization. She had reached the point where she was attempting to choke her youngest sister and when I asked her about it, the first time she did it was when we were all riding in the car, well, me and the kids, we're in the car. She has her hands around the littlest's neck, and I was like, "Move your hands; sit on them." We were on our road, almost to our house, but there is nowhere to pull off on that little stretch of road. The kids are watching. We made it up to the house. I got her out of the car first, I had to pick her up, made sure that our youngest was fine. She was okay, she was just screaming, but she was fine. Got her inside and said, "Meredith, what were you doing?" And she said, "I was choking her." And I said, "Why?" She said, "Because I wanted to kill her." I was like, "Well, okay." We had been back and forth consulting with everybody and finally they're, "You need to do this. You need to figure out what's going on." We made that decision to do that hospitalization at that point, just to see if we could get a handle on what we were dealing with. (12/11/14)

Some parents struggled to commit their child to inpatient services, arguing they did not want to consider hospitalization, which for some led to delayed treatment. For example, Catelyn was initially apprehensive about psychiatric care and hospitalization for her son Kevin. She thought he was struggling with a recent breakup with his high school girlfriend. Kevin had been an engaged and happy teenager; he was in a band and had close friends. But after the breakup, Kevin became withdrawn and rarely left his bedroom. She explained that, in hindsight, her son was suffering from major depression and the beginning stages of obsessive-compulsive disorder. By age 18, Kevin was unable to eat food that his mother prepared because of his fear of germs, he was not showering, and he began writing notes to his mother that were threatening in nature. In the following quote, Catelyn explained her eventual decision to commit her son and how the delay damaged their relationship.

I knew that because I had taken *Family-to-Family* at Community Alliance, which saved me. It did not save my relationship with Kevin because I took it too late and by then, we had already had too many difficulties, but it saved me. When Kevin was going through this breakdown and not washing everything [i.e., personal hygiene], so the Region One guy says commit him. I can't do that. I went to Jackson [Kevin's psychologist] and spoke to him. He said he needed to be on anti-psychotics and commit him. I couldn't do it. He has no good psychiatrist and we have not had a good psychiatrist in seven years. This has been going on in some degree in seven years. I can't talk about psychiatrists and the horrible experiences we have had, horrible. Anyway, I got three professionals telling me to commit him. This was in December. I could not commit him until Easter when he finally wrote [a letter threatening to cut off my hands]…. He was screaming at me all the time. (4/13/14)

Delayed treatment has been investigated in a variety of arenas, including persons suffering from sexually transmitted diseases (Lichtenstein, Hook, & Sharma, 2005), alcoholism (Luoma et al., 2007), and tuberculosis (Eastwood & Hill, 2004). Fear of stigmatization was often a reason to delay treatment across these populations. This finding is also consistent with decisions to delay treatment among persons with mental illness and their family members (Compton & Esterberg, 2005; Franz et al., 2010; McGorry & Killackey, 2002; Okazaki, 2000). Franz and colleagues (2010) interviewed 12 family members directly involved in a relative's treatment initiation during a first episode of psychosis. The researchers found the time between psychosis onset and first psychopharmacological treatment was prolonged if family members were fearful of stigma, labeling, and resulting stereotypes for themselves and their family member with mental illness.

Other family members tried a long list of alternative treatments to avoid hospitalization. Courtney explained how her mother and father avoided institutionalization for their son by trying different pharmaceuticals, and even getting him involved in different activities and changing schools. Despite these efforts over the course of two years when he was in high school, Courtney's parents eventually made the tough decision to commit him to a state hospital in 1966. He stayed there for more than 12 months.

> They were trying everything; trying the psychiatry, different drugs that they had at the time. This was like…. When he was diagnosed as a paranoid schizophrenic, he was 16 and it was 1966. I remember my mother crying all the time. She was taking me to college one morning, and she was sobbing. She couldn't even get herself ready, she was so broken. She was a very beautiful, beautiful lady, my mom was, and very sweet, very sensitive. She was crying all the way to college and she said, "He's my little boy, and they're saying I should institutionalize him, and I can't do that." All this torment. I just watched her life go downhill. I watched her really drink to help herself, and I have that tendency. (12/5/14)

The decision to hospitalize is extremely difficult for many family caregivers of children with mental illness. Unfortunately, after family members either recognized the possibility that there was an issue with mental illness or after they made the decision to pursue hospitalization, they were confronted with new barriers, including outsiders who either denied there was a problem and/or professionals who delayed hospitalization. For example, some parents were told their child would grow out of it, characterizing the behavior as "typical boy or girl stuff," while other family members were told they were ineffective parents. This was especially present among parents of preteen children. Denial and/or blaming would further delay hospitalization and minimize the parents' ability to help themselves and their loved ones. For example, Linda reported looking for help and access to services long before her son's first inpatient hospitalization. The delayed hospitalization was attributed to Linda's experience of mother-blaming. Both extended family members and professionals identified poor parenting as the cause of her son's deviant behavior, rather than it being a manifestation of mental illness. Linda described how professional support finally materialized after emergency room staff witnessed her son's suicidal behavior.

> The day he was first hospitalized, he ... I don't even remember exactly what triggered it, but he became violent.... I was able to push him out on the patio and lock the doors. He really had no place to go.... He decided to rip off the fence line and start beating at the door, yelling that he wanted to kill me. I went to call the police. They came and they restrained him, and they brought him to crisis intervention. By the time they talked to him, he had calmed down. I'm sitting in the room with the worker and she had the paperwork in talking to me, and I was just at my wit's end.... He [my son] proceeded to very calmly walk over to the blinds in the room and wrap the cord around his neck. That got him hospitalized. At that point then, suddenly my family went, "You weren't kidding. There's really something wrong with him." I got more sympathy, and nobody really accused me of poor parenting anymore. (5/4/14)

Interestingly, Linda reflected on how hospitalization had an immediate effect on her family's perceptions and their gradual acceptance that her son had a "real" mental health problem.

These experiences are consistent with prior research that suggests parent or mother blaming (Caplan & Hall-McCorquodale, 1985) is a result of the socially constructed notion of the ideal family. Generally speaking, an ideal family is represented as a White, middle-class, heterosexual couple with children in a self-contained family unit (Thorne, 1993). Families with children with mental illness who have been violent deviate from this norm. Mother blaming has been present in studies of mental illness for decades and early explanations of the etiology of a child's psychosis or mental illness tended to place blame on the mother. For example, Bateson, Jackson, Haley, and Weakland (1956) argued that the mother would place the child in a double bind, in which the mother presented the child with contradictory expectations that could not be resolved. The child in a double bind would develop schizophrenia as a result. In a content analysis, Caplan and Hall-McCorquodale's (1985) found mothers of children with mental illness were overrepresented as targets of blame and were described as having mental health problems themselves and as being neglectful or manipulative. Mothers were also five times more likely than fathers to be cited as part of the patient's problem.

Issues with *The System*: From Finding a Bed to Paying for It

This section is organized into two parts. First, I describe two systemic issues that make psychiatric commitment difficult: namely, finding an available hospital bed and paying for treatment. Second, I describe the programs and policies that family members have found to be helpful.

Family members reflected on how minimal access to beds was a source of frustration, particularly when a child with mental illness was in crisis. In the following quote, Lily reflected on how she wanted a shorter time frame for receiving professional help. She explained how her daughter waited both for hospital intake and a psychiatrist, despite her daughter reporting suicidal ideation.

> We couldn't get help right away. The only answer for a parent going through that is to go sit in the emergency room, sometimes for days while they find a bed. Then you get a bed and the facility is useless. The kids are running wild. They just release them after a couple days.... Then to wait for a psychiatrist, we were on the waiting list for eight months before. This is all the while that we're in and out of the hospital. Cutting and doing all this stuff and I had to take her home and hide everything. We couldn't get in to see a psychiatrist for eight months. I think that they need to make more services available for the amount of people they're serving and realize that these are urgent issues, not issues that can wait eight months. (12/14/14)

In the next narrative, Katherine focused on the need for long-term services and their unavailability. She understood the historical context and how the asylums were sometimes inhumane; however, evident in her narrative is the desperation she and her brother felt over the impossibility of living with their brother who was diagnosed with schizophrenia. She believed long-term inpa-tient services might be the only safe option for families that have a child with mental illness who has been violent.

> Honestly I think the only way it could have been managed differently than it was is if there was somewhere to send him to get out of the house. There's nowhere … people's hands are tied. What are they going to do? There is nowhere to go.… I think it [the mental illness and violence] started earlier than when he attacked [me and my brother] and I was already out of the house at college. It started earlier than that, but you're a kid. You can't go anywhere. You can't do any-thing.… They say it's inhumane to lock these people up, but that's the only way Michael [my brother] and I would have been safe is if he [my other brother who has mental illness] could have been locked up. Given the circumstances, I think it's a miracle that Michael and I turned out as normally as we did. (10/17/13)

Policies associated with deinstitutionalization—transfer of asylum-based care into comprehensive community support—were well intentioned and viewed as both liberal and enlightened (Chaimowitz, 2011). However, because Congress failed to provide sufficient financial support to communities affected by deinstitutionalization (Sharfstein, 2000), community-based support systems were either not implemented or were so poorly organized that they were unable to manage the huge number of patients being discharged and moved into the communities (Greenberg & Rosencheck, 2008).[3]

Even when long-term hospitalization was an option, services received were viewed as inadequate, or patients were prematurely discharged. Grace described the system as "insane." She said, "That's why I'm an advocate. It's got to change. It's going to take a lot of people making that happen" (12/5/14). Grace described an event during which she transported her son to the hospital during a psychotic episode. After waiting four hours for an evaluation, her son did not meet ad-mission criteria, and they were told to go home. It took her another two months before he was officially admitted to an inpatient psychiatric facility. In a second example, Samantha explained her brother's many hospitalizations, during which he would inevitably be discharged too early for treatment to actually work.

> He would go to hospitals, to the mental hospitals and stuff and it was just pathetic.… They were just like, "Yes, in fact you are suicidal and

---

3. For more on the treatment of people with mental illness throughout history, see that chapter in *The Criminalization of Mental Illness*.

you do have severe mental illness, so we'll just keep you here for two weeks and then that should be good." That's just ridiculous.... They just think they can lock you up for a week and let you go and then hopefully he'll be okay.... I know that sounds ridiculous, but actually understanding or having programs that last longer than two weeks with people who are trained to get to the heart of the matter and not just putting it off and send you on your way. (4/29/14)

Family members also discussed financial barriers to treatment. Financial barriers included issues with out-of-pocket expenses, health insurance, and government funding. Treatment for mental health issues can be costly, especially when health insurance does not cover certain medications or specialized treatments and services, such as electroconvulsive treatment and long-term inpatient hospitalizations. A national survey on drug use and health found that approximately four million Americans who received mental health services identified themselves as the primary payer for services. The cost of those services ranged between $100 and $5,000 in out-of-pocket expenses (Kliff, 2012).

When asked what she would ask for if she could receive any one service, Dina said, "Affordable treatment that works" (12/15/14). She explained how affordable care "just doesn't exist" in her state and that quality care "is out there" but "it's hard to find and really expensive." She had been battling the health insurance company to help pay for her daughter's many medical bills.

Linda also had a hard time paying for her son's mental health treatment. She explained how her income put her in a bracket too high to receive state-sponsored services, thus forcing a decision between maintaining a job in order to afford high health care costs or being unemployed in order to receive financial assistance.

The hard part is that I have worked through all this.... I was making a few thousand dollars over the limit for getting any sort of public assistance. Programs that offered care, income counseling, and support were out there, but not for someone who works for a living. You have to actually find a group and pay for it, which unless you're at a level making a whole lot of money, it's not affordable.... Really, I actually paid a pretty heavy price for being a working parent. It would be really, really nice to figure out a way to fix that. (5/4/14)

In addition to treatment-related expenses, family caregivers are often responsible for paying adult children's housing costs, especially when government income, including Social Security Disability Income (SSDI) and Supplemental Nutrition Assistance Program (SNAP) benefits, is unable to cover living expenses, such as housing, food, and transportation. Casey, for example, applied for a state-sponsored individual care grant designed to pay for either intensive outpatient community-based services or residential treatment for children with severe mental illness. In the following narrative, she explained the difficulty in the application process.

> When Tim was 12 we applied and were denied, which we thought was weird since he was just diagnosed with schizophrenia. When he was 14, I managed to find some people around who had gotten the grant for their kids before. They helped us with our application; we applied and were denied again. We appealed and then he was accepted.... With all of the violence we had at home and how many times we had to send him to the hospital for his own safety and everyone else's, he went through residential treatment the month before his 15th birthday and he was in residential treatment for three and a half years. (1/12/14)

Another barrier to treatment is related to the bureaucratic complexity of state and local programs that are federally funded. This complex structure makes it difficult to determine whether a person qualifies for a particular program. One father explained how his son's dual diagnosis, psychiatric illness and drug addiction, made it impossible for his son to be accepted into treatment facilities or community-based supports. That struggle was especially frustrating for Gary because he was a case manager for the State Department of Mental Health, where his job involved finding services for clients with mental illness. Even so, Gary was unable to make the system work for his own child.

> I think the unique perspective and unique piece that I would lend is that I'm not only in it in terms of having had raised a child with these issues but I had also worked in the field for as many years. I really see both sides and that has affected and impacted everything through the years, and how actually unfortunately it's I think increased my level of frustration. It's given me a clear vision of how empty the system is in terms of tangible strategies for people with children like ours. The prevalence is so incredible. The stats are out there. The needs analysis has been done. It's all about funding. (10/17/13)

Gary is correct that the issues with the mental health system are all about funding. A recent investigation into the United States mental health system found that the U.S. federal government eliminated approximately $4 billion in mental health funding between 2009 and 2012 (Szalavtiz, 2012). Indeed, the National Alliance on Mental Illness (NAMI) claimed that long-term, impatient psychiatric facilities were the primary victims of budget cuts during the recession

(Kliff, 2012). Suffice it to say, increased local and federal funding for mental health care is a critical need for persons with mental illness and their families.

Conclusion

In 2010, the Bureau of Labor Statistics estimated that 89.3 million Americans were living in geographic locations designated as mental health professional shortage areas (Kliff, 2012). According to the Department of Health and Human Services (2015), an additional 2,800 psychiatrists are needed to satisfy the needs of underserved areas and populations. Data from the National Co-morbidity Survey showed that only 15.3 percent of respondents with serious mental illness received "minimally adequate treatment" (Wang, Demler, & Kessler, 2002). The need for easier access to mental health treatment and services in the United States is critical and expanding.

In general, policy suggestions tend to focus on improved communication between mental health professionals and family members, easier access to psychiatric care, including improved care at emergency rooms and inpatient facilities, and better trained criminal justice agents in crisis situations (Clarke & Winsor, 2010; Huang, Sun, Yen, & Fu, 2008; Johnson, 2000; Slate et al., 2013). Currently, family members are often dependent on themselves, other family members, and/or friends for support and guidance. Perhaps the policy and program discrepancies are a result of policy makers being unsure of what works for this unique population.

Family caregivers would benefit from a variety of services and programs. Education, respite, and continuation of care are three core features of what has helped these participants and what could help others (Sporer & Radatz, 2017). First, participants explained the benefits of learning about different parenting techniques and coping strategies. Programs that teach parents different disciplinary strategies or crisis management techniques can help them be prepared for a difficult situation. For example, effective education programs can help family members learn necessary skills and approaches to the management of a chronic stressor situation.

Second, respite is a therapeutic option for both the child with mental illness and family members. This type of caregiving can be an emotional burden that leads family members into exhaustion (Bernheim & Leham, 1985; Harper & Hoopes, 1990; Karp, 2001; Vine, 1982), making respite an important option for family members of persons with mental illness.

Last, participants were afraid their child would lose services as an adult or that the adult child would no longer follow treatment recommendations, (for example, would stop taking medications). Adults with mental illness have a legal right to control their treatment, but their family caregivers have unique insight and knowledge into the adult child's warning signs and needs. It seems warranted that caregivers continue to play some sort of role in the treatment of their family member with mental illness.

Discussion Questions

1. What are the risk factors for increased violence and aggression by persons with mental illness against family caregivers?

2. How are family members negatively affected by caring for a child with mental illness who exhibits violence?

3. Relying on the comments by family members, describe how mental health professionals can help family members be better prepared to assist their children and siblings with mental illness.

4. What reforms are needed to bring about meaningful and positive change in the mental health system? What types programs in particular will help both persons with mental illness and their family caregivers?

5. What are the challenges in implementing the programs that would be most useful to families who care for a relative with mental illness?

References

Akhtar, S., & Kramer, S. (Eds.). (1999). *Brothers and sisters: Developmental, dynamic, and technical aspects of the sibling relationship.* Northvale, NJ: Jason Aronson Inc.

Aschbrenner, K., Greenberg, J., Allen, S., & Seltzer, M. M. (2010). Subjective burden and personal gains among older parents of adults with serious mental illness. *Psychiatric Services, 61*(6), 605–611.

Atkin, K., & Ahmad W. I. U. (2009). Family care-giving and chronic illness: How parents cope with a child with a sickle cell disorder or thalassaemia. *Health and Social Care in the Community, 81*(1), 57–69.

Bateson, G., Jackson, D., Haley, J., & Weakland, J. (1956). Toward a theory of schizophrenia. *Behavioral Science, 1*, 251–264.

Bebbington, P., & Kuipers, L. (1994). The clinical utility of expressed emotion in schizophrenia. *Acta Psychiatrica Scandinavica, 89* (Suppl. 382), 46–53.

Bernheim, K. F., & Leham, A. F. (1985). *Working with families of the mentally ill.* New York, NY: W.W. Norton Company.

Binder, R., & McNeil, D. (1986). Victims and families of violent psychiatric patients. *Bulletin of American Academy of Psychiatry and Law, 14,* 131–139.

Brekke, J. S., Prindle, C., Bae, S. W., & Long, J. D. (2001). Risks for individuals with schizophrenia who are living in the community. *Psychiatric Services, 52*(10), 1358–1368.

Brett, K. M. (1988). Sibling response to chronic childhood disorders: Research perspectives and practice implications. *Issues in Comprehensive Pediatric Nursing, 11,* 43–57.

Caplan, P., & Hall-McCorquodale, I. (1985). Mother-blaming in major clinical journals. *American Journal of Orthopsychiatry, 55,* 345–353.

Chaimowitz, G. (2011). The criminalization of people with mental illness. *The Canadian Journal of Psychiatry, 57*(2), 1–7.

Clark, D., & Winsor, J. (2010). Perceptions and needs of parents dueling a young adult's first psychiatric hospitalization: "We're all on this little island and we're going to drown real soon." *Issues in Mental Health Nursing, 31,* 242–247.

Compton, M. T., & Esterberg, M. L. (2005). Treatment delay in first-episode nonaffective psychosis: A pilot study with African American family members and the theory of planned behavior. *Comprehensive Psychiatry, 46*(4), 291–5.

Cox, A. H., Marhall, E. S., Mandleco, B., & Olson, S. F. (2003). Coping responses to daily life stressors of children who have a sibling with a disability. *Journal of Family Nursing, 9,* 397–413.

Dobson, R. (1998, July). Are schizophrenics the lepers of our time? *Independent Review, 21,* 11.

Doornbos, M. (2002). Family caregivers and the mental health care system: Reality and dreams. *Archives of Psychiatric Nursing, 16*(1), 39–46.

Eastwood, S. V., & Hill, P. C. (2004). A gender-focused qualitative study of barriers to accessing tuberculosis treatment in The Gambia, West Africa. *The International Journal of Tuberculosis and Lung Disease, 8*(1), 70–75.

Elbogen, E. B., & Johnson, S. C. (2009). The intricate link between violence and mental disorder: Results from the National Epidemiological Survey on Alcohol and Related Conditions. *Archives of General Psychiatry, 66*(2), 152–161.

Estroff, S. E., Swanson, J. W., Lachicotte, W. S., Swartz, M., & Bolduc, M. (1998). Risk reconsidered: Targets of violence in the social networks of people with serious psychiatric disorders. *Social Psychiatry and Psychiatric Epidemiology, 33*(Suppl. 1), 95–101.

Faux, S. A. (1993). Siblings of children with chronic physical and cognitive disabilities. *Journal of Pediatric Nursing, 8*(5), 305–317.

Ferriter, M., & Huband, N. (2003). Experiences of parents with a son or daughter suffering from schizophrenia. *Journal of Psychiatric and Mental Health Nursing, 10*(5), 552–560.

Franz, L., Carter, T., Leiner, A. S., Bergner, E., Thompson, N. J., & Compton, M. T. (2010). Stigma and treatment delay in first-episode psychosis: A grounded theory study. *Early Intervention in Psychiatry, 4*, 47–56.

Gondolf, E., Mulvey, E., & Lidz, C. (1990). Characteristics of perpetrators of family and nonfamily assaults. *Hospital and Community Psychiatry, 41*, 191–193.

Greenberg, G., & Rosencheck, R. (2008). Jail incarceration, homelessness and mental health: A national survey. *Psychiatric Services, 59*, 170–177.

Greenberg, J. S., Seltzer, M. M., & Judge, K. (2000). Another side of the family's experience: Learning and growing through the process of coping with mental illness. *The Journal of the California Alliance for the Mentally Ill, 11*, 8–10.

Harper, J. M., & Hoopes, M. H. (1990). *Uncovering shame: An approach integrating individuals and their family systems.* New York, NY: W.W. Norton & Company.

Huang, W., Sun, F., Yen, W., & Fu, C. (2008). The coping experiences of carers who live with someone who has schizophrenia. *Journal of Clinical Nursing, 17*, 817–826.

Johnson, E. D. (2000). Differences among families coping with serious mental illness: A qualitative analysis. *American Journal of Orthopsychiatry, 70*(1), 126–134.

Karp, D. A. (2001). *The burden of sympathy: How families cope with mental illness.* Oxford, UK: Oxford University Press.

Kinsella, K. B., Anderson, R. A., & Anderson, W. T. (1996). Coping skills, strengths, and needs as perceived by adult offspring and siblings of people with mental illness: A retrospective study. *Psychiatric Rehabilitation Journal, 20*(2), 24–32.

Kliff, S. (2012, December 17). Seven facts about America's mental health-care system. *The Washington Post.* Retrieved from https://www.washingtonpost.com/news/wonk/wp/2012/12/17/seven-facts-about-americas-mental-health-care-system/.

Koocher, G. P., & O'Malley, J. E. (1981). Interviews with brothers and sisters. In G. P. Koocher & J. E. O'Malley (Eds.), *The Damocles syndrome: Psychosocial consequences of surviving childhood cancer* (pp. 101–111). New York, NY: McGraw-Hill.

Labrum, T., & Solomon, P. L. (2015). Rates of victimization of violence committed by relatives with psychiatric disorders. *Journal of Interpersonal Violence*. Retrieved from https://doi.org/10.1177/0886260515596335.

Leith, J. E., & Stein, C. H. (2012). The role of personal loss in the caregiving experiences of well siblings of adults with serious mental illness. *Journal of Clinical Psychology*, 68(10), 1075–1088.

Lichtenstein, B., Hook III, E. W., & Sharma, A. K. (2005). Public tolerance, private pain: Stigma and sexually transmitted infections in the American Deep South. *Culture, Health & Sexuality*, 7(1), 43–57.

Lukens, E. P., Thorning, H., & Lohrer, S. P. (2004). Sibling perspectives on severe mental illness: Reflections on self and family. *American Journal of Orthopsychiatry*, 74, 489–501.

Luoma, J. N., Twohig, M. P., Waltz, M., Hayes, S. C., Roget, N., Padilla, M., & Fisher, G. (2007). An investigation of stigma in individuals receiving treatment for substance abuse. *Addictive Behaviors*, 32, 1331–1346.

Mandleco, B. L., Olsen, S. F., Robinson, C. C., Marshall, E. S., & McNeilly-Choque, M. K. (1998). Social skills and peer relationships of siblings of children with disabilities. In P. T. Slee & K. Rigby (Eds.), *Children's peer relations* (pp. 106–120). London, UK: Routledge.

Marsh, D. T., & Dickens, R. M. (1997). *Troubled journey: Coming to terms with the mental illness of a sibling or parent.* New York, NY: Penguin.

Marsh, D. T., Lefley, H. P., Evans-Rhodes, D., Ansell, V. I., & Doerzbacher, B. M. (1996). The family experience of mental illness: Evidence for resilience. *Psychiatric Rehabilitation Journal*, 20, 3–12.

Maurin, J. T., & Boyd, C. B. (1990). Burden of mental illness on the family: A critical review. *Archives of Psychiatric Nursing*, 4, 99–107.

McCampbell, S. W. (2001). Mental health courts: What sheriffs need to know. *Sheriff*, 53(2), 40–43.

McGorry, P. D., & Killackey, E. J. (2002). Early intervention in psychosis: A new evidence based paradigm. *Epidemiological Psychiatry*, 11(4), 237–247.

Nathiel, S. (2007). *Daughters of madness: Growing up and older with a mentally ill mother.* Westport, CT: Praeger.

Nordström, A., & Kullgren, G. (2003). Victim relations and victim gender in violent crimes committed by offenders with schizophrenia. *Social Psychiatry & Psychiatric Epidemiology*, 38(6), 326–330.

Okazaki, S. (2000). Treatment delay among Asian-American patients with severe mental illness. *American Journal of Orthopsychiatry*, 70(1), 58–64.

Pearlin, L. I. (1983). Role strain and personal stress. In H. B. Kaplan (Ed.), *Psychosocial stress: Trends in theory and research* (pp. 3–32). New York, NY: Academic Stress.

Phillips, D. A., Bowie, B. H., Wan, D. C., & Yukevich, K. W. (2016). Sibling violence and children hospitalized for serious mental and behavioral health problems. *Journal of Interpersonal Violence*. Retrieved from https://doi.org/10.1177/0886260516628289.

Rosenblatt, P. C. (1994). *Metaphors of family systems theory: Toward new constructions*. New York, NY: The Guilford Press.

Safer, J. (2002). *The normal one: Life with a difficult or damaged sibling*. New York, NY: The Free Press.

Seligman, M., & Darling, R. B. (1997). *Ordinary families, special children: A systems approach to childhood disability* (2nd ed.). New York, NY: The Guilford Press.

Sharfstein, S. S. (2000). Whatever happened to community mental health? *Psychiatric Services, 51*, 616–620.

Slate, R. N., Buffington-Vollum, J. K., & Johnson, W. W. (2013). *The criminalization of mental illness: Crisis and opportunity for the justice system* (2nd ed.). Durham, NC: Carolina Academic Press.

Solomon, P. L., Cavanaugh, M. M., & Gelles, R. J. (2005). Family violence among adults with severe mental illness: A neglected area of research. *Trauma, Violence, & Abuse, 6*(1), 40–54.

Solomon, P., & Draine, F. (1994). Subjective burden among family members of mentally ill adults: Relation to stress, coping, and adaptation. *American Journal of Orthopsychiatry, 65*(3), 419–427.

Solomon, P., & Marcenko, M. (1992). Families of adults with severe mental illness: Their satisfaction with inpatient and outpatient treatment. *Psychosocial Rehabilitation Journal, 16*(1), 121–134.

Sporer, K. (2016a). *Families and their violent children with mental illness* (Doctoral dissertation). Retrieved from ProQuest. (Publication number 10113708).

Sporer, K. (2016b). Aggressive children with mental illness: A conceptual model of family-level outcomes. *Journal of Interpersonal Violence*. Retrieved from https://doi.org/10.1177/0886260516641283.

Sporer, K., & Radatz, D. (2017). Mothers of violent children with mental illness: How they perceive barriers to effective help. *Journal of Family Violence, 32*, 683–697.

Stengard, E., Honkonen, T., Koivisto, A., & Salokangas, R. K. (2000). Satisfaction of caregivers of patients with schizophrenia in Finland. *Psychiatric Service, 51*, 1034–1039.

Straznickas, K., McNiel, D., & Binder, R. (1993). Violence toward family caregivers by mentally ill relatives. *Hospital and Community Psychiatry, 44*, 385–387.

Swanson, J., Holzer, C., Ganju, V., & Jono, R. (1990). Violence and psychiatric disorders in the community: Evidence from Epidemiological Catchment Area Survey. *Hospital and Community Psychiatry, 41F,* 761–770.

Szalavitz, M. (2012, December 20). America's failing mental health system: Families struggle to find quality care. *TIME.* Retrieved from http://healthland.time.com/2012/12/20/americas-failing-mental-health-system-families-struggle-to-find-quality-care/.

Szmukler, G. (2000). Homicide enquiries: What sense do they make? *Psychiatric Bulletin, 24,* 6–10.

Thompson, E., & Doll, W. (1982). The burden of families coping with the mentally ill: An invisible crisis. *Family Relations, 31,* 379–388.

Thorne, B. (1993). Feminism and the family: Two decades of thought. In B. Thorne & M. Yalom (Eds.), *Rethinking the family: Some feminist questions* (2nd ed., pp. 3–30). New York, NY: Longman.

Torrey, E. F. (2006). Violence and schizophrenia. *Schizophrenia Research, 88,* 3–4.

Torrey, E. F. (2008). *The insanity offense: How America's failure to treat the seriously mentally ill endangers its citizens.* New York, NY: W. W. Norton & Company.

Tritt, S. G., & Esses, L. M. (1988). Psychosocial adaptation of siblings of children with chronic medical illness. *American Journal of Orthopsychiatry, 58,* 211–220.

U.S. Department of Health and Human Services. (1999). *Mental health: A report of the surgeon general.* Rockville: MD: U.S. Department of Health and Human Services. Retrieved from https://profiles.nlm.nih.gov/ps/access/NNBBHS.pdf.

U.S. Department of Health and Human Services. (2015). *Shortage designation: Health professional shortage areas & medically underserved areas/populations.* Rockville, MD: U.S. Department of Health and Human Services. Retrieved from https://bhw.hrsa.gov/shortage-designation.

Vaddadi, K. S., Soosai, E., Gilleard, C. J., & Adlard, S. (1997). Mental illness, physical abuse and burden of care on relatives: A study of acute psychiatric admission patients. *Acta Psychiatrica Scandinavica, 95*(4), 313–317.

Vine, P. (1982). *Families in pain: Children, siblings, spouses, and parents of the mentally ill speak out.* New York, NY: Pantheon Books.

Wang, P. S., Demler, O., & Kessler, R. C. (2002). Adequacy of treatment for serious mental illness in the United States. *American Journal of Public Health, 92*(1), 92–98.

Williams, P. D. (1997). Siblings and pediatric chronic illness: A review of the literature. *International Journal of Nursing Studies, 34,* 312–323.

Williams, P. D., Lorenzo, F. D., & Borja, M. (1993). Pediatric chronic illness: Effects on sibling and mothers. *Maternal-Child Nursing Journal*, *21*, 111–121.

Yee, J., & Schultz, R. (2000). Gender differences in psychiatric morbidity among family caregivers: A review and analysis. *Gerontologist*, *40*, 147–64.

6

Discovering CIT across the CJS

Ken Kerle

Introduction

This chapter traces the development of the connection between the mental health and criminal justice systems generally and the use of Crisis Intervention Teams (CIT) by law enforcement and corrections through the lens of my personal and professional experiences. I grew up in Topeka, Kansas, in the 1940s. When I was in high school, my friend was taken to Topeka State Hospital, a state mental institution, to serve an indeterminate sentence. I visited my friend some Saturdays and observed that patients got up at 5:30am and got their exercise by scrubbing and waxing the floors. Breakfast in the dining hall followed and after eating, patients had time on their hands. If visitors occasionally brought reading material or games, this was permitted, but neither activities nor treatment, or anything recreational, occurred. Lunch in the same dining hall at noon offered a brief escape from the dorm living quarters. At 5pm, the dinner hour ended their nourishment for the day. This dreary, endless, boring repetition consumed all of the patients' waking hours and every tedious evening concluded with lights out at 8:30pm.

Ironically, my friend suffered from epilepsy rather than mental illness and his seizures first struck him when he became a teenager. His incarceration in the mental hospital occurred soon after a relative on a family visit to his home discovered rifles under the front porch. Apparently, my friend had burglarized a nearby gun store in the neighborhood, roughly a block from his house. A visiting uncle who discovered the weapons called the police; eventually a local judge sentenced my friend to the mental hospital. The closure of the Topeka

State Hospital in 1997 came during deinstitutionalization, the process of closing psychiatric facilities in favor of community-based mental health care that never really materialized, leaving people with mental illness at risk of homelessness, victimization, and incarceration (Torrey, 2008, 2014).

My Unexpected Introduction to the CJS

On June 5, 1968, Robert Kennedy was assassinated in Los Angeles, which concluded his effort to become Democratic Party nominee for president of the U.S. I had been offered a position on his campaign team. A few minutes after I heard this disturbing news about his death over the radio, my phone rang. A voice inquired if I would consider teaching two college classes and working with a power and light company on a project to educate the community about the need for community planning in Washington County, Maryland. The school was Hagerstown Junior College and needing money, I accepted the position. Little did I know, this would be the start of my journey through an unanticipated career. Just two short years later, I received a letter from the department chair at Hagerstown letting me know it was my turn to teach at the prison. I immediately thought of all the prison movies I had seen where muscle-bound inmates physically subdued others, including the staff, and started doing push-ups. After the third one, I decided there were probably better ways for me to prepare for this duty.

When I arrived at Maryland Correctional Institution, I was charged with teaching 30 male inmates who had qualified for college courses funded from a federal grant. My approach to teaching remained unchanged and included lectures and participation in discussions of key issues of American government. Several weeks into the class, one student suggested I make trips to visit foreign prisons in order to compare them with American prisons. This sounded a little unusual, but still a fine idea and I sketched out a prison visitation plan.

Over the next 16 years, periodic travel took me to Europe, Asia, Australia, New Zealand, and Canada to visit correctional facilities. As a result of this travel, I later became acquainted with several British prison governors and invited them to the annual conference of the American Jail Association. For seven successive years, attending the annual British Prison Governors Conference and visiting different prisons in the United Kingdom became a regular part of my travel schedule.

Eventually, I taught American government in both medium-security prisons in the Hagerstown area and even developed a class for inmates and staff that focused on prisoners' rights. But perhaps my biggest challenge was teaching at

Patuxent, a psychiatric prison just outside of Baltimore. Inmates at Patuxent had indeterminate sentences, so they could not be released until the psychiatrist heading the prison determined they were not a danger to the community and could be paroled.

The first story I heard upon my arrival at Patuxent was that a number of inmates had recently seized control of the building. Soon, the Army-based staff at Ft. Meade, Maryland, was contacted for assistance and loaned several large trucks to local law enforcement. At a prearranged signal, these trucks rammed the entrances of the Patuxent education building with such force that chunks of concrete plummeted from its ceiling. A correctional officer inside this building got hit by one of the concrete chunks and sustained a head injury severe enough to gain early retirement. However, this unforeseen entry by military vehicles snuffed out the inmate takeover and correctional staff regained control.

The incident reiterated for me that work in a correctional environment differs dramatically from work in the outside world. Rebellion always remains a viable option for unhappy inmates. A friend at Patuxent described to me his experience during the inmate takeover. Some rebelling inmates grabbed him and tied him to his office chair. These inmates explained that they needed to convince the prison management that they meant business, so the teacher would be executed. While bound in his chair, one inmate dialed the teacher's home number to permit a final goodbye to his family. Fortunately, the outside assault on the prison education building erupted and succeeded in quelling the takeover before the inmates had time to kill him.

The Switch from Prisons to Jails

In 1973, Francis R. Ford (Dick Ford), a retired police officer from Washington, D.C., moved to Hagerstown and accepted a job at the college to teach criminal justice courses. During his first spring semester, he asked me to work as his campaign manager in the race for sheriff. I agreed but cautioned him that his chances of success were limited. Though Ford was experienced and educated, he grew up in Maine, not western Maryland, and his status as a newcomer would make it more difficult to win an election. His opponent had always lived in Maryland and the fact he was campaigning for his fourth consecutive term seemed ample evidence of public approval of his performance in office.

However, two days before the September primary election, the popular sheriff unexpectedly committed suicide with his own weapon in his courthouse office. This gruesome act altered the political climate and Dick Ford won a victory following a short five-week campaign. I was offered and agreed to accept a position in the sheriff's department and terminated my faculty position effective the end of that fall semester. I agreed to be an unpaid consultant for the sheriff and could come and go as I pleased (Kerle, 1998, 2003).

My new position introduced me to the working world of criminal justice. When the opportunity presented itself, the new sheriff encouraged me to do the 13 weeks of training for Maryland police officers and sheriff's deputies. Thanks to this opportunity, I gained greater perspective on what is expected in law enforcement as a Maryland police officer. I eventually took the job of jail deputy and worked there managing and supervising inmates. One of the first things I noticed when I started my position in the early 1970s was the constant arrival of people with mental illness or substance abuse issues, and often both, to our local jail.

The Maryland legislature appropriated a sum of money for each of the state's 23 counties to bring criminal justice and mental health staff together on friendlier terms, since predictions had proved true about the closure of the mental hospitals bringing increased numbers of people with mental illness into the criminal justice system. I helped set up a meeting for criminal justice and mental health staff to start the dialogue between these groups. The Washington County mental health director did not come to the meeting and when I asked him why, he told me he was not interested in meeting any criminal justice officials or employees. Once back in my office, I telephoned a state employee in Annapolis connected with this project and she called the county mental health director to remind him that if the mental health system did not participate, there would be no money from the state. From that point on, both criminal justice and mental health system staff participated in the project and these systems started to work together, at least in Washington County, Maryland.

The National Sheriffs' Association and the Jail Audit

Although Sheriff Ford did an outstanding job managing the Washington County Sheriff's Department, he lost the next election. However, the National Sheriffs' Association (NSA) selected him as the NSA Director of Jail Operations. His first assignment was the development of a training manual of guidelines and standards for jail officers and I was invited to participate. This written material provided the basis for conducting jail audits. As chief auditor, I conducted onsite visits with those jails requesting audits. I traveled to the jails and met with staff and with inmates to determine the degree of compliance with these newly issued guidelines and standards. At the end of the audit, I conferred with the sheriff and jail administrator to discuss findings and make helpful suggestions. Frequently, I found that written jail policies did not even exist. When they did, it was apparent that specialized officer training for managing inmates with mental illness was absent.

Jails with completed audits were encouraged to share them with their elected county boards and use the audits as justification for additional jail funding. Much of a jail's budget involves money to pay staff salaries. If staff were not hired because the money was not available, the county in question risked lawsuits when inmates charged that their constitutional rights were ignored or violated. The refusal of county governments to spend money to hire sufficient jail staff proved to be a serious problem, followed by the problem of a lack of training. Bluntly stated, if not enough jail staff are on duty to supervise inmates, the prisoners will run the jail. One can only imagine what that implied for prisoners with mental illness.

In 1981, Dick Ford became the first executive director of the newly formed American Jail Association (AJA), which combined the National Jail Association and the National Jail Managers' Association. Upon his appointment, Director Ford asked me to develop a magazine for the AJA. The first issue of *American Jails* appeared in the spring of 1987 and was soon published every other month. The Summer 1989 issue was focused on people with mental illness in jails. I appeared on the cover as a person with mental illness being booked into a local jail. The director's remarks got to the heart of the problem: "Police are often asked to correct a community nuisance for which there is no criminal statute. Bag ladies or mental patients are a good example. Hospitals refuse to take them and so they end up in a jail because it is a 24-hour institution" (Ford, 1989, p. 4). My editorial focused on diversion efforts: "In fact, The American Jail Association, the National Sheriffs' Association, The American Correctional Association, NACO (National Association of County Officials) and thirty plus other national associations worked as members of the National Jail Coalition to divert the mentally ill, public inebriates, and juveniles from our nation's jails. The activity of the coalition subsided dramatically when federal funding ceased" (Kerle, 1989, p. 6).

My Introduction to CIT

Though CIT began in Memphis, Tennessee, in 1988,[1] my first introduction to it was in 2008 in Topeka, Kansas,[2] where I had returned after nearly 50 years away. I was intrigued by the 40-hour CIT training to which I had been invited. I noticed that participants came from law enforcement, the local jail, Valeo Mental Health (the equivalent of the county mental health authority), parole and probation, court employees, the district attorney's office, the local hospital, alcohol/drug treatment staff, the homeless shelter, et cetera. All these people involved represented different agencies committed to the challenge of reducing the number of people with mental illness in the criminal justice system. The CIT training provided different agencies an unusual opportunity to train together to improve the management and treatment of people with mental illness that proved challenging in many Kansas communities.

From a personal vantage point, the term criminal justice system seemed theoretical. Up to this time, I never found criminal justice agencies in dialogue with other community agencies about solving the challenges brought on by the management of the people with mental illness or those with substance abuse issues. With CIT, I finally encountered a program where criminal justice and mental health system staff trained together and where the emphasis was on cooperation. Furthermore, I am convinced that I would have ignored CIT without the introduction to criminal justice that I have described in this chapter. Prison teaching, world travel, my introduction to Dick Ford, police training, visiting hundreds of jails, employment as a jail officer, and developing *American Jails* magazine for the AJA changed my adult working life in ways that would have been inconceivable to me when I first started out. CIT training became a significant step in understanding how committed people and agencies could improve life in the community for the people with mental illness caught up in the criminal justice system. In the next section, I examine CIT and related initiatives in Kansas so that a clearer picture of the state's handling (or lack thereof) of people with mental illness emerges.

---

1. For more on law enforcement response to people with mental illness, including CIT, see that chapter in *The Criminalization of Mental Illness*.
2. As with Memphis, the impetus to start CIT in Topeka was a tragedy involving a person with mental illness. See Kerle (2016).

CIT and Related Initiatives in Kansas

Kansas, a state of 105 counties, resembles a square box over 400 miles in length and over 200 miles in width in the center of the country, with a population of less than three million. About 70 percent of the population resides in the eastern counties of Johnson, Wyandotte, Shawnee, Douglas, and Sedgwick (Wichita) in south central Kansas, 40 miles from the Oklahoma border.

The first CIT training class in Kansas was held in the largest populated county, Johnson County, in 2004, which has since continued its strong interest in the CIT approach. Less populated counties have adapted an approach similar to CIT to cover more rural areas. For example, in Thomas County, the High Plains Mental Health Center delivers services to 20 counties covering 19,000 square miles. Agencies in the area have received training in mental health responding. The course provides eight hours of training for law enforcement, but it is also offered to social workers, clergy, and other civic leaders. In addition, the High Plains Mental Health Center uses telemedicine systems, which allow contact with mental health professionals, which is especially helpful because rural areas lack psychiatrists and other medical professionals (Shorman, 2016). CIT is also a lasting feature in Topeka, as discussed below, and was codified as a best practice by the state legislature in 2012 (Committee, 2012).

However, about 75 percent of the police departments in Kansas have fewer than 10 officers and some of these small departments decline CIT training, noting "We don't need that stuff, we know how to talk to people," ultimately resulting in lawsuits because of mistakes by officers (Shorman, 2016). Moreover, some counties, such as Reno County, used to employ CIT, but it was discontinued later from lack of support.

In the Topeka Police Department, which has about 300 sworn officers, almost three-quarters of patrol officers have been CIT trained. In 2016, the Topeka CIT team made 78 calls during a three-month period. The average length of each call was 87 minutes. Of the people who were the subject of the calls, only one had to be transported to the Shawnee County Detention Center (Moore, 2016). The Topeka CIT team is an excellent example of a CIT program in action, where a community-based service provided the needed assistance in addition to saving the taxpayers money by avoiding detention. In fact, the CIT approach may be more effective at encouraging people with mental illness to start and maintain treatment than a more coercive approach that implicitly or explicitly threatens jail.

As seen above, Valeo Mental Health is the agency responsible for the provision of mental health services in Shawnee County, where Topeka is located, and has been since 1967. Even with Valeo in existence, it took the advent of

Table 6.1 Training Topics for Topeka Police Department CIT

Day of the Week	Topics
Monday	Lifespan development; Child and adolescent brain development; Stigma; Developmental disorders; Autism spectrum disorders; Child and adolescent psychiatric disorders
Tuesday	Psychotropic medication; Parents of children with mental illness; Substance abuse and co-occurring disorders; Management of self in crisis intervention; Self-harm and mutilation; Violence interruption process; Personal story
Wednesday	Trauma informed care; Yellow ribbon program; Juvenile de-escalation
Thursday	Crisis intervention skill and risk assessment; Excited delirium; Parents of children with mental illness; Cultural competency; Minimizing childhood stress and supporting them during a caregiver's arrest; Classroom management of children with disorders
Friday	Bullying and cyberbullying; Increasing awareness of intellectual and developmental disabilities; Juvenile intake; Local justice agencies' presentations

Source: Topeka Police Department CIT Training schedule provided to author.

CIT to better meet the challenges of people with mental illness. For example, the Topeka Police Department used to take people with mental illness in crisis on a 75-mile trip to the psychiatric hospital in Osawatomie, only to be turned away for lack of beds. Law enforcement noted that these trips often proved a fruitless waste of time, with people with mental illness often ending up in the local jail anyway.

Valeo has worked in collaboration with criminal justice agencies for a number of years, including providing staff to serve as trainers for the Topeka Police Department CIT training. Table 6.1 provides a list of topics that are covered in current CIT training for the Topeka Police Department.

In addition, Valeo has assigned a mental health practitioner to work at the Shawnee County Detention Center and with grant money, has also placed two mental health personnel in the Topeka Police Department. These individuals accompany CIT-trained officers on two of the three daily shifts and help divert people with mental illness in crisis from the criminal justice system where appropriate. CIT-trained officers and Valeo mental health staff then follow up with those who are brought to Valeo after an encounter with police, providing some continuity of care.

The CIT Advisory Group in Topeka has backed a number of other initiatives to better meet the challenges that people with mental illness can pose to the criminal justice system. One such initiative was the Alternative Sentencing Court, which was the local name for the mental health court.[3] The CIT Advisory Group in Topeka had been long-time supporters to get one started, and three of its members drove to Wichita, Kansas, to see the first mental health court in the state in action. As a result of the Wichita mental health court's success, Valeo later received a $50,000 state grant to support the mental health court concept. A Valeo representative in Topeka indicated that so far 60 people had benefited from this court and new funding will support another 20 people participating. Individuals charged with a misdemeanor will be part of a one-year program and will work with a clinician and peer support staff to avoid jail (Moore, 2016; Ranker, 2016).

Another important initiative is the Family-to-Family Program. Sponsored by the National Alliance on Mental Illness (NAMI), the 12-week program is run by trained nurses with backgrounds in mental health whose families had been tragically touched by mental illness. Participants are able to hear firsthand about attempts to cope with the challenges of family members with mental illness. I had the opportunity to observe this program for myself and it provided deep insights into struggles, successes, and failures, which broadened my own limited horizons considerably.

Another key initiative is the implementation of CIT at the local jail. Inmates with mental health problems are often incarcerated due to a lack of community services. The people with mental illness who are incarcerated get their meds on a daily basis at a high cost to the taxpayer. An ordinary inmate without mental illness can be housed for $95 per day. If an inmate has a mental illness, the cost at least triples to $270 to $300 per day, because psychotropic medicines are expensive. Even with the provision of medications, many inmates with mental illness may come back to jail once released due to a lack of, or lack of access to, community services.[4] As seen above, Valeo has provided the jail with a psychiatrist and psychiatric nurse practitioner to assist the jail staff with the provision of mental health services. This has proved beneficial to both the staff and the community to have these individuals on site as a regular source of advice and assistance.

The Shawnee County Detention Center has also provided CIT training to about two-thirds of its jail staff. CIT International has modified CIT training

---

3. For more on mental health courts, see that chapter in *The Criminalization of Mental Illness*.

4. For more on the needs of offenders with mental illness that medication alone cannot address, see Chapter 2 in this reader.

Table 6.2 Training Topics for Shawnee County Detention Center CIT

Day of the Week	Topics
Wednesday	Introduction and overview; *New Asylums* video; The culture of corrections; Legality and mental health programs; Suicide prevention programs in jails
Thursday	Crisis intervention and de-escalation techniques; Alternative sentencing and discharge planning; The commitment process; Jail tour; NAMI representative and families living with mental illness

Source: Shawnee County Detention Center CIT Training schedule provided to author.

specifically for jail staff. Since 2016, the hours of mental health training that Shawnee County jail staff receive has jumped from just six to 48, thanks in large part to the addition of the aforementioned psychiatric nurse practitioner (Hrenchir, 2018). As seen in Table 6.2, the issues the training covers on the middle two days of the week are specific to the jail setting.

Lingering Challenges

On the heels of discussing CIT implementation in the local Topeka jail, a key lingering challenge is the fact that jail inspections are not required in Kansas. Cutting jail inspections was a purely financial move ordered by the governor back in the mid-1990s. Kansas is also one of the few states to leave jail training up to the local county governments. As a result, some of the more populated jails do require jail training, but many of the small jails in this state of 105 counties do not. This casual attitude about jails does little credit to the state's elected and appointed officials.

Frankly, states today have no business operating jails without laws that mandate jail training and jail inspection on at least a yearly basis. The fact that jails now have replaced nearly all state mental hospitals and the fact that many people with mental illness end up in jails due to a lack of adequately funded community mental health treatment facilities makes training more imperative. Jail standards must be modernized and updated, and jail staff must receive additional training and education in regard to the management of inmates with mental illness. Or, as a jail deputy put it over two decades ago after her survey of 35 county jails in Kansas, "officials need to cooperate with one another to form a jail officer training academy. Kansas counties have had relatively few lawsuits brought against them. But many jail administrators agree that it seems to be only a matter of time before the lack of jail officer training in Kansas is brought to the forefront of jail problems" (Cortright, 1993, p. 40). Indeed, a decade before Kansas destroyed its state jail standards, an editorial observed that the push to do the same in Washington State would attract more inmate lawsuits and allow politicians to decimate budgets while seeking cover under the guise of developing county-level standards (Kerle, 1987).

Conclusion

In my opinion, CIT programming has had a positive impact on the criminal justice systems in the Kansas communities that have employed the approach, as well as on the people with mental illness who encounter the police or jails in those jurisdictions. In fact, Kansas now has its own statewide CIT organization, which is currently involved in persuading counties and cities to provide CIT training to their criminal justice system staff, especially in law enforcement and corrections.

But CIT is just one approach that can play a helpful and significant role for people with mental illness. When a community is committed to involving all the agencies needed to cooperate together to meet challenges, real improvements can be made. The state of Kansas, beset by recent lackluster politicians, has made the road to improvement more difficult than it needs to be. However, many of these lawmakers failed to regain their seats in the November 2016 election, and today's Kansas legislative body has the potential to offer more hope to people with mental illness and those with substance abuse issues while slowing the revolving door of incarceration and reducing cost to the taxpayers.

Discussion Questions

1. Find out if any jurisdictions in your state have CIT training for law enforcement (see http://www.cit.memphis.edu/). Do any of those jurisdictions have CIT training for correctional officers? Should the way that CIT is evaluated for effectiveness be the same for law enforcement as for corrections? Why or why not?

2. What other agencies or institutions do you think could benefit from CIT training? For example, would you support CIT training at your college or

university? Why or why not?

3. Describe the role the criminal justice system in your community plays in confronting issues surrounding mental health. How successful is collaboration between criminal justice agencies, mental health facilities, and substance abuse treatment organizations? What, if anything, hinders collaboration?

4. Discuss the politics surrounding mental health and mental illness at the state and local level where you live. Be sure to address the role of NAMI (http://www.nami.org), if any, and to include the successes and failures of keeping people with mental illness out of the criminal justice system.

5. What role do you think the families and friends of people with mental illness play in getting initiatives like CIT training for law enforcement and correctional officers implemented? How do you think that role could be more pronounced?

References

Committee on Corrections and Juvenile Justice. (2012). Kansas State House Concurrent Resolution No. 5032. Retrieved from http://kslegislature.org/li_2012/b2011_12/measures/documents/hcr5032_01_0000.pdf.

Cortright, J. (1993). Jail officer training in Kansas. *American Jails, 7*, 36–40.

Ford, D. (1989). Executive director's remarks. *American Jails, 3*, 4–5.

Hrenchir, T. (2018, May 7). Shawnee County corrections steps up efforts to deal with mental illness. *The Topeka-Capital Journal.* Retrieved from: http://www.cjonline.com/news/20180506/shawnee-county-corrections-steps-up-efforts-to-deal-with-mental-illness.

Kerle, K. (1987). The jail tragedy of Washington State. *American Jails, 1*, 2–3.

Kerle, K. (1989). Editorial. *American Jails, 3*, 6–7.

Kerle, K. (1998). *American jails: Looking to the future.* Waltham, MA: Butterworth-Heinemann.

Kerle, K. (2003). *Exploring jail operations.* Hagerstown, MD: American Jail Association.

Kerle, K. (2016). The mentally ill and crisis intervention teams: Reflections on jails and the U.S. mental health challenge. *The Prison Journal, 96,* 153–161.

Moore, K. (2016, October 26). NAMI Topeka honors leaders in mental health services, advocacy Wednesday night. *The Topeka Capital-Journal.* Retrieved from http://cjonline.com/news/2016-10-26/nami-topeka-honors-leaders--mental-health-services-advocacy-wednesday-night.

Ranker, L. (2016, October 17). Valeo receives grant to continue supporting Topeka Municipal Court program. *The Topeka Capital-Journal*. Retrieved from http://cjonline.com/news/2016-10-17/valeo-receives-grant-continue-supporting-topeka-municipal-court-program.

Shorman, J. (2016). Handling Kansans with mental illness a matter of training for law enforcement. *KHI News Service*. Retrieved from http://www.khi.org/news/article/crisis-intervention-training-a-new-focus-for-law-enforcement.

Torrey, E. F. (2008). *The insanity offense: How America's failure to treat the seriously mentally ill endangers its citizens*. New York, NY: W. W. Norton & Company.

Torrey, E. F. (2014). *American psychosis: How the federal government destroyed the mental illness treatment system*. New York, NY: Oxford University Press.

7

Practicing in Corrections

*Maria "Maite" Silva, Philip Magaletta &
Alix McLearen*[1]

Introduction

Corrections is a growing field for psychologists and other mental health professionals due to an increase in incarceration rates and a decrease in hospital-based care for people with chronic mental illnesses (Mobley, 2008). People who might otherwise be receiving psychiatric care in hospitals are now housed in correctional settings due to the lingering effects of deinstitutionalization and the fact that individuals with mental health issues are more likely to be arrested (Steadman & Ribner, 1980; Teplin, 1984). Correctional facilities are now the largest inpatient treatment settings in the United States and house more individuals with mental illness than psychiatric hospitals (Lamb & Weinberger, 2005; Torrey, Kennard, Eslinger, Lamb & Pavle, 2010). To understand the extent to which psychologists are needed in correctional settings, one simply needs to consider the facts: all forms of mental illness are between two to four times higher in incarcerated populations, and approximately 8–16 percent of offenders have a severe mental illness, including schizophrenia or bipolar disorder (Diamond, Wang, Holzer, Thomas, & Cruser, 2001).

In meeting the needs of the offenders in correctional settings, psychologists may take on various job roles, such as serving as staff and chief psychologists,

---

1. The views expressed in this chapter are those of the authors only and do not reflect the official policy or opinions of the Department of Justice, Federal Bureau of Prisons, or any of their academic affiliates.

specialty psychology treatment program coordinators, crisis negotiators, employee assistance program managers, training and internship directors, and forensic evaluators. Owing to their broad, versatile, and diverse skill set, psychologists are also selected for other, non-service delivery roles in correctional organizations such as commissioner, superintendent, warden, director, or other administrative leader. However, for the purposes of this chapter, we focus on the roles and competencies that are foundational to the delivery of psychological services to offenders with mental illness in correctional settings, describe the challenges of providing such care, and propose solutions to these challenges alongside the benefits of a career working with underserved populations.

The Correctional Psychologist: Roles and Competencies

The overarching goal of correctional psychology, namely to evaluate and treat offenders in confined settings, has a documented history dating back more than a century (Maglaetta, Butterfield, & Patry, 2016). Since its beginning, correctional psychology has consistently grown toward deeper understandings of behavior, enhancing psychological functioning, and assisting offenders with societal adjustment (Wicks, 1974). Starting in the 1950s, psychologists began experiencing significant role expansion within correctional systems. Psychologists went from being viewed by some as "assistants to psychiatrists" (Knowles, 1949, p. 174)[2] to complementary and equal partners of medical providers, and from being limited to only making suggestions and recommendations for policies to now developing and implementing these alongside wardens and other agency leaders (Hawk, 1997). Additionally, while some therapeutic and advocacy work overlaps with those of social workers and case managers, psychologists' roles have expanded to include reentry tasks involving connecting offenders to community resources (Mobley, 2008).

Despite an increasingly diverse staff composition, there are various characteristics that mental health providers in corrections generally share. Among some of the major commonalities, these providers tend to share an interest in offenders and legal issues and have solid interpersonal boundaries that facilitate work with offenders (Boothby & Clements, 2002). In the words of Mobley

---

2. While psychologists and psychiatrists provide many of the same services, including but not limited to diagnosis and therapy, a key difference between the two is that only psychiatrists may prescribe medications.

(2008), the individuals providing psychological services must be "fair, firm, and consistent." We add that they must also possess the requisite foundational competencies that are broad and general in their application across the wide range of offenders they will be expected to work with. It is worth noting that in most jurisdictions, those with serious mental illness are only one segment of the offender population who require services. In fact, many of the psychological services delivered in contemporary correctional settings are aimed at the other 70 percent of offenders without serious mental illness, but who require services mandated by policy, such as screening, housing review, risk assessment, or transition planning (Faust & Magaletta, 2010). These services are all grounded in the following foundational competencies.

Competency 1: Screening and Assessment

Psychologists juggle various responsibilities in correctional settings. A unique task reserved solely for psychologists is conducting psychological screening, assessments, evaluations, and testing. While other staff members may be trained to conduct intakes and screenings, such as to determine offender custody and treatment programming and placement, offenders often need to be referred to psychologists for specialized individual mental health assessments. Mental status evaluations, for instance, may include face-to-face interviewing and include questions about immediate needs, problems, or medications. A record review might also be included. Psychological evaluations may be conducted to assess for issues including cognitive impairment or developmental disability, for which intelligence or ability testing may be warranted. Offenders may also be referred for mental health concerns, which may include risk assessments, such as when there is evidence, suspicion, or report of safety issues regarding the offender or others, such as potential suicidality or violence.

For example, psychologists may be asked to determine necessity and/or appropriateness of restrictive or protective housing; in fact, at times a mental health review is required for offenders with mental health issues to assess whether their inappropriate behavior suggesting a need for segregated housing may actually be resulting from a mental health problem (Mobley, 2008). Psychologists may have to conduct periodic assessments for those in restrictive housing to determine whether these offenders continue to require that placement. These decisions are made by tracking any mental health changes or decompensation, and then reporting the findings through proper documentation.

Findings may also be communicated by offering verbal input, such as by attending classification or review committee meetings. In communicating findings, behavioral observations and evidenced-based recommendations are key. The most commonly used instruments are the Minnesota Multiphasic Personality Inventory-2 Restructured Form (MMPI-2-RF) and the Wechsler Adult Intelligence Scale-Fourth Edition (WAIS-IV) and based on the results of these assessments, psychologists provide feedback and recommendations around decisions such as classification and treatment planning (Boothby & Clements, 2000).

Competency 2:
Psychotherapy and Interventions

Given the high rates of mental health issues among offenders, psychotherapy is often a necessary component of offenders' treatment plans while incarcerated. Some of the major diagnoses offenders present with include depression, psychosis, anxiety, and adjustment disorders, as well as substance use disorders (Boothby & Clements, 2000). In addition to carrying a therapy caseload, psychologists must also commit their time to crisis intervention and management (Mobley, 2008). During an offender crisis, the first task is to de-escalate the crisis. This step often involves active listening and exploration of the precipitants of the event. After it is determined that the offender is safe and secure, the psychologist helps the offender develop and practice adaptive coping strategies, while delivering psychosocial interventions that might yield more long-term coping benefits.

When psychologists are able to conduct therapy that does not revolve around crisis management, cognitive-behavioral therapy (CBT) has been proven quite effective (Landenberger & Lipsey, 2005), and both long and short-term interventions may be offered. Most therapy is delivered to address mental health treatment needs, and in many instances, to increase the potential for successful reentry while decreasing likelihood of future criminality. Of course, therapy ideally is conducted in a manner that respects the multicultural needs of the diverse populations being treated.[3]

---

3. For more on the use of CBT with sexual offenders in particular, see Chapter 4 in this reader. For more on the importance of cultural competency in treating offenders with mental illness, see Chapter 1 in this reader.

Andrews and Bonta (2003) have conducted and summarized extensive research that identifies effective, empirically supported principles for therapy that are elucidated in their Risk-Need-Responsivity (RNR) Model.[4] Their findings indicate that long-term, intensive treatment for high-risk offenders has positive effects, whereas treatment for low-risk offenders may actually demonstrate negative effects (Risk Principle). They argue that treatment should focus on the needs that are associated with illegal behavior, also known as criminogenic needs (i.e., substance abuse, anger management, sexual deviance), as per the Need Principle. Finally, their Responsivity Principle stresses an individualized approach to determining the methods that are likely to work for each offender, usually with a CBT focus. Beyond utilizing RNR principles, psychologists are also expected to utilize effective interpersonal skills, to model appropriate behavior, and to offer positive reinforcement in therapy (Gendreau, French, & Gionet, 2004).

Many of these approaches to change can be conducted in a group setting. This is beneficial given that mental health providers at institutions are limited in number and the group modality, where multiple offenders receive treatment simultaneously, allows them to extend their reach. Of groups offered, psychoeducational, cognitive skills, anger management, and process groups have historically been most popular in correctional settings (Boothby, 2000).

Competency 3:
Administration and Management

Since the 1980s, psychologists have been playing an increasingly administrative role in correctional settings, with administration accounting for approximately 30 percent of their work time (Boothby & Clements, 2000; Garland, McCarty, & Zhao, 2009). A major administrative role they are assigned involves supervision and consultation; these are growing fields for which specific training is required. Supervision consists of two core parts: structure performance and showing employees/supervisees consideration (Hersey, Blanchard, & Johnson, 2001; Magaletta & Verdeyen, 2005; Stogdill & Coons, 1957). Components of supervision include providing feedback, recognition, performance evaluation, and role clarification (Saylor & Wright, 1992). Supervision is key in shaping attitudes and outcomes in both job sat-

---

4. For more detail on the Risk-Need-Responsivity Model and its use with offenders with mental illness, see Chapter 2 in this reader.

isfaction and organizational commitment in correctional institutions, which bestows psychologists with significant power and responsibility (Garland et al., 2009).

Furthermore, psychologists' involvement in administrative and management roles has shifted intervention implementation from being almost solely client-focused to interventions that are also systemic in nature (Hawk, 1997). In particular, psychologists are now responsible for program development and evaluation, as well as for the management and oversight of staff (Boothby & Clements, 2000).

Competency 4:
Training and Research

While psychologists in correctional settings generally spend minimal time conducting research, they have expressed that they would like to allocate more time to this area (Boothby & Clements, 2000), and some certainly manage to. Research is crucial for the development of evidence-based practices that can be both feasible and effective in correctional settings; however, it has been difficult for psychologists to be able to conduct research, given that they are too often tasked with responsibilities that take priority, particularly crisis management (Mobley, 2008).

In contrast, psychologists are now spending increased amounts of time conducting staff trainings and in-services. For instance, they may offer workshops or trainings on topics such as referring offenders for suicide risk or mental health screening, as well as referring staff for employee assistance program services. Additionally, psychologists may be required to train interns and other staff, such as doctoral interns who lack experience using certain assessment instruments utilized for psychological testing, or nurses who must be able to recognize symptoms of severe mental illness and/or suicidal warning signs.

Competency 5:
Interdisciplinary Communication

Psychologists in correctional institutions are one ingredient of many on the interdisciplinary teams that exist in these settings. In order to be effective, they must be able to work as team players with other staff at the institutions, including security staff and psychiatrists, among others. Psychologists and other staff must understand each other's lines of work in order to productively work toward similar goals and outcomes for success, despite taking dissimilar avenues at times. Collaboration with security staff is absolutely essential, given that they spend significantly more time with offenders than do most other staff, including psychologists. For this reason, effective psychologists support offenders and staff by practicing what has been called "management by walking around" (Carlson & DiLulio, 2008), which allows them to see the reality of the institution from an involved, "in the trenches" perspective and not simply from the office. In the context of this style, psychologists have the opportunity to project themselves as proactive, assertive, and humble individuals and professionals who can build relationships with staff that are grounded in trust. Fostering these alliances may facilitate the teams' use of the psychologists' clinical judgements. These collaborative and trusting relationships allow correctional staff to be more receptive and responsive to the clinical recommendations made by psychologists, who advocate for the treatment of incarcerated individuals experiencing mental illness. Conversely, it allows the psychologists to remain teachable and learn from the experience of others on the teams. Overall, offenders with severe mental illness benefit from the therapeutic and collaborative relationships that psychologists establish not only with the offenders themselves, but also with the correctional staff that are most frequently in contact with them.

Psychologists must also be able to partner with other medical professionals to offer offenders the comprehensive psychiatric treatment that they often require. In part, this means that psychologists must develop not only a deep understanding for psychopathology but for psychopharmacology as well (Magaletta, Patry, Dietz, & Ax, 2007). This knowledge may become especially important during crisis intervention. Additionally, offenders in restraints require observation and assessment by both mental health and medical staff to monitor not only psychological state but physical health, including circulation (Mobley, 2008). It has also been shown that a combination of both medical and CBT approaches appears to be promising for specific issues, such as self-mutilation (Muehlenkamp, 2006).

In working with security, medical personnel, and other correctional staff in an interdisciplinary manner, psychologists are expected to cautiously monitor the climate of the institution by "keeping [their] finger on the pulse of the inmate population" (Wicks, 1974, p. 160) so as to skillfully detect unrest as it brews. They are charged with communicating with wardens about such matters and any concerns as they arise and must balance their duties as protectors of the safety and security of a vulnerable population against doing the same for staff.

Challenges, Solutions, and the Value of Being a Correctional Psychologist

While psychologists face various difficulties in their work due to the nature of the services that they provide, there are some challenges that are unique for correctional psychologists and which should be taken into account by those entering the field. It goes without saying that these challenges are only compounded when staff is not properly trained in the basic, foundational competencies of general clinical and counseling psychologist skills. When there are problems in that area, the addition of the following challenges may require immediate action.

Working conditions and the professional atmosphere in correctional settings are typically paramilitary in nature. This can represent a significant shift in culture for many psychologists, beyond issues of overcrowding and understaffing (Mobley, 2008). This culture may breed a sense of mistrust between security staff and psychologists, and psychologists may encounter communication difficulties with other staff. Additionally, aside from being exposed to a different culture, psychologists unfamiliar with a non-clinical environment may face disappointment in the ways that their actual time is spent at the workplace relative to how they may ideally wish to spend their time on various job duties. In reality, psychologists in correctional settings allocate about a third of their time to administrative demands, despite their reported desire to decrease this time by half to attend to intervention and offender contact (Garland et al., 2009).

For those who are able to spend more time with offenders, an additional challenge is presented, namely, working with a difficult population that often lacks insight, evidences significant behavioral and thinking problems, displays high rates of trauma, and is culturally diverse in a way that providers may not be fully prepared for (Mobley, 2008). Further, there are the particular issues and difficulties associated with all human service work, including a heavy focus on the negative or dysfunctional sides of people, lack of positive feedback, emotional strain, and, some might argue, limited hope for recovery and/or improvement (Maslach, 1982). Simply put, work with offenders can be tiring (Gerstein, Topp, & Correll, 1987).

Also, the field has shifted towards evidence-based treatment approaches that are standardized and even manualized, especially those utilizing CBT approaches. Some psychologists may perceive or experience this as a loss of autonomy in working with offenders. Lastly, while there are opportunities for promotion or recognition within the profession, psychologists have raised concerns about the limited number of such opportunities. Some voice a need to relocate and to pursue other avenues in achieving professional advancement in the field (Boothby & Clements, 2002; Hawk, 1997).

Despite the undeniable challenges associated with being a correctional psychologist, there are many advantages that not only draw individuals into the field but that also manage to keep them there, often creating a lifelong career in corrections. It is worthwhile to note that psychologists in corrections do report overall satisfaction in their careers, comparable to those working in other settings (Boothby & Clements, 2002). This may be due to factors such as being in a stimulating environment, having a solid sense of job security, and/or having the opportunity to engage in various tasks and functions within one's work roles as a correctional psychologist. There are tremendous advantages to working with a population that is broadly diverse and demographically rich, not only in terms of identity and background factors but also with regard to pathology. This is appealing for psychologists who enter the field with an interest in such matters. Unlike other practice settings, correctional facilities are usually able to offer extensive clinical information, including readily accessible records and documentation of constant observations, which makes it possible to develop a more complete conceptualization of offenders. The environment is fast-paced and frequently offers new challenges, which many find more appealing than working in an office setting.

Additionally, there are clear opportunities for continuity of care, as psychologists are able to see offenders from the beginning to the end of their treatment, and as a result, to gain an adequate perspective on what was and was not effective in working on a particular case. Further, offenders pending release may have additional motivational factors that incentivize them to engage in treatment in the hopes of achieving lasting change. Perhaps for these reasons, psychology staff in particular have reported job satisfaction above and beyond that of other correctional staff (Garland et al., 2009). Research indicates that psychologists perceive their therapeutic relationships with offenders as a major influence on job satisfaction, particularly if the psychologist demonstrates efficacy in working with these individuals (Boothby & Clements, 2002; Garland et al., 2009). Psychologists also report significant satisfaction from working with others on their interdisciplinary teams (Boothby & Clements, 2002).

Despite some stereotypes about the dangerousness of or risks in working at a correctional setting, psychologists have indicated that they value the sense of safety they experience in having intact security systems in their work spaces (Boothby & Clements, 2002). In fact, psychology staff shows more satisfaction in this regard at higher security institutions, which offer safety features in a way that many public health work settings do not (Garland et al., 2009). This is likely to continue, as new laws and policies are created to further protect psychologists in law enforcement settings, for example, allowing correctional staff to carry and use pepper spray or to wear stab resistant vests.

Correctional settings also offer psychologists unique and ongoing educational opportunities, beyond the rich learning opportunities that come from working with the incarcerated. Even before entering correctional institutions, some sites offer pre- and postdoctoral training that prepare psychologists in the making for clinical careers in corrections (Magaletta & Verdeyen, 2005). For psychologists already in the field, learning opportunities range from intensive trainings to frequent in-service opportunities and workshops that serve to broaden the learning experience (Magaletta et al., 2007).

Finally, certain human resource benefits may be available to those working in correctional settings. These may range from seemingly minor perks, such as receiving transit subsidies that offset commuting costs to work, to certain retirement benefits. One factor that is appealing to psychologists familiar with the challenges of work schedules and issues associated with these (e.g., overtime, no shows), is the quality of life that a correctional schedule allows. For example, hours may be set from 7:30 AM to 4:00 PM, allowing correctional psychologists to preserve a work-life balance.

Conclusion

As prison work has evolved, the role of the mental health professional in promoting not only wellness, but in reducing recidivism and strengthening adaptive behavior, has grown. Correctional psychologists engage in meaningful clinical work that includes assessment, crisis management, and CBT, with a population of individuals facing complex lifestyle, criminal justice, and mental health needs. Because this work is so challenging, five competencies are recommended to support best practices: screening and assessment, psychotherapies and intervention, administration and management, training and research, and interdisciplinary communication. While correctional psychology certainly has challenges, proper practice is highly rewarding to the clinician and beneficial to society.

Discussion Questions

1. Do you think anything is missing from the list of foundational competencies in this chapter? If so, how would practitioners gain practice exposure to these areas?

2. In what specific ways can you envision changes to the community mental health services system that could influence correctional practice settings of the future?

3. How do you envision technology influencing the future of psychology service delivery in correctional settings?

4. What aspects of correctional psychology are appealing to you and why? Which ones are unappealing to you and why?

5. What self-care strategies would you envision needing to put in place for you to have a satisfying and fulfilling career delivering psychological services in a correctional setting?

References

Boothby, J. L., & Clements, C. B. (2000). A national survey of correctional psychologists. *Criminal Justice and Behavior, 27*, 716–732.

Boothby, J. L., & Clements, C. B. (2002). Job satisfaction and correctional psychologists: Implications for recruitment and retention. *Professional Psychology: Research and Practice, 33*, 310–315.

Carlson, P., & DiLulio, J. J. (2008). Organization and management. In P. Carlson & J. Simon Garrett (Eds.), *Policy and jail administration practice and theory* (2nd ed., pp. 193–211). Sudbury, MA: Jones and Bartlett.

Diamond, P. M., Wang, E. W., Holzer III, C. E., Thomas, C. R., & Cruser, D. A. (2001). The prevalence of mental illness in prison: Review and policy implications. *Administration and Policy in Mental Health, 29*, 21–40.

Faust, E., & Magaletta, P. R. (2010). Factors predicting levels of female inmates' use of psychological services. *Psychological Services, 7*, 1–10.

Garland, B. E., McCarty, W. P., & Zhao, R. (2009). Job satisfaction and organizational commitment in prisons. *Criminal Justice and Behavior, 36*(2), 163–183.

Gendreau, P., French, S. A., & Gionet, A. (2004). What works (what doesn't work): The principles of effective correctional treatment. *Journal of Community Corrections, 13*(3), 4–6.

Gerstein, L. H., Topp, C. G., & Correll, G. (1987). The role of the environment and person when predicting burnout among correctional personnel. *Criminal Justice and Behavior, 14*(3), 352–369.

Hawk, K. M. (1997). Personal reflections on a career in correctional psychology. *Professional Psychology: Research and Practice, 28,* 335–337.

Hersey, P., Blanchard, K. H., & Johnson, D. E. (2001). *Management of school behavior: Leading human resources* (8th ed.). Upper Saddle River, NJ: Prentice Hall.

Knowles, J. A. (1949). The role of the prison psychologist. In *Proceedings of the Oklahoma Academy of Science for 1949* (pp. 172–175). Edmond, OK: Oklahoma Academy of Science.

Lamb, H. R., & Weinberger, L. E. (2005). The shift of psychiatric inpatient care from hospitals to jails and prisons. *Journal of the American Academy of Psychiatry and the Law, 33*(4), 529–534.

Landenberger, N. A., & Lipsey, M. W. (2005). The positive effective of cognitive-behavioral programs for offenders: A meta-analysis of factors associated with effective treatment. *Journal of Experimental Criminology, 1,* 451–476.

Magaletta, P. R., Butterfield, P., & Patry, M. (2016). Correctional Settings. In J. C. Norcross, G. R. VandenBos, & D. K. Freedheim (Eds.), *The APA handbook of clinical psychology: Roots and branches* (Vol. 1, pp. 539–549). Washington, D.C.: American Psychological Association.

Magaletta, P. R., Patry, M. W., Dietz, E. F., & Ax, R. (2007). What is correctional about clinical practice in corrections? *Criminal Justice and Behavior, 34,* 7–21.

Magaletta, P. R., & Verdeyen, V. (2005). Clinical practice in corrections: A conceptual framework. *Professional Psychology: Research and Practice, 36,* 37–43.

Maslach, C. (1982). *Burnout: The cost of caring.* Englewood Cliffs, NJ: Prentice Hall.

Muehlenkamp, J. J. (2006). Empirically supported treatments and general therapy guidelines for non-suicidal self-injury. *Journal of Mental Health Counseling, 28*(2), 166–185.

Saylor, W. G., & Wright, K. N. (1992). Status, longevity, and perceptions of the work environment among federal prison employees. *Journal of Offender Rehabilitation, 17*(3–4), 133–160.

Steadman, H. J., & Ribner, S. A. (1980). Changing perceptions of the mental health needs of inmates in local jails. *The American Journal of Psychiatry, 137*(9), 1115–1116.

Stogdill, R. M., & Coons, A. E. (1957). *Leader behavior: Its description and measurement.* Columbus. OH: The Ohio State University.

Teplin, L. A. (1984). Criminalizing mental disorder: The comparative arrest rate of the mentally ill. *American Psychologist, 39*(7), 794–803.

Torrey, E. F., Kennard, A. D., Eslinger, D., Lamb, R., & Pavle, J. (2010). *More mentally ill persons are in jails and prisons than hospitals: A survey of the states.* Arlington, VA: Treatment Advocacy Center.

Wicks, R. J. (1974). *Applied psychology for law enforcement and correction officers.* New York, NY: McGraw-Hill.

Media Coverage of
People with Mental Illness

Katti Gray

Introduction

The Internet permanently altered the flow of news and the types of news that get reported—with varying degrees of clarity, efficiency, and accuracy—during the 24/7 news cycle. To be sure, high quality, reliable journalism still is being done by an array of legacy newsrooms and newer digital-only news organizations, even as many of those organizations fight to balance their finances, pay staffers and other contributors, and encourage the broader public to actually underwrite the journalism it relies upon. However, these less lucrative times for the news industry have yielded fewer full-time paid journalists, an increasing reliance on independent freelance journalists and, some critics contend, a pool of news professionals that is less diverse demographically and sometimes less nuanced in its approach to newsgathering and delivery.

Layered atop those challenges is the 24-hour, 7-day-a-week, non-stop news cycle itself: When being the first to get on air, online, and/or into print with a big, breaking news story becomes a primary goal, some essential explanatory and contextual facts, opinions, and truths can get left on the cutting floor. Coverage of mental health, mental illness, and persons hamstrung by or flourishing amid mental illness are areas where journalism and journalists could stand to be shored up, observers say. This is especially critical, given that stories linking crime and mental illness disproportionately make headlines.

Indeed, the news business can do harm on this front, but also has the potential to reverse that troubling trend in headlines. Journalists are aware of this. For example, the Association of Health Care Journalists, whose membership includes physician journalists, researcher journalists, and other journalists who are not scientists, has increasingly added mental health topics—including criminogenic factors and mental illness, among others[1]—to its annual conference workshop line-up. The largest group of its kind in the world, the Association of Health Care Journalists helps its members to more accurately cover health issues by providing instruction on medical nomenclature, on what makes for legitimate and illegitimate scientific research or medical care, and on how to parlay that mother lode of information into news that the average person can understand and put into practical use. Additionally, the organization tracks where mental illness has been given undue attention in crime stories or has been insufficiently or inaccurately couched in general news stories.

Inaccuracies in Reporting on Mental Illness

Those and other efforts notwithstanding, news coverage of mental illness frequently misses the mark, according to Dr. Colleen Barry, chair of the Department of Health Policy and Management at the Johns Hopkins University Bloomberg School of Public Health. Too often, it grossly mischaracterizes people with mental health diagnoses and those who are suspected of being mentally ill and who find themselves in the news for their alleged or actual role in crime.

"I would assume that, just like [in many other] professions, folks go into journalism to improve the world and do a good job and get the story right. And that raises the question of what creates an environment for getting the story right," said Barry,[2] a lead researcher or co-researcher on several key studies parsing news coverage of persons with mental illness.

"Journalists," she continued, "are not so different from the rest of us. If there are broader societal stereotypes that are a form of misinformation, the journalist community is not immune to those stereotypes. If the broader public thinks people with mental illness are far more dangerous than people in the general public, it's reasonable that [some] journalists would, as well, hold the same view."

---

1. For more on criminogenic factors among people with mental illness and how those factors facilitate their justice system involvement, see Chapter 2 in this reader.

2. This and the other quotations featured in the chapter come from direct communication with the author.

Strong evidence for her assertion is found in McGinty, Kennedy-Hendricks, Choksy, and Barry (2016). The study analyzed a random sample of 400 news articles about mental illness. Barry and others on that research team concluded that 55 percent of those articles homed in on violence committed by persons with mental illness, while just 14 percent spotlighted recovery from mental illness or persons who were thriving largely because their mental illness was being well treated medically. Publication of those violence-focused stories was more frequent in the study's second 10 years than in its first 10 years. The researchers conclude that "news media's continued emphasis on interpersonal violence is highly disproportionate to actual rates of violence among those with mental illnesses. Research suggests that this focus may exacerbate social stigma and decrease support for public policies that benefit people with mental illnesses" (McGinty et al., 2016, p. 1121).

The ways in which journalists frame and deliver mental health news sometimes reinforces inherent, pre-existing stigma, Barry added.[3] Preceding that 2016 analysis was her investigation comparing medical insurance for bodily ailments to less comprehensive insurance coverage for people with mental illness. "That got me to the role of the news media and the profound impact the news media has on our lives and, in particular, the way the public sees different groups in the society who are beneficiaries of or hurt by policies enacted by Congress, state legislatures, insurance companies," Barry said. "I've been interested both in documented ways the news media portrays the population of people with mental illness but also studying how changes in those portrayals may change the public view in a way that is more humanizing … and that leads to a more equitable, helpful public policy."

Certainly, we are a nation grappling still with the bare medical facts of what constitutes mental illnesses but also how to view mental illness on par with bodily impairments, as well as with how to shape a reasoned, heavily news-driven public discourse about the science of mental illness, its related policy concerns, and the nation's collective handling of individuals diagnosed with a mental health issue.

Journalists do not bear sole responsibility for shaping medical and public policy on mental illness or the rules and regulations on persons with mental illness who become involved with the criminal justice system; the primary job of journalists is reporting the news, and that news often is dictated by police, the courts, and correctional agencies logging persons with mental illness into the system.

---

3. For more on stigmatization of mental illness and people with mental illness, see Chapter 3 in this reader.

Mental Health Reporting Resources for Journalists

Nevertheless, journalists are obligated to report mental health issues accurately and optimally. There are tools for getting there. The Carter Center (2015), partnering with Emory University, has published The Carter Center Journalism Resource Guide on Behavioral Health.[4]

In addition to schooling journalists on preferred language to describe persons with mental illness—"a person with a substance use disorder" versus "an addict" or "a person is hallucinating" versus "a person is crazy"—the guide provides other ground-level advice. "Consider," the Carter guide suggests, "three important questions" in coverage:

1) Is mental illness or substance use relevant to the story? If it is not meaningfully linked to the story, there is no need to mention it. Avoid speculation and the generalized belief that behavioral health conditions explain unusual acts or behavior.

2) What is your source for the mental illness and substance use diagnosis? Don't rely on hearsay. If someone's mental and substance use disorder is relevant, make sure your source is authorized to share information about the person's lived experience and that the information is accurate. Often individual circumstances have much more impact on events, such as violence or homicide covered in breaking news, than the presence of behavioral health conditions.

3) What is the most accurate language to use? Using terms like "crazy," "lunatic," or "psycho" can perpetuate stereotypes and the discrimination experienced by people living with behavioral health conditions. Describe the individual first as a person who also is living with a specific behavioral health issue. It is important to note that the most accurate term to use is "substance use," not "substance abuse" or "substance misuse" (Carter Center, 2015, p. 3).

---

4. Former First Lady Rosalynn Carter has championed mental health issues for decades. She has launched the annual Rosalynn Carter Fellowships for Mental Health Journalism, which includes a database of fellows' news projects, including ones exploring the arrests of persons of mental illness, adjudication of their cases, and the disproportionate tally of persons with mental illness who linger behind bars, including during in pre-trial detention, because there are not enough psychiatric beds available so that their competency to stand trial can be assessed. The searchable database is available here: https://www.cartercenter.org/health/mental_health/fellowships/archive/index.html.

"It's very hard to evaluate some of this.... The broader trend is that, in some ways, coverage of mental illness has gotten better ... except when it comes to mental illness and crime and violence," said clinical psychologist Dr. Caroline Clauss-Ehlers, Rutgers University professor, former Rosalynn Carter Mental Health Journalism Fellow, and member of the fellowship's advisory board. "For some reason, when mental illness and violence are mentioned, the basic tenets of reporting often are thrown out the door and these stories become, almost, entertainment news. But, really, reporting should dig in. Stick to the facts. Don't speculate. Give the context: Was this person in treatment? Ever in treatment? Exposed to violence when they were growing up, an issue that effects people whether or not they have mental illness?"

She continued: "We don't need journalists to be advocates, but we need to show the domino effect. If reporting continues in this [superficial, sometimes error-filled] way, it keeps people from treatment. It promotes stigma that mental illness is linked to violence or that violent people all have mental illness.... Who would want to be connected to that idea? You will not share with anyone and you will not get treatment. You're afraid it will affect your life, your relationship, your job. Tweets, headlines, images, all of this is important to look at."

Researchers, she noted, have concluded that 3% to 5% of violent crimes are committed by people with serious mental illness (Metzl & MacLeish, 2015).

Getting—and Reporting—the Facts

Like Clauss-Ehlers, Doris A. Fuller is a journalist-turned-researcher and advocate. In 2017, she left the Treatment Advocacy Center, a national non-profit think tank, reform and advocacy center, where she had been at the helm of its communications and research arms. Where, why, and how the media have stereotyped the mentally ill as more prone to violence than persons without mental illness is a complex, concerning issue, she said. "I come at these questions from so many different points of view," added Fuller, whose former agency is tackling, among other issues, the lack of psychiatric beds for diagnosing criminally charged persons being held in jail pre-trial. Its recent analysis concluded that in 2016, 90,000 of 400,000 pre-trial inmates could not have their cases adjudicated because "they were too disordered to understand the charges under which they had been detained" and were still awaiting either an initial or follow-up psychiatric evaluation (Fuller, Sinclair, Lamb, Case, &

Snook, 2017). "In some states, people had been waiting for over a year to be restored to competency," Fuller said, so they could have their court cases heard.

Regarding her work with journalists probing those and related issues, Fuller said, "When I came to the Treatment Advocacy Center in mid-2010 as communications director, the questions I commonly got from reporters at every experience level showed that their base of knowledge about mental illness was pretty low. They were not asking the right questions at all.... And I do not remember many of them asking about the role of mental illness in incarceration." While there remains much room for reporters to improve their fundamental knowledge of mental illness, many of them are getting up to speed, said Fuller, whose daughter, diagnosed with bipolar disorder and psychosis, committed suicide when she was 28. "Back then, there would be reporters who called who really didn't know what psychosis was," she said of her early years at the Treatment Advocacy Center. "Many of them didn't have basic knowledge of what is serious mental illness and its symptoms, or of aspects of mental illness that result in people being homeless or arrested or violent," Fuller said. Among other appearances before journalists, Fuller has been an expert panelist at John Jay College Center on Media, Crime and Justice conferences that launch fellowships for journalists nationwide as they cover cutting-edge criminal justice and justice policy topics, including mental health care in prisons, jails and community-based projects for the formerly incarcerated who are reentering mainstream society.

"But in the years since then [2010]," she added, "it's like the media went to university. The overall level of understanding of mental illness among general reporters, not just those who are specialists, has continued to improve. Now, they come to me having read and having done a lot of homework. They are well up to speed. It has been interesting and exciting from an advocacy or communications standpoint. Now, you can get into more nuanced, new topics. You can take the conversation from centering on the very most basic things to questions of why someone with mental illness is in contact with police, of the role of mental illness in police shootings, of why the federal government [until recently], wasn't collecting data on the role of mental illness in law enforcement homicide, and mental illness is a factor in 30 percent of all those homicides;" Tindy, Tate, Jenkins, Rich, Alexander, and Lowery (2015) place the rate higher, at 50 percent.

Room for Improvement

One factor currently placing mental illness higher on the radar of the general public, policymakers, and legislators is the sheer, rising cost of having a disproportionately large number of people with mental illness confined to jails and prisons (Steinberg, Mills, & Romano, 2015). Another factor, according to Fuller, has been the surge in high-profile mass killings and other gun violence by persons with mental illness; as alluded to above, studies continue to show that the vast majority of persons with mental illness are not violent (Beckett, 2014).

"There were tragic shootings ... including of Congresswoman Gabrielle Giffords. A congresswoman and a federal judge getting shot was a big story," Fuller said. "And before that, we'd had the Virginia Tech shootings by someone with untreated mental illness.... There was one episode after another, with mass shootings in Newtown and Santa Barbara as bookends. We were getting telephone calls from media: 'What's this thing with mental illness and violence?' It's unfortunate that we have these treatment issues and trends and that it takes these acts of violence to get everyone's attention. Be that as it may ... we're talking about people with profound mental illness and a system that sometimes fails people like that."

Those failures do get minimized, including by some journalists—the aforementioned strides among the most referenced and researched news reporters, notwithstanding, "If I would fault the media for anything, right now—and I do see less of this today than I did five years ago, seven years ago—is that there are reporters who accept faulty, oversimplified answers. Some reporters do get attached to some part of the ideological spectrum, including people in the anti-psychiatry movement, and miss some of the good information out there," Fuller said.

Added to those challenges facing journalists covering mental illness among people involved in the criminal justice system is a tendency of some mental health advocates to be so fixated on not further stigmatizing those with mental illness that they refuse to address what, for journalists and others, are unequivocal facts.

"It's a given that this population has suffered enough without being further, gratuitously stigmatized by police, media.... But there is not a lot of agreement of how to avoid stigma altogether, which leads to some of the worst mistakes," Fuller said.

> There's this notion that the way to not stigmatize people is not to talk about anything bad, to not report on violence committed by people with mental illness. You've got some academics and whomever else saying people with mental illness are no more likely to be violent than anyone else. That is not entirely true; the National Institutes Mental Health and [Substance Abuse and Mental Health Services Administration] will tell you that.... But you have people who feel that if we can stop people from believing this fact, the fact will go away and the media will go out and report that. The reality is we don't know how to elim-

inate stigma.... So, what I would prefer talking about is the idea that there is no health without mental health, and that we have in this country a small subset of profoundly ill people who use a grossly disproportionate amount of public resources because they are so sick, so much more likely to be in jail, in court, in a police car.... This is the higher-level view that the body politick, the news media, and the rest of us, should be looking at if we are going to come up with any real solutions to avoid criminalizing people with mental illness.

Discussion Questions

1. What is the fundamental role and duty of journalists?

2. How do you think journalism should intersect with the lived experiences of persons with mental illness involved with the criminal justice system?

3. In what ways might journalists better convey the myriad stories involving the criminal justice system's handling of persons with mental illness?

4. Which individuals, throughout and outside of the criminal justice system, should be interviewed for those stories? Why do you think so?

5. Find a story about a person with mental illness who is justice involved from a local or national media outlet. What stands out to you as responsible or irresponsible reporting in the story, and why?

References

Beckett, L. (2014). Myth v. fact: Violence and mental illness. *ProPublica*. Retrieved from https://www.propublica.org/article/myth-vs-fact-violence-and-mental-health.

The Carter Center. (2015). *The Carter Center journalism resource guide on behavioral health*. Retrieved from https://www.cartercenter.org/resources/pdfs/health/mental_health/2015-journalism-resource-guide-on-behavioral-health.pdf.

Fuller, D. A., Sinclair, E., Lamb, H. R., Case, J. D., & Snook, J. (2017). *Emptying the new asylums*. The Treatment Advocacy Center. Retrieved from http://www.treatmentadvocacycenter.org/storage/documents/emptying-new-asylums.pdf.

McGinty, E. E., Kennedy-Hendricks, A., Choksy, S., & Barry, C. L. (2016). Trends in news media coverage of mental illness in the United States: 1995–2014. Health Affairs, 35, 1121–1129.

Metzl, J. M., & MacLeish, K. (2015). Mental illness, mass shootings, and the politics of American firearms. *American Journal of Public Health*, *105*, 240–249.

Steinberg, D., Mills, D., & Romano, M. (2015). When did prisons become acceptable mental healthcare facilities? Stanford Law School Three Strikes Project. Retrieved from https://law.stanford.edu/wp-content/uploads/sites/default/files/publication/863745/doc/slspublic/Report_v12.pdf.

Tindy, K., Tate, J., Jenkins, J., Rich, S., Alexander, K. L., & Lowery, W. (2015, May 30). Fatal police shootings in 2015 approaching 400 nationwide. *The Washington Post*. Retrieved from https://www.washingtonpost.com/national/fatal-police-shootings-in-2015-approaching-400-nationwide/2015/05/30/d322256a-058e-11e5-a428-c984eb077d4e_story.html?utm_term=.de39f1d3e47d.

Mental Health Courts: Therapeutic Jurisprudence for Offenders with Mental Illness

Arthur J. Lurigio

Introduction

Fundamental changes in mental health laws and policies have brought criminal justice professionals into contact with people with serious mental illnesses (PWSMI) at every stage of the criminal justice process (Lurigio & Swartz, 2000). Police arrest PWSMI because few other options are readily available to handle their disruptive public behavior or to obtain much-needed treatment or housing for them (Teplin, 2000). Among the 11 million people arrested in the United States annually, 600,000 are likely to suffer from an acute mental illness, and another six million suffer from substance use and other psychiatric illnesses (James & Glaze, 2006). Jail and prison administrators often struggle to treat and protect PWSMI. Judges grapple with limited sentencing alternatives for PWSMI who fall outside of specific forensic categories (e.g., guilty but mentally ill). Probation officers scramble to obtain scarce community services and programs for PWSMI and often cannot fit them into standard correctional categories or monitor them successfully with traditional case management strategies (Lurigio & Swartz, 2000). When PWSMI are sentenced to prison, their disorders complicate and impede their ability to comply with institutional rules and norms and increase their vulnerability to victimization. After they are placed on parole, they have difficulties adhering to the conditions of release, compounding the already onerous challenges of prisoner reentry (Council of State Governments, 2002).

The presence of mental disorders among justice-involved individuals complicates the supervision and custodial responsibilities of the criminal justice system. PWSMI who are incarcerated in jail or prison require costly treatments and impose a burden on correctional supervision. They also spend more time incarcerated and are more likely to be victimized while incarcerated than those without serious mental illnesses (Ditton, 1999; James & Glaze, 2006).[1]

Offenders with mental illnesses are three times more likely than those with no mental illness to have histories of arrest, probation sentences, and incarcerations (James & Glaze, 2006). PWSMI on probation or parole supervision are highly likely to violate the terms of their supervision, placing them at heightened risk of reincarceration (Skeem, Emke-Francis, & Louden, 2006). The penetration of offenders with mental illnesses into deeper levels of criminal justice involvement adversely affects public safety, public health, and public spending (Prins & Draper, 2009). Indeed, "as PWSMI continue to come in contact with the criminal justice system, communities across the United States struggle to develop interventions and supports that improve outcomes for these individuals, their service providers, and the public" (Almquist & Dodd, 2009, p. 3). The current chapter focuses on a popular strategy for dealing with the challenges of PWSMI during the pre- and post-adjudication stages of the criminal justice process: the mental health court (MHC).

The Development of Mental Health Courts (MHCs)

PWSMI in the Criminal Justice System

MHCs emerged out of a growing awareness that substantial numbers of PWSMI were appearing before the judiciary (Bernstein & Seltzer, 2004). Evidence suggests that 15–20 percent of those in correctional populations suffer from a serious mental illness—a percentage that is substantially higher than the representation of PWSMI in the general population (Ditton, 1999). Few of these individuals met the standards for incompetency or insanity or had their illnesses addressed in sentencing or court supervision plans. "People with

---

1. For more on the challenges PWSMI face in prison, see Chapter 10 in this reader. For more on the challenges PWSMI face when reentering the community after incarceration, see Chapter 11 in this reader.

mental illness [have been] falling through the cracks of this country's social safety net and are landing in the criminal justice system at an alarming rate" (Council of State Governments, 2002, p. 3). PWSMI often cycle repeatedly through the criminal justice system, in part because of the court's failure to recognize that psychiatric illness contributes to their continued criminal activity (Lurigio & Swartz, 2000).

Advocates, researchers, and legal scholars called for the creation of specialized programs that could respond justly, fairly, and humanely to PWSMI at every stage of the legal process—from arrest to reentry after prison (Lurigio & Swartz, 2000). Two converging legal trends spurred the development of MHCs as an appropriate mechanism for handling the problems of criminally involved PWSMI: therapeutic jurisprudence (TJ) and the drug court movement. The former laid the philosophical groundwork for specialized courts, and the latter developed and tested the basic elements for successful specialized court operations (Watson, Hanrahan, Luchins, & Lurigio, 2001).

MHC and its forerunner, drug treatment court (DTC), are examples of problem-solving courts, which are predicated on the notion that offender change can be best effectuated when underlying behavioral healthcare problems are addressed. Such courts operate in a non-adversarial climate that involves multidisciplinary teams of professionals that share the goal of client recovery and rehabilitation through treatment and ancillary services that reduce recidivism. Problem-solving courts involve partnerships between public agencies (e.g., courts and probation departments) and social service providers (e.g., substance abuse, mental health, employment, and housing agencies). As discussed below, problem-solving courts require participants[2] to have regular contact with judges and other program stakeholders and subject participants to high levels of monitoring (e.g., home visits, status hearings, drug testing); they also provide graduated sanctions for rule breaking (e.g., stepped-up curfews and jail stays), and increasing rewards for program compliance (e.g., early termination).

Therapeutic Jurisprudence (TJ)

TJ first appeared in the law literature in the late 1980s, in the context of mental health law. TJ is defined as "the study of the extent to which substantive rules, legal procedures, and the roles of lawyers and judges produce therapeutic or antitherapeutic consequences for individuals involved in the legal process"

---

2. The terms participant/participants and client/clients are used interchangeably in this chapter to refer to those who are enrolled in mental health courts.

(Hora, Schma, & Rosenthal, 1999, p. 440). TJ has emerged as an approach for examining an extensive array of legal subjects, including the response of the criminal court system to the problems and needs of PWSMI and the effect of legal decisions on therapeutic outcomes.

Legal scholars view TJ as the application of social scientific theories and methodologies from a wide variety of disciplines for the purpose of understanding and promoting the psychological wellbeing of participants in the legal process. TJ recognizes that the law and legal actors, as well as legal rules and procedures, can all have therapeutic (favorable and healthy) or antitherapeutic (unfavorable and unhealthy) consequences for those who are affected by the court's activities and decisions (Wexler & Winick, 1996). The concept of TJ favors the court's adoption of a problem-solving, proactive, hands-on, results-oriented posture that is responsive to the emotional and social problems of legal consumers.

TJ conceptualizes the law as a social force and judges as therapeutic agents who exercise the court's authority to promote clients' psychological health and social interests, protect their due process rights, and ensure that justice is served in every case (Wexler & Winick, 1996). The National Association for Court Management and the National Center for State Courts widely touted TJ as an effective approach for delivering court services (Schema, 2005). Furthermore, the National Trial Court Performance Standards incorporated the TJ concept in Standard 4.5, which states that:

> The trial court anticipates new conditions and emergent events and adjusts its operations as necessary. Effective trial courts are responsive to emergent public issues, such as drug abuse, child and spousal abuse, AIDS, drunken driving, child support enforcement, crime and public safety, consumer rights, gender bias, and more efficient use of fewer resources. A trial court that moves deliberately in response to emergent issues is a stabilizing force in society and acts consistently with its role in maintaining the rule of law.

"Mental illness" clearly falls within the purview of the TJ framework. Before the court turned its therapeutic attention to PWSMI, however, it first employed TJ in its handling of drug cases.

Drug Treatment Courts (DTCs)

The most recent war on drugs, launched with the passage of the Anti-Drug Abuse Act of 1988, led to a massive influx of offenders at every stage of the criminal justice process, contributing to overtaxed court dockets and massive prison overcrowding (Lurigio, 2003). Specialized DTCs were implemented in response to an unprecedented wave of drug offenders and their tendency to cycle through the criminal justice and treatment systems (Lurigio, 2000). Drug courts are based on several major premises and include key components that have been adapted by MHCs, such as specialized court dockets and a team approach to handling cases (e.g., Cooper, 1998; Drug Courts Program Office, 1997). The 10 essential elements of DTCs are as follows:

- The integration of alcohol and other drug treatment services with justice system case processing.
- The adoption of a non-adversarial approach that promotes public safety and protects participants' due process rights.
- Early identification of eligible participants and prompt placement into DTC programming.
- Access to a continuum of alcohol, drug, and other related treatment and rehabilitation services.
- The monitoring of abstinence through frequent alcohol and other drug testing.
- A coordinated strategy to respond consistently to participants' compliance and noncompliance with program conditions.
- Regular and immediate judicial interactions with each DTC participant.
- The implementation of program monitoring and evaluation measures to gauge program effectiveness and attainment of goals.
- Continuing education to promote effective drug court planning, implementation, and operations.
- The formation of partnerships among drug courts, public agencies, and community-based organizations to generate local support and enhance DTC effectiveness (National Association of Drug Court Professionals, 2015).

DTC's basic philosophy views addiction as a chronic brain disease that precipitates or intensifies criminal behavior. Relapses are expected during recovery, but they also afford opportunities for personal growth and eventual sobriety. DTCs integrate treatment with other rehabilitative services and criminal justice case processing. When successfully treated, persons with addiction are less likely to recidivate in terms of rearrest, reincarceration, and readmission (Lurigio, 2000). DTCs use formal leverage or coercion to encourage offenders to begin and remain engaged in treatment programs. Judges exercise their moral and legal authority in overseeing the recovery process, and they take a strong professional interest in each offender's recovery.[3]

The creation of MHCs benefited from the political groundwork, successful implementation, and purported successes of DTCs. Although the quality of some of the research undertaken to evaluate DTCs has been questionable, most reviews have touted the accomplishments of DTCs in decreasing recidivism, saving taxpayer dollars, and increasing retention in treatment (National Drug Court Institute, 2004; Rossman et al., 2011). One review of research on drug courts concluded, "we know that drug courts outperform virtually all other strategies that have been attempted for drug-involved offenders" (Marlowe, DeMatteo, & Festinger, 2003, p. 11).

As the number of DTCs increased, so did the number of defendants in those courts who had comorbid mental health problems. In response to the growing presence of PWSMI on court dockets, several jurisdictions—Honolulu, Hawaii, and Ithaca, New York, for example—developed mental health tracks within their DTCs. Similarly, the DTC in Lane County, Oregon, developed two mental health tracks; one for PWSMI and another for persons with personality disorders. These disorders consist of characterological problems and destructive behavioral patterns that affect people's relationships and overall functioning (American Psychiatric Association, 2013). San Bernardino County, California, has separate drug and mental health courts, with the same judge presiding over both (Rabasca, 2000). In the late 1990s, other jurisdictions began implementing independent MHCs.

In summary, the DTC model transformed specialized criminal courts from adversarial and legalistic to therapeutic and rehabilitative and laid the foundation for MHCs (Fulton-Hora, 2002). DTCs adopt a common mission and team approach to working with drug-involved offenders. Judges, prosecutors, defense attorneys, probation officers, and treatment providers execute a coordinated case management plan that holds offenders accountable through graduated sanctions for rule infractions and rewards them through stepwise reductions in sentences and dismissals of charges for successful program completion (Belenko, 1998).

Model MHCs

Inaugural MHCs. According to proponents, specialized MHCs hold great promise for diverting PWSMI from the criminal justice system and ensuring

---

3. Astute readers may be curious about the role drug courts play in reversing the opioid epidemic. For one such investigation, see Westervelt (2017).

that they receive psychiatric treatment and other services (Bazelon Center for Mental Health Law, 2004). Pioneering MHC initiatives were implemented in response to three critical problems: the perceived public health risk posed by offenders with serious mental illnesses, the challenges and costs of housing PWSMI in crowded local jails, and the criminal justice system's pervasive inability to respond effectively and humanely to PWSMI (Goldkamp & Irons-Guynn, 2000). The first three jurisdictions to establish MHCs were Broward County, Florida; King County, Washington; and Anchorage, Alaska. However, MHC historians point to the specialized mental health docket, which was developed in 1980 in Marion County, Indiana, as the country's first *de facto* MHC. The court was dissolved in 1992 and later revived as a formal MHC in 1996 (Steadman, Davidson, & Brown, 2001).

Early MHC Funding. Since the inception of these and other bellwether courts, interest in MHCs has grown tremendously. Numerous jurisdictions have implemented their own mental health models, tailored to local needs, resources, and political exigencies. In November 2000, President Clinton signed into law the Law Enforcement and Mental Health Project Act, sponsored in the Senate by Mike DeWine (R-Ohio) and in the House of Representatives by Ted Strickland (D-Ohio). The law authorized the allocation of funds to support the implementation of MHCs at the county level (Council of State Governments, 2008).

In fiscal years 2002 and 2003, Congress appropriated $5 and $4 million, respectively, for seed grants to help inchoate MHC programs become operational. However, the House of Representatives allocated no funds in fiscal year 2004 for the support of MHCs. Furthermore, the Senate's Commerce, Justice, State, and Judiciary Appropriations Subcommittees also allocated no dollars to launch MHCs. With limited federal funding, MHCs rely on competitive federal and state grants to help support administrative costs and personnel (Council of State Governments, 2008).

The Mentally Ill Offender Treatment and Crime Reduction Act, which President George W. Bush signed into law in 2004 and Congress reauthorized in 2008, has awarded many MHC development grants. This law created the Justice and Mental Health Collaboration Program and authorized a $50 million grant program to be administered by the Department of Justice. Some courts utilize sales taxes, grants, and other county-based funding sources to support the program (Council of State Governments, 2008).

Despite the paucity of these allocations, the number of MHCs in the United States ballooned from four in 1997 to over 300 in 2017. MHCs are now located in nearly every state (Council of State and Local Governments, 2006; Council of State Governments Justice Center, 2018; Steadman, Redlich, Griffin, Petrila, & Monahan, 2005). MHCs rely on state and federal grants and local funding sources to support their operations (Redlich, 2005). Given the current budget restrictions at all three levels of government, MHCs have been unable to grow at the same pace as they did in the first decade of the century (Castellano & Anderson, 2013).

MHC Operations and Policies

Benefits and Goals. MHCs are purported to achieve several goals. The courts were created to respond to PWSMI's specific behavioral health problems by delivering intensive supervision and services through dedicated dockets and specialized caseloads. The presumption of these and other problem-solving courts is that untreated criminogenic needs increase the likelihood of offending. At the pre-adjudication level, MHCs deflect PWSMI from jails and into psychiatric care facilities, where their disorders can be treated, and they can avoid the deleterious effects of detention. Similarly, at the post-adjudication level, MHCs offer judges a service-oriented alternative to prison, which protects public safety and helps PWSMI to achieve stability and sobriety and to adjust productively to life in the community.

Common Elements. MHCs are designed within a particular court jurisdiction with its own working group culture and caseload volume, nature, and complexity, as well as various arrest levels and jail capacities. Notwithstanding these structural differences, MHCs ascribe to general principles of design and operations, known as the common core elements (Council of State Governments, 2007). Participation in an MHC is voluntary. Potential clients who meet the eligibility requirements are identified and approached for program screening and assessment. All must first give informed consent before yielding to the evaluation process and can decline program participation even if they meet program requirements. Informed choice by defendants and their defense attorneys must also include procedures for determining defendant competency. Moreover, the confidentiality rights of defendants are maintained even in cases in which they return to standard court processing due to ineligibility or refusal to enter MHC programming.

Thus, eligible clients are afforded the option of MHC. All potential participants must be fit to stand trial, and formal entry into the MHC has to be in open court, on the record. Potential participants are informed of program requirements and the consequences of noncompliance with conditions and asked to sign a consent form prior to participation (Administrative Office of the Illinois Courts, 2015).

The hallmarks of the MHC are the pronounced role of the judge as the leader of an interdisciplinary team of professionals assigned to an exclusive

MHC caseload. MHC judges are highly involved in each individual case, closely following clients' progress and responding promptly to any setbacks in treatment or nonadherence to other court-ordered conditions. These highly involved and proactive judges preside over frequent court hearings and non-adversarial proceedings (Council of State Governments, 2007). Research shows that MHC participants experience TJ in their interactions with the judge during court sessions (Frailing, 2010; Wales, Hiday, & Ray, 2010).

Other members of the MHC team typically include a state's attorney, public defender, probation officer, court liaison, and behavioral healthcare provider. Clients' progression through the program is discussed at case staffing meetings, and the team decides about changes in supervision or treatment plans. Satisfactory program completion is defined by predetermined criteria. Clients are motivated to succeed by the threat of sanctions and the promise of rewards (Council of State Governments, 2007).

Client Eligibility

Only arrestees and defendants with a diagnosed mental illness are eligible for MHC programming. Some programs accept people with serious mental illness alone; others will accept people with serious mental illness and substance use or personality disorders. Public safety considerations are paramount; clients with no violent charges or histories are privileged for admission (e.g., Frailing, 2011). Many MHCs restrict participation to people with nonviolent, misdemeanor charges; a smaller portion of such courts accepts people with felony charges. Increasingly, courts have been accepting a combination of misdemeanor and felony charges or individuals with only felonies (Redlich, 2005; Erickson, Campbell, & Lamberti, 2006). Many first-generation MHCs (before 2000) accepted only defendants with misdemeanor charges and utilized pre-conviction programs that diverted defendants from the criminal justice system or expedited a release from jail and a referral to mental health services. Such programs offered the possibility for suspended sentences upon the completion of treatment and usually admitted only nonviolent offenders (Redlich, Steadman, Monahan, Petrila, & Griffin, 2005).

The second generation of MHCs (post-2000) is more likely to accept individuals with felonies and violent charges (Erickson et al., 2006). Programs with felony offenders are usually post-conviction, probation programs that mandate mental health treatment and other interventions as conditions of release. MHC offenders are often supervised on a more frequent schedule of contacts, compared with those on standard probation, and they are subject to graduated sanctions for noncompliance and accorded with progressive rewards for compliance with their conditions of release (Redlich, Steadman, Monahan, Robbins, & Petrila, 2006).

Effectiveness of MHCs

After 20 years of operations, the effects of MHCs on participants, the court system, and the community continue to be investigated. The outcome measures in MHC studies include client recidivism rates, symptoms, quality of life, and use of services. Numerous studies have suggested that MHCs reduce recidivism among participants both during and after programming compared with non-participants (i.e., those processed through traditional court protocols) (Almquist, & Dodd, 2009; Christy, Poythress, Boothroyd, Petrila, & Mehra, 2005; Council of State Governments Justice Center, 2008; Frailing, 2010; Gurrera, 2005; Herinckx, Swart, Ama, Dolezal, & King, 2005; Hiday, Wales, & Ray, 2013; McNiel, & Binder, 2007; Moore & Hiday, 2006; Trupin & Richards, 2003; Sarteschi, Vaughn, & Kim, 2011; Steadman, Redlich, Callahan, Robbins, & Vesselinov, 2011).

Not only do MHCs reduce recidivism, they also reduce the severity of criminal activity following program participation (Cosden, Ellens, Schnell, Yamini-Diouf, & Wolfe, 2003; Gurrera, 2005; Moore & Hiday, 2006). The crimes of MHC participants who are rearrested are more likely to be nonviolent offenses or probation violations rather than serious violent crimes (Cosden et al., 2003; Gurrera, 2005; McNiel & Binder, 2007). MHC participants also report fewer violent acts during both MHC supervision and follow-up periods, compared with matched samples of traditional court participants (Christy et al., 2005).

The findings of a randomized experiment of MHCs in Santa Barbara County, California, showed that 47 percent of clients were convicted of a new crime in the year following programming, compared with 60 percent of those processed through standard court proceedings. Moreover, among MHC probationers who were convicted of a new offense, 51 percent were also adjudicated for violations of probation, compared with 65 percent of the standard probationers in the study (Cosden et al., 2003). Another investigation found that MHCs reduced rearrests for new offenses and probation violations. Specifically, one year after program participation, 54 percent of MHC graduates had no new arrests, their probation violations were 62 percent lower, and they were four times less likely to reoffend, compared with non-MHC offenders (Herinckx et al., 2005).

MHCs have also been found to enhance participants' quality of life. In a meta-analysis, MHC participants, on average, were more likely than nonparticipants to report significant improvements in their overall state of health and their sense of fulfillment with family, occupational, and social obligations (Sarteschi, 2009).

Service utilization was also higher for MHC participants compared with nonparticipants with mental disorders. In one study, MHC participants accessed more services and accessed them more quickly than similar nonparticipants (Keator, Callahan, Steadman, & Vesselinov, 2013). In another investigation, MHC participants increased their service use by 62 percent in the eight months following MHC participation, compared with the eight months prior to MHC participation (Boothroyd, Poythress, McGaha, & Petrila, 2003). Other studies have reported that MHC clients were more successful in treatment and had greater access to housing and other supportive services than nonclients (Trupin, Richards, Wertheimer, & Bruschi, 2001). One of the few studies to examine cost effectiveness indicated that MHCs produced no substantial short-term costs over traditional court processing and could potentially yield long-term savings by reducing recidivism and hospitalizations (Ridgely, Greenberg, DeMartini, & Dembosky, 2007).

An overarching goal of MHCs is to alleviate participants' psychiatric symptoms. However, to date, no studies have shown that MHCs are achieving this goal (Boothroyd, Mercado, Poythress, Christy, & Petrila, 2005). One of the few studies that measured psychiatric symptoms found that participants' symptoms worsened during programming in both traditional courts and MHCs. The researchers noted that although individuals were engaged in treatment, the type and quality of services were never examined. These results suggest that treatment and MHC participation alone might be insufficient to reduce symptoms (Boothroyd et al., 2005).

The overwhelmingly favorable results in MHC research must be tempered by several methodological considerations, which diminish the validity of the findings. For example, few studies of MHCs have employed a randomized experimental design, which is the most powerful method for definitively establishing a causal connection between programs and outcomes. Relatedly, many studies either lack a comparison group or use "treatment as usual" as the basis for comparison, which produces an invidious or biased appraisal in favor of the intervention. PWSMI are often handpicked for MHC programs and might already be less inclined to relapse or recidivate. Moreover, in evaluations of MHCs, sample sizes have been small and follow-up periods too limited to allow for explorations of long-term impact on offenders (Epperson, Canada, & Lurigio, 2013).

Conclusions and Critiques

The MHC is a fairly widespread and popular type of problem-solving court. Based on the principles of TJ and the prototypic DTC model, such courts focus on the challenges and needs of PWSMI and are a promising alternative to standard court processing for people with behavioral health disorders. Nonetheless, critics have challenged their usefulness and cost effectiveness. Studies have shown that the link between mental illness alone and criminal behavior is highly questionable. Hence, the development of courts to treat mental illness as a mechanism for reducing recidivism rests on a faulty premise with no empirical substantiation (Keator et al., 2013; Skeem, Manchak, & Peterson, 2010). However, most PWSMI are comorbid for substance use disorders, and addiction is highly criminogenic. Thus, the integrated treatment of substance use and other psychiatric disorders in MHC clients could lower rates of reoffending (Lurigio, 2009).

The selection of misdemeanants for MHCs might be an instance of net widening, causing unnecessary and iatrogenic penetration into the criminal justice system (Wolff & Pogorzelski, 2005). By selecting mostly "good risk" clients (i.e., "creaming"), MHCs are spending money and investing resources on offenders who are the least likely to recidivate—a strategy that is neither cost effective nor in the interests of public safety (Wolff, 2003). Moreover, the conditions of MHC supervision are onerous, and violations can result in harsher punishments than regular court processing and sentencing for lower-level offenders (Bonnie & Monahan, 2005). Consequently, MHCs could be an unbidden pathway to incarceration rather than a diversion from confinement.

Another concern is whether candidates for MHC are properly evaluated for the ability to provide informed consent. Serious mental illness can impair cognitive and decision-making capacities, rendering clients unable fully to accept and understand the terms of their participation in the program and adding an element of hidden coercion, especially among those whose mental illness is particularly debilitating (Redlich, Hoover, Summers, & Steadman, 2010). Entry into the program requires a guilty plea, thereby establishing or lengthening a criminal record, which increases the risk of future arrests and convictions and exposes clients to the pernicious collateral consequences of a criminal record (Erickson et al., 2006; Griffin, Steadman, & Petrila, 2002).

Finally, critics of problem-solving courts are concerned that allocating scarce behavioral healthcare resources for criminally involved PWSMI could draw services away from PWSMI with no criminal involvement (Stefan & Winick, 2005). The latter might be more likely to take advantage of such services. In short, the receipt of mental health services should not privilege those who have committed crimes over those have not. "Overall, if [mental health treatment] funds are limit and must be targeted, targeting treatment resources to individuals who have the greatest criminal risk may take money away from those for whom treatment is most effective" (Wolff, 2003, p. 165).

Discussion Questions

1. Should criminal courts be involved in providing mental health services to clients? If so, how do these services align with the goals of punishment?

2. In what ways might therapeutic justice be manifested in court sessions?

3. How can defendants benefit from the practice of therapeutic jurisprudence?

4. Should most courts be able to handle PWSMI or is the specialized court model the best (or only) approach for such offenders?

5. How is mental illness related to criminal behavior? What treatments do you think are most important to reduce criminal behavior among those with mental illness?

6. What are the strengths and weaknesses of MHCs? Do you think the strengths outweigh the weaknesses, or vice versa?

7. What conclusions can be drawn so far from the evidence regarding MHC effectiveness?

References

Administrative Office of Illinois Courts. (2015). *Problem-solving court standards.* Springfield, IL: Author. Retrieved from http://www.illinoiscourts.gov/ Probation/Problem-Solving_Courts/P-SC_Standards_2015.pdf.

Almquist, L., & Dodd, E. (2009). *Mental health courts: A guide to research-informed policy and practice.* New York, NY: Council of State Governments Center.

American Psychiatric Association. (2013). *Diagnostic and statistical manual of mental disorders: Fifth edition (DSM-5).* New York: Author.

Bazelon Center for Mental Health Law. (2004). *The role of specialty mental health courts in meeting the needs of juvenile offenders.* Washington, D.C.: Judge David L. Bazelon Center for Mental Health Law.

Belenko, S. (1998). *Research on drug courts: A critical review.* New York: National Center on Addiction and Substance Abuse, Columbia University.

Bernstein, R., & Seltzer, T. (2003). Criminalization of people with mental illnesses: The role of mental health courts in system reform. *University of the District of Columbia Law Review, 7*, 143–162.

Bonnie, R. J., & Monahan, J. (2005). From coercion to contract: Reframing the debate on mandated community treatment for people with mental disorders. *Law and Human Behavior, 29*, 485–503.

Boothroyd, R. A., Mercado, C. C., Poythress, N. G., Christy, A., & Petrila, J. (2005). Clinical outcomes of defendants in mental health courts. *Psychiatric Services, 56*, 829–834.

Boothroyd, R. A., Poythress, N. G., McGaha, A., & Petrila, J. (2003). The Broward mental health court: Process, outcomes, and service utilization. *International Journal of Law & Psychiatry, 26*, 55–71.

Casey, P. M., & Rottman, D. B. (2005). Problem-solving courts: Models and trends. *The Justice System Journal, 26*, 35–56.

Castellano, U., & Anderson, L. (2013). Mental health courts in America: Promise and challenges. *American Behavioral Scientist, 57*, 163–173.

Christy, A., Poythress, N. G., Boothroyd, R. A., Petrila, J., & Mehra, S. (2005). Evaluating the efficiency and community safety goals of the Broward County mental health court. *Behavioral Sciences & the Law, 23*, 227–243.

Cooper, C. S. (1998). *1998 Drug court survey: Preliminary findings.* Washington, D.C.: Drug Court Clearinghouse and Technical Assistance Project, American University.

Cosden, M., Ellens, J. K., Schnell, J. L., Yamini-Diouf, Y., & Wolfe, M. M. (2003). Evaluation of a mental health treatment court with assertive community treatment. *Behavioral Sciences & the Law, 21*, 415–427.

Cosden, M., Ellens, J., Schnell, J., & Yamini-Diouf, Y. (2004). Efficacy of a mental health treatment court with assertive community treatment. *Behavioral Sciences and the Law, 23*, 199–214.

Council of State Governments. (2002). *Criminal Justice-Mental Health Consensus Project Report.* New York, NY: Council of State Governments. Retrieved from https://www.ncjrs.gov/pdffiles1/nij/grants/197103.pdf.

Council of State Governments. (2006). *Mental health courts: A national snapshot.* Washington, D.C.: Bureau of Justice Assistance. Retrieved from https://www.bja.gov/Programs/MHC_National_Snapshot.pdf.

Council of State Governments. (2007). *Improving responses to people with mental illnesses: The essential elements of a mental health court.* Washington, D.C.: Bureau of Justice Assistance. Retrieved from https://www.bja.gov/publications/mhc_essential_elements.pdf.

Council of State Governments. (2008). *Mental health courts: A primer for policymakers and practitioners.* New York, NY: Council of State Governments.

Retrieved from https://csgjusticecenter.org/wp-content/uploads/2012/12/mhc-primer.pdf.

Council of State Governments Justice Center. (2018). Mental health courts. Retrieved from https://csgjusticecenter.org/mental-health-court-project/.

Ditton, P. (1999). *Mental health and treatment of inmates and probationers.* Washington, D.C.: Bureau of Justice Statistics. Retrieved from http://www.ojp.usdoj.go/bjs/abstract/mhtip.htm.

Drug Courts Program Office. (1997). *Defining drug courts: The key components.* Washington, D.C.: Office of Justice Programs.

Epperson, M. W., Canada, K. E., & Lurigio, A. J. (2013). Mental health court: One approach for addressing the problems of persons with serious mental illnesses in the criminal justice system. In J. B. Helfgott (Ed.), *Criminal psychology* (pp. 367–392). Haverhill, MA: Praeger Press.

Erickson, S. K., Campbell, A., & Lamberti, S. (2006). Variations in mental health courts: Challenges, opportunities, and a call for caution. *Community Mental Health Journal, 42,* 335–344.

Frailing, K. (2010). How mental health courts function: Outcomes and observations. *International Journal of Law and Psychiatry, 33*(4), 207–213.

Frailing, K. (2011). Referrals to the Washoe County mental health court. *International Journal of Forensic Mental Health, 10*(4), 314–325.

Goldkamp, J., & Irons-Guynn, C. (2000). *Emerging judicial strategies for the mentally ill in the criminal caseload: Mental health courts in Fort Lauderdale, Seattle, San Bernardino, and Anchorage: A report on community justice initiatives.* Philadelphia, PA: Crime and Justice Research Institute.

Griffin, P. A., Steadman, H. J., & Petrila, J. (2002). The use of criminal charges and sanctions in mental health courts. *Psychiatric Services, 58,* 1285–1289.

Gurrera, M. M. (2005). *An evaluation of a mental health court: Process, procedure, and outcome.* Retrieved from Dissertations and Theses database (AAT 3269390).

Herinckx, H. A., Swart, S. C., Ama, S. M., Dolezal, C. D., & King S. (2005). Rearrest and linkage to mental health services among clients of the Clark County mental health court program. *Psychiatric Services, 56,* 853–857.

Hiday, V. A., Wales, H. W., & Ray, B. (2013). Effectiveness of a short-term mental health court: Criminal recidivism one-year post-exit. *Law & Human Behavior, 37,* 401–411.

Hora, P., Schema, W., & Rosenthal, J. (1999). Therapeutic jurisprudence and the drug court movement: Revolutionizing the criminal justice system's response to drug abuse and crime in America. *Notre Dame Law Review, 74,* 439–555.

James, D. J., & Glaze, L. E. (2006). *Mental health problems of prison and jail inmates*. Washington D.C.: U.S. Department of Justice. Retrieved from https://www.bjs.gov/content/pub/pdf/mhppji.pdf.

Keator, K., Callahan, L., Steadman, H. J., & Vesselinov, R. (2013). The impact of treatment on the public safety outcomes of mental health court participants. *American Behavioral Scientist, 57*, 231–243.

Lurigio, A. J. (2000). Drug treatment availability and effectiveness: Studies of the general and criminal justice populations. *Criminal Justice and Behavior, 27*, 495–528.

Lurigio, A. J. (2003). Racial disparities in sentencing for drug crimes: The national scene. *Research Bulletin, 2*, 1–8.

Lurigio, A. J. (2009). Comorbidity. In N. A. Piotrowski (Ed.), *Encyclopedia of psychology and mental health* (pp. 439–442). Pasadena, CA: Salem Press.

Lurigio, A. J., & Swartz, J. A. (2000). Changing the contours of the criminal justice system to meet the needs of persons with serious mental illness. In J. Horney (Ed.), *NIJ 2000 Series: Policies, processes, and decisions of the criminal justice system* (Vol. 3, pp. 45–108). Washington, D.C.: National Institute of Justice.

McNiel, D. E., & Binder, R. L. (2007). Effectiveness of a mental health court in reducing criminal recidivism and violence. *American Journal of Psychiatry, 164*, 1395–1403.

Moore, M. E., & Hiday, V. A. (2006). Mental health court outcomes: A comparison of re-arrest and rearrest severity between mental health court and traditional court participants. *Law & Human Behavior, 30*, 659–674.

National Association of Drug Court Professionals. (2015). *Adult drug court best practice standards, Vol. 1*. Retrieved from http://www.nadcp.org/sites/default/files/nadcp/AdultDrugCourtBestPracticeStandards.pdf.

National Drug Court Institute. (2004). *Drug court benefits*. Alexandria, VA: Author.

National Trial Court Performance Standards. *Trial court performance standards with commentary*. Washington, D.C.: Bureau of Justice Assistance. Retrieved from https://www.ncjrs.gov/pdffiles1/161570.pdf.

Prins, S. J., & Draper, L. (2009). *Improving outcomes for people with mental illnesses under community corrections supervision: A guide to research-informed policy and practice*. New York, NY: Council of State Governments Justice Center.

Rabasca, L. (2000). Demand overwhelms San Bernardino Mental Health Court. *Monitor on Psychology, 7*, 10.

Redlich, A. D. (2005). Voluntary, but knowing and intelligent? Comprehension in mental health courts. *Psychology, Public Policy, & Law, 11*, 605–619.

Redlich, A., Hoover, S., Summers, A., & Steadman, H. J. (2010). Enrollment in mental health courts: Voluntariness, knowingness, and adjudicative competence. *Law and Human Behavior, 34*, 91–104.

Redlich, A. D., Steadman, H. J., Monahan, J., Petrila, J., & Griffin, P. A. (2005). The second generation of mental health courts. *Psychology, Public Policy, & Law, 11*, 527–538.

Redlich, A. D., Steadman, H. J., Monahan, J., Robbins, P. C., & Petrila, J. (2006). Patterns of practice in mental health courts: A national survey. *Law & Human Behavior, 30*, 347–362.

Rossman, S., Rempel, M., Roman, J., Zweig, J., Lindquist, C., Green, M., ... Farole, D. (2011). *The Multi-Site Adult Drug Court Evaluation: The impact of drug courts* (Vol. 4). Washington, D.C.: The Urban Institute. Retrieved from https://www.ncjrs.gov/pdffiles1/nij/grants/237112.pdf.

Sarteschi, C. M. (2009). Assessing the effectiveness of mental health courts: A meta-analysis of clinical and recidivism outcomes. Unpublished doctoral dissertation. University of Pittsburgh. Retrieved from http://d-scholarship.pitt.edu/9275/.

Sarteschi, C. M., Vaughn, M. G., & Kim, K. (2011). Assessing the effectiveness of mental health courts: A quantitative review. *Journal of Criminal Justice, 39*, 12–20.

Schema, W. (2005). *Therapeutic jurisprudence. Knowledge and information service.* Washington, D.C.: The National Center for State Courts.

Skeem, J. L., Emke-Francis, P., & Louden, J. E. (2006). Probation, mental health, and mandated treatment: A national survey. *Criminal Justice & Behavior, 33*, 158–184.

Skeem, J. L., Manchak, S., & Peterson, J. K. (2010). Correctional policy for offenders with mental illness: Creating a new paradigm for recidivism reduction. *Law and Human Behavior, 35*, 110–136.

Steadman, H. J., Davidson, S., & Brown, C. (2001). Mental health courts: Their promise and unanswered questions. *Psychiatric Services, 52*, 457–458.

Steadman, H. J., Redlich, A. D., Callahan, L., Clark Robbins, P., & Vesselinov, R. (2011). Effect of mental health courts on arrest and jail days: A multisite study. *Archives of General Psychiatry, 68*, 167–172.

Steadman, H. J., Redlich, A., Griffin, P., Petrila, J., & Monahan, J. (2005). From referral to disposition: Case processing in seven mental health courts. *Behavioral Sciences and the Law, 23*, 215–226.

Stefan, S., & Winick, B. J. (2005). A dialogue on mental health courts. *Psychology, Public Policy, and Law, 11*, 507–526.

Teplin, L. A. (2000). *Keeping the peace: Police discretion and mentally ill persons.* Washington, D.C.: National Institute of Justice.

Trupin, E., & Richards, H. (2003). Seattle's mental health courts: Early indicators of effectiveness. *International Journal of Law & Psychiatry*, *26*, 33–53.

Trupin, E., Richards, H., Wertheimer, D. M., & Bruschi, C. (2001). *City of Seattle mental health court evaluation report*. Seattle, WA: Seattle Municipal Court.

Wales, H. W., Hiday, V. A., & Ray, B. (2010). Procedural justice and the mental health court judge's role in reducing recidivism. *International Journal of Law and Psychiatry*, *33*(4), 265–271.

Watson, A., Hanrahan, P., Luchins, D., & Lurigio A. J. (2001). Mental health courts and the complex issue of mentally ill offenders. *Psychiatric Services*, *52*, 477–481.

Westervelt, E. (2017). To save opioid addicts, this experimental court is ditching the delays. *NPR*. Retrieved from https://www.npr.org/sections/health-shots/2017/10/05/553830794/to-save-opioid-addicts-this-experimental-court-is-ditching-the-delays.

Wexler, D., & Winick, B. (Eds.). (1996). *Law in a therapeutic key*. Durham, NC: Carolina Academic Press.

Wolff, N. (2003). Courting the courts: Courts as agents for treatment and justice. In W. H. Fisher (Ed.), *Community-based interventions for criminal offenders with severe mental illness* (pp. 143–198). Boston, MA: JAI Press.

Wolff, N., & Pogorzelski, W. (2005). Measuring the effectiveness of mental health courts: Challenges and recommendations. *Psychology, Public Policy, and Law*, *11*, 539–569.

10

The Plight of Long-Term Prisoners with Mental Illness

Craig Haney, Sarah Camille Conrey & Roxy Davis

Introduction

Imprisonment is a painful experience. Depending on where and for how long someone is incarcerated, it can be psychologically damaging as well. As the National Research Council (2014, p. 200) summarized it, "some poorly run and especially harsh prisons can cause great harm and put prisoners at significant risk." Beyond the basic pains and potential harms of imprisonment per se, "long-term" prison confinement (which, as noted below, we will define here as a term of 10 years or more) presents prisoners with a host of especially difficult psychological challenges (e.g., Frank & Gill, 2015; Maschi, Viola, & Koskinen, 2015).

Although long-term prisoners may exist in a kind of "behavioral deep freeze" (Zamble, 1992, p. 420), at least in some very limited respects, most of them are significantly changed by prison life. Moreover, the greater the length of their incarceration, the deeper the transformations that are likely to occur. These changes and transformations often impede prisoners' eventual transition back to free society. Many of them struggle to readjust to the norms and routines of the free world once returned to it, having adapted to the structure of prison life and having become "prisonized" (e.g., Liem, 2016; Price, 2015). Beyond the gradual accommodation to the unique and atypical nature of prison life, the traumatic nature of the experience can create or exacerbate pre-existing symptoms of posttraumatic stress disorder (PTSD) (Goff, Rose, Rose, & Purves, 2007; Heckman, Cropsey, & Olds-Davis, 2007; Herman, 1992), as well as instilling what some researchers have termed a "post-incarceration syndrome" (Liem & Kunst, 2013). In addition to the nature and duration of confinement, the characteristics of the prisoners themselves can affect the nature and magnitude of the prison effects that befall them. Vulnerable prisoners are, of course, more susceptible to the potential negative effects of prison life.

In this chapter, we consider the plight of a particularly vulnerable group of prisoners—prisoners with mental illness who are subjected to "long-term" confinement. In discussing their experiences, it is useful to borrow the concept of "intersectionality" from feminist psychology, to recognize that oppressed people, especially, experience the effects of "multiple, complex social inequalities" (Collins, 2015, p. 5) and to underscore the need for prison policy that is "grounded in lived experiences and captures the complexities of interdependent social locations" (Hankivsky & Cormier, 2011, p. 218). We note that any discussion of long-term prisoners who also have mental illness should take both of these statuses into account. They each compound the painful and potentially harmful nature of prison life. It is important to note, also, that the system of prison oppression will be experienced in significantly different ways by long-term prisoners with mental illness who are of color, women, and/or LGBT, as well as by those who are confined in especially harsh, overcrowded, or badly run institutions and/or ones that operate with poorly functioning mental health systems, and by prisoners who have little or no outside support from family and friends.

Long-Term Imprisonment

The definition of what constitutes "long-term" prison confinement varies among researchers and is admittedly somewhat arbitrary. Increased sentence lengths during the "era of mass incarceration" in the United States (e.g., Alexander, 2010) have changed our understanding of normative sentence lengths. In this chapter, we have chosen 10 years or more, in part to acknowledge a "trend reflective of the significant shifts that have occurred in American correctional policy during the last four decades and [which] suggests a higher threshold for what is regarded as excessive punishment" (Kazemian & Travis, 2015, p. 361).

Long before the movement toward mass incarceration had begun to gather momentum, Flanagan (1980, p. 148) observed that: "In the United States sentences of imprisonment are imposed at a rate that is the highest in the free world. In addition, the lengths of sentences meted out by American courts are generally recognised as among the longest in the world." Comparisons along both dimensions—rate and length of confinement—between the United States and the rest of the world have worsened over subsequent decades. Mass incarceration not only resulted in an unprecedented influx in the number of persons incarcerated but also significant increases in the length of their prison sentences (Pew Research Center, 2012), including increases in the already large numbers of prisoners who were serving very long prison terms, including life.

In 2002, for example, the average sentence meted out by state courts that sentenced prisoners for felony convictions was 53 months, or approximately 4½ years. The median sentence (the number at which approximately half were sentenced to more and half to less) was 36 months, or 3 years (Durose & Langan, 2005). However, the actual time served (as opposed to time sentenced to be served) was considerably less, estimated at an average of approximately 27 months, or just over two years. Based on these statistical comparisons alone, it seems reasonable to conclude that any prison sentence that is double the average sentence of about 5 years (and is considerably beyond the median sentence) and is more than four times the average amount of time actually served by felons in the United States can be considered a "long-term"—if not extremely long-term—period of prison confinement. It is important to note also that the number of people serving very long-term sentences in the United States is substantial. As of 2016, the number of prisoners serving life sentences, with or without parole, was at an all-time high since 1984, when national life sentence records are first available (Nellis, 2017). One in every seven prisoners was serving a life or "virtual life" sentence of 50 years or more and in several states, more than one in every five prisoners was serving a sentence of life, with or without parole, or virtual life.

Of course, long-term confinement can also be defined psychologically, in terms of the developmental period(s) during which a person is incarcerated and the maturational stages that have passed (or would ordinarily have passed) during the period in which the person was imprisoned. Thus, the same period of long-term confinement might be experienced differently and have a different kind of impact for a younger prisoner as compared to an older prisoner because of the greater number or significance of the developmental milestones that passed during the period of incarceration for the younger prisoner. For example, in a study of young male and female prisoners with mandatory life sentences in the United Kingdom, prisoners expressed having to grapple with challenges such as the prospect of being incarcerated for more time than they had been alive, the likelihood of friends or family passing away before they were released, and missing the experience of becoming a parent (Wright, Crewe, & Hulley, 2017). Of course, long-term imprisonment also presents older prisoners with a special set of life course-related developmental challenges.

Thus, very long-term periods of imprisonment begin to implicate aging-related issues (such as physical disability and mortality) for older prisoners in ways that would not be expected to impact younger prisoners serving the same term.

The Plight of Long-Term Prisoners

Long-term prisoners tend to be underserved in most prison systems, as if their far off release dates lessen the need to provide them with programming and other services (e.g., Kazemian & Travis, 2015). In addition, and for perhaps obvious reasons, their time in prison is likely to have a more profound negative impact on them than on other prisoners. The length of time during which prisoners are subjected to the pains of imprisonment, the accumulated stresses of prison life, the gradual but persistent process of prisonization, and the ever-increasing likelihood that they will lose meaningful connections to loved ones in the outside world combine to exacerbate the negative effects of incarceration. Among other things, one's ability to preserve a positive social identity other than as a "prisoner" is jeopardized by mounting years of incarceration and forced adaptations and prolonged accommodations made to the rigors of prison life. As Flanagan (1980, p. 155) put it, "the element of time" not only exacerbates the pains and deprivations of imprisonment, but also transforms them from the "noxious characteristics" of day-to-day life that can be tolerated in the short run to "major problems of survival over the duration of a long prison sentence."

A number of studies have confirmed the basic proposition that long-term imprisonment can have especially negative psychological consequences for prisoners. For example, psychiatrist Adrian Grounds (2005, p. 45) summarized the changes experienced by a sample of long-term prisoners whom he studied this way: "Long-term imprisonment entailed psychological adaptation to prison and losses—of separation, life opportunities, a generation of family life for some, and years of their expected personal life history. These are … intrinsic features of long-term confinement."

Among a relatively large sample of prisoners from a variety of European Union nations, who were serving long-term prison sentences (defined, in the European context, as five years or more), half or more reported subjective feelings of distress of the sort that would warrant psychiatric treatment, and the treatment needs of those long-term prisoners were 50 percent greater than those of prisoners serving short-term sentences (Dudeck et al., 2011).

Certain groups entering prison may be more likely to have experienced traumatic pre-prison events, making them more vulnerable to the pains of imprisonment. Female prisoners have higher rates of mental illness than their male counterparts (James & Glaze, 2006). Dye and Aday (2013) found that among a sample of women serving life sentences, most had experienced physical or sexual abuse prior to prison. Nearly half had thought about suicide prior to incarceration, and of that group, most had also attempted suicide at some point in their lives. The authors found current suicidal ideation to be associated with factors relating to prison adjustment, such as prison support and family connections. Similarly, Leigey and Reed (2010) found that among a sample of females serving life sentences, female prisoners were more likely than life-sentenced male prisoners to report having made a suicide attempt, to have experienced physical and sexual abuse, to have more extensive histories of abuse, and to have been diagnosed with PTSD.

Traumatic pre-prison histories tend to be more common among prisoners with mental illness in general. According to a 2006 survey, prisoners with mental illness in state facilities were more likely than those prisoners classified as not having a mental illness to have experienced homelessness, past physical or sexual abuse, to have had parents or guardians who abused drugs or alcohol, to have been in foster care growing up, and to have had a family member be incarcerated (James & Glaze, 2006).

The experience of long-term imprisonment for prisoners with mental illness interacts with another increasingly important issue: aging. Obviously, long-term prisoners age in prison and their psychological well-being and mental health status may be impacted by a variety of aging-related issues. Older prisoners are the fastest growing demographic segment of the U.S. prisoner population (e.g., Luallen & Cutler, 2015). Physical and mental aging may be accelerated by the stress of the prison environment which, in certain cases, brings on aging-related challenges at a younger age than for non-incarcerated adults (e.g., Maschi, Gibson, Zgoba, & Morgen, 2011; Maschi et al., 2015).

In addition to the increased likelihood of physical health-related problems, aging in prison is itself a risk factor for psychiatric problems including depression and suicidality (e.g., Barry, Wakefield, Trestman, & Conwell, 2016). Among the other challenges they face and maladies from which they disproportionately suffer (e.g., Williams, Stern, Mellow, Safer, & Greifinger, 2012), older prisoners are at greatest risk of suicide (e.g., Noonan, 2015). For example, one study found that, perhaps not surprisingly, prisoners who experienced difficulties performing the "activities of daily living" that prison demands of them were more likely to report depression and more severe suicidal ideation (Barry et al., 2016). The measures of the particular activities of daily prison living that these researchers used to determine whether individual older prisoners were disabled or impaired serve as stark reminders not only of the challenges of aging in prison but also of the nature of mundane, day-to-day prison routines. They included: dropping to the floor for alarms, climbing on/off the top bunk, hearing orders, walking while wearing handcuffs, standing in line for medications, and walking to the "chow hall" for meals.

Older prisoners also tend to have complex trauma histories for which they are unlikely to have received treatment in prison (e.g., Luallen & Cutler, 2015; Courtney & Maschi, 2012). The trajectory of PTSD can also be more complicated for older prisoners due to factors relating to aging, such as chronic pain, cognitive decline, and increased stress levels (Courtney & Maschi, 2013).

Finally, the trauma of long-term imprisonment may, in and of itself, result in PTSD-like mental health symptoms. Liem and Kunst (2013) identified what they termed a "post-incarceration syndrome" among released life prisoners who had served, on average, nearly 19 years in a state correctional institution. Symptoms included chronic PTSD symptoms, such as sleep disturbances, hyperarousal, avoidance of crowded spaces, panic attacks, emotional numbing, paranoia, difficulty trusting others and feeling vulnerable to attack, and an inability to engage in relationships, leading the authors to conclude that long-term incarceration may result in a special subtype of PTSD that stems specifically from long-term incarceration.

Mental Illness in Prison

The plight of prisoners with mental illness is widely recognized as a very serious problem in the United States (e.g., Kupers, 1999; Lee & Prabhu, 2015), and one that has been deemed "a modern prison crisis" (Haney, 2017, p. 311). In fact, however, the task of determining precisely *how many* prisoners with mental illness are housed in any given correctional facility or prison system is more challenging than it first appears. Estimates vary widely, depending on the methodology and data sources used, as well as the definitions employed. For example, studies that focus on "serious mental disorder" such as psychosis and major depression (e.g., Fazel & Danesh, 2002) report lower prevalence rates than those that focus on any mental disorder.

One summary of existing studies on the prevalence of mental illness in various prison systems found that, depending on how "mental illness" was defined and assessed, the estimates ranged from 12 percent to 43 percent (Haney, 2006, p. 250). However, a Bureau of Justice Statistics report on the topic, published that same year, yielded a much higher figure. Specifically, James and Glaze (2006) relied on actual interviews conducted with a sample of more than 20,000 prisoners in state and federal prisons and local jails around the country. Using the criteria of having either (a) been given a clinical mental health diagnosis,

(b) received mental health treatment by a mental health professional or (c) having suffered from symptoms of a mental disorder, any time within the last 12 months of having been interviewed, they found that an estimated 56 percent of state prisoners reported suffering from "mental health problems." This included nearly 25 percent who were suffering from major depression and 15 percent with symptoms of psychosis. Rates are even higher among female prisoners, with an estimated 73 percent of women in state prison suffering from a mental health problem (James & Glaze, 2006).

Proactive, direct assessments that rely on properly drawn representative samples of prisoners are likely to produce more accurate estimates of the prevalence of mental illness in prisons than official reports from correctional systems or facilities. There are several reasons why this is true. For one, there are general and longstanding concerns about the poor quality and reliability of the data collection undertaken by prison systems in general (e.g., National Research Council, 2014, p. 164–166). Moreover, mental health prevalence data are only as reliable the mental health care systems that produce them. Poor prison mental health care systems typically lack adequate personnel and procedures with which to reliably detect mental illness among prisoners. Hence, the very worst systems are likely to significantly *undercount* their prisoners with mental illness.

In addition, the unreliability and likely undercounting in most estimates of the prevalence of mental illness in prison may be exacerbated by the counter-therapeutic nature of the environment itself and the problematic fact that prisoners are reluctant to discuss psychological problems with correctional officers and even, under many circumstances, with mental health staff. For example, one study found that despite high levels of suicidal ideation among different groups of prisoners, nearly half of general population prisoners and nearly a third of those housed in a residential therapy unit said they were unlikely to tell even the mental health staff about their suicidal thoughts (Way, Kaufman, Knoll, & Chlebowski., 2013). One likely explanation is that the typical correctional response to prisoners' expressions of suicidal ideation is to place them in barren suicide "watch" or "observation" cells, where they are stripped of their clothing and kept naked or placed in a "suicide smock," and also stripped of their property, privacy, and, as many report, their dignity. Not surprisingly, this most common but draconian correctional response is the one that is least desired by the prisoners (Way et al., 2013), creating a built-in disincentive to report suicidal thoughts.

Among the estimates based entirely on data sources coming from U.S. correctional systems themselves, data from California may be the most reliable. This is because legal scrutiny of the state prison system's mental health care began decades ago, when the state legislature initiated a proactive, direct assessment of the prevalence of mental illness among a representative sample of prisoners (Haney & Specter, 2001). The study found that there were many more inmates with mental illness than prison officials were aware of, and many more than the prison system had the capacity to treat. Statewide litigation over the unconstitutional level and quality of mental health care soon followed (see *Coleman v. Brown*, 1995). Some 20 years later, the litigation remains ongoing, and has included a U.S. Supreme Court decision (*Brown v. Plata*, 2011) concluding that the state's prisoners with mental illness were still suffering from a lack of constitutionally adequate care.

In the course of this decades-long litigation process, the reform of the prison mental health care system has been overseen by a federal district court, which implemented elaborate monitoring procedures to evaluate the quality of mental health care that is being delivered throughout the state's very large prison system, a system that at one point in the process held nearly 200,000 inmates. Thus, the recent report from the California system that more than 30 percent of its inmates are now on the mental health caseload (California Department of Corrections and Rehabilitation, 2016) appears to be as reliable an estimate of the number of state prisoners who actually have a mental illness as exists, at least among those that are based on correctional system data alone.

The Plight of Prisoners with Mental Illness

Mental illness represents a special kind of vulnerability in prison. Prisoners with mental illness are more sensitive to the day-to-day pains of imprisonment, perhaps as a result of their more extensive trauma histories (e.g., Dudeck et al., 2011; Schnittker, Massoglia, & Uggen, 2011). Unfortunately, they are also especially vulnerable to various forms of harm during their incarceration (e.g., Johnston, 2013).

In addition to the risk of deterioration or decompensation that exposure to especially dangerous, degrading, and dehumanizing prison conditions can cause, prisoners with mental illness are more likely to be physically and sexually victimized in prison (e.g., James & Glaze, 2006; Blitz, Wolff, & Shi, 2008; Wolff, Blitz, & Shi, 2007; Wolff, Shi, Blitz, & Siegel, 2007). For example, a 2011–2012 Bureau of Justice Statistics report found higher rates of reported sexual victimization by both other prisoners and staff among prisoners with anxiety and mood disorders, compared to those who reportedly did not suffer from a mental illness, and even higher rates of sexual victimization among prisoners with serious psychological distress (Beck, Berzofsky, Caspar, & Krebs, 2013).

Not surprisingly, a study measuring subjective feelings of unsafety among prisoners found that prisoners who suffered from depression, anxiety, or PTSD were more likely to report feeling unsafe, especially if they had recently been victimized (Wolff & Shi, 2009). For prisoners with mental illness, the trauma of victimization can contribute to worsening symptoms and trigger the onset of PTSD for those prisoners who do not already suffer from it (Johnston, 2013; Neal & Clements, 2010). The high rates of past physical and sexual victimization among prisoners with mental illness (James & Glaze, 2006), coupled with their increased likelihood of experiencing further trauma once incarcerated and a greater subjective sense of unsafety all contribute to the need for trauma-related treatment while incarcerated (e.g., Wolff, Blitz et al., 2007).

Prisoners with mental illness are also more likely to be found to have violated prison rules and regulations (e.g., Toch & Adams, 1986), receive disciplinary infractions, and to be subjected to the uniquely counter-therapeutic sanction of punitive isolation (e.g., Hafemeister & George, 2012; Johnston, 2013; Wolff, Blitz et al., 2007; Wolfe, Shi et al., 2007b; SpearIt, 2009). Prisoners with mental illness have higher rates of being charged with assault-based rules violations, both physical and verbal, and of being injured in a fight, compared to those prisoners who reportedly do not have a mental illness (James & Glaze, 2006).

Prison rules violations often stem from symptoms of mental illness (Fellner, 2006; Metzner & Fellner, 2013; Johnston, 2013). A prisoner who is yelling, refusing to follow orders, or being disruptive or belligerent may be viewed as engaging in intentional misconduct, and be treated as such by correctional staff, rather than as exhibiting the symptoms of a mental illness. This is particularly likely in cases where prison staff has not been adequately trained in recognizing and responding to mental illness (e.g., Fellner, 2006; Metzner & Fellner, 2013). One study found that prisoners with lifetime PTSD diagnoses and those who reported having been assaulted or abused before prison had been charged with a greater number and variety of disciplinary infractions which, in turn, may be associated with features of PTSD, such as hypervigilance and irritability (Wood, 2014). Additionally, rates of substance abuse disorders are higher among prisoners with mental illness (James & Glaze, 2016), which can both exacerbate symptoms of mental illness and lead to a greater likelihood of rules violations (Houser & Belenko, 2015; Wood, 2014).

For those prisoners experiencing severe mental illness, with features such as delusions, hallucinations, and loss of contact with reality, imprisonment is likely to be especially difficult. A study of long-term prisoners with mental illness in France concluded that prisoners with severe mental illness may have an "increased sense of persecutory threat" and be less able to understand the intended objectives of their imprisonment (Yang, Kadoun, Revah-Levy, Mulvey, & Falissard, 2009, p. 302). As the authors note, this would likely worsen certain features of their illness (such as withdrawal and the tendency to misconstrue others' intentions), and correspondingly heighten the effects of long-term confinement.

Unfortunately, mental illness often goes unidentified and untreated for many prisoners (e.g., Haney, 2017). Only a third of state prisoners who had mental health problems had received treatment since they began their incarceration (James & Glaze, 2006). Taken together, this contributes to the danger that symptoms of mental illness in a prisoner will be punished as a disciplinary infraction in ways that exacerbate it, rather than treated with appropriate medical care.

Two commentators accurately summarized the problem: the "growth in the number of inmates with a mental disorder, combined with the recent rise of prolonged solitary confinement and the increasingly punitive nature of American penology" has resulted in a disproportionate number of inmates with mental illness being housed in supermax-type prisons where "harsh restrictions ... often significantly exacerbate these inmates' mental disorders or otherwise cause significant additional harm to their mental health, as well as preclude proper mental health treatment" (Hafemeister & George, 2012, p. 53).

Long-Term Confinement, Mental Illness, and Isolation

Because the destabilizing effects of mental illness can result in higher rates of disciplinary write-ups among prisoners with mental illness, these inmates are at risk of suffering disproportionate placement in disciplinary segregation units. Obviously, the longer their terms of prison confinement, the more likely this is to occur. Although prison isolation places all prisoners at serious risk of harm, its adverse psychological effects are expected to vary as a function not only of the specific nature and duration of the isolation (such that more deprived conditions experienced for longer amounts of time are likely to have more detrimental consequences) but also as a function of the vulnerabilities of the prisoners subjected to it. Prisoners with mental illness are particularly at risk in these isolated environments. There are several reasons why this is so.

For one, solitary or isolated confinement subjects prisoners to significantly more stress and psychological pain than other forms of imprisonment. Prisoners with mental illness are generally more sensitive and reactive to psychological stressors and emotional pain. In many ways, the harshness and severe levels of deprivation that are imposed on them in isolation are the antithesis of the kind of benign and socially supportive atmosphere that mental health clinicians seek to create within genuinely therapeutic environments. Not surprisingly, prisoners with mental illness are more likely to deteriorate and decompensate when they are subjected to the harshness and stress of prison isolation.

Some of the deterioration and decompensation that prisoners with mental illness suffer in isolated confinement results from the critically important role that social contact and social interaction play in maintaining psychological equilibrium. The esteemed psychiatrist Harry Stack Sullivan once summarized the clinical significance of meaningful social contact by observing that "[w]e can't be alone in things and be very clear on what happened to us, and we … can't be alone and be very clear even on what is happening in us very long— excepting that it gets simpler and simpler, and more primitive and more prim- itive, and less and less socially acceptable" (Sullivan, 1971, p. 326). Social contact and social interaction are essential components in the creation and maintenance of normal social identity and social reality.

Thus, the experience of isolation is psychologically destabilizing, because it undermines a person's sense of self or social identity and erodes his or her con- nection to a shared social reality. Isolated prisoners have few if any opportunities to receive feedback about their feelings and beliefs, which become increasingly untethered from any normal social context. In extreme cases, a related pattern emerges: isolated confinement becomes so painful, so bizarre, and so impossible to make sense of that some prisoners create their own reality—they live in a world of fantasy instead of the intolerable one that surrounds them.[1]

Finally, many of the direct negative psychological effects of isolation mimic or parallel specific symptoms of mental illness. Even though the direct effects of isolation, experienced in reaction to adverse conditions of confinement, are generally less chronic than those that are produced by a diagnosable mental illness, they can nevertheless add to and compound the outward manifestation of symptoms as well as the internal experience of the disorder among prisoners with mental illness. For example, many studies have documented the degree to which isolated confinement contributes to feelings of lethargy, hopelessness, and depression (e.g., Haney, 2003). For already clinically depressed prisoners, these acute situational effects are likely to exacerbate their pre-existing chronic condition and lead to worsening of their depressed state. Similarly, the mood swings that some prisoners report experiencing in isolation would be expected to amplify the pre-existing emotional instability that prisoners diagnosed with bipolar disorder suffer. Prisoners who suffer from disorders of impulse control would likely find their pre-existing condition made worse by the frustration,

---

1. For a vivid description of the effects of isolation in prison, see Binelli (2015).

irritability, and anger that many isolated prisoners report experiencing. And prisoners prone to psychotic breaks may suffer more in isolated confinement due to conditions that deny them the stabilizing influence of social feedback that grounds their sense of reality in a stable and meaningful social world.

In fact, widespread recognition of the heightened vulnerability of prisoners with mental illness to the adverse psychological effects of isolated confinement has led numerous corrections officials, professional mental health groups, and human rights organizations to prohibit their placement in such units or, if it is absolutely necessary as a last resort to confine them there, to very strictly limit the duration of such confinement and to provide prisoners with significant amounts of out-of-cell time and augmented access to care. For example, the American Psychiatric Association (APA) has issued a Position Statement on Segregation of Prisoners with Mental Illness, stating:

> Prolonged segregation of adult inmates with serious mental illness, with rare exceptions, should be avoided due to the potential for harm to such inmates. If an inmate with serious mental illness is placed in segregation, out-of-cell structured therapeutic activities (i.e., mental health/psychiatric treatment) in appropriate programming space and adequate unstructured out-of-cell time should be permitted. Correctional mental health authorities should work closely with administrative custody staff to maximize access to clinically indicated programming and recreation for the individuals (American Psychiatric Association, 2012).

The APA's position on this issue reflects the accepted fact that prisoners with mental illness are especially vulnerable to isolation- and stress-related regression, deterioration, and decompensation that worsen their psychiatric conditions and intensify their mental health-related symptoms and maladies (including depression, psychosis, and self-harm).

This widely accepted fact about the heightened vulnerability of prisoners with mental illness to isolated confinement is acknowledged in the standard operating procedures that govern their admission and retention in a number of such units. Mental health staff in some prison systems screen out prisoners with mental illness in advance of their possible placement in isolation and exclude them from such confinement. Moreover, they are routinely required to monitor isolated prisoners with the same intended purpose—to identify any prisoners who may be manifesting the signs and symptoms of emerging mental illness or other serious psychological reactions and to remove them from these harmful environments.

Courts that have been presented with evidence on this issue have reached the same conclusions about the vulnerability of inmates with mental illness to severe forms of prison isolation. One such court noted that those prisoners for whom the psychological risks of isolated confinement were "particularly"— and unacceptably—high included anyone suffering from "overt paranoia, psychotic breaks with reality, or massive exacerbations of existing mental illness as a result of the conditions in [solitary confinement]" (*Madrid v. Gomez*, 1995, p. 1265). The judge elaborated, noting that the group of prisoners to be excluded from isolation should include:

> [T]he already mentally ill, as well as persons with borderline personality disorders, brain damage or mental retardation, impulse-ridden personalities, or a history of prior psychiatric problems or chronic depression. For these inmates, placing them in [isolated confinement] is the mental equivalent of putting an asthmatic in a place with little air to breathe. The risk is high enough, and the consequences serious enough, that we have no hesitancy in finding that the risk is plainly "unreasonable" (*Madrid v. Gomez*, 1995, p. 1265).

The accumulated weight of the scientific evidence demonstrates the painful nature of isolated confinement, and the serious risk of significant psychological harm at which it places prisoners. When persons are deprived of normal social contact for extended periods of time, they experience mental pain and suffering, are more susceptible to severe stress-related maladies and disorders, are subject to deterioration and dysfunction along a number of mental, emotional, and physical dimensions, and are placed at risk of even more serious harm, including the loss of their sanity and even their lives.

The broad range of adverse effects that derive from social deprivation underscores the fundamental importance of meaningful social contact and interaction and, in essence, establishes these things as identifiable human needs. Over the long term, meaningful social contact and interaction may be as essential to a person's psychological well-being as adequate food, clothing, and shelter are to his or her physical well-being. This appears to be true for prisoners in general, but especially true for prisoners with mental illness who are particularly vulnerable to the pains of isolated confinement and susceptible to its harmful effects.

Conclusion

To summarize the implications of what is known about this especially vulnerable group of long-term prisoners with mental illness: the increasingly aging prisoner population in the United States, approximately one-third or more of whom have mental illness, are susceptible to a number of damaging stressors that may include physical and sexual assault, the loss of outside social support, inadequate psychiatric and other treatment services, greater risk of solitary-type confinement and its extremely deleterious effects, and the lack of appropriate reentry services to manage their challenging transition to free society if and when they are eventually released.

Discussion Questions

1. What are some ways that prisons could better respond to prisoners with mental illness who are serving long-term sentences? What are some challenges to implementing those solutions?

2. What are some possible reasons why prisoners with mental illness might be more likely to be victimized while in prison?

3. Based on what you have learned in this chapter, what classes of long-term prisoners with mental illness do you think might be especially vulnerable to harm while incarcerated? Why?

4. What other statuses or vulnerabilities not discussed here might be likely to be present in the lives of prisoners with mental illness serving who are serving long-term sentences? How might those statuses or vulnerabilities interact with some of the challenges described in this chapter?

5. What interventions might increase the likelihood of successful reentry by prisoners with mental illness after serving a long-term sentence? What events or experiences over the course of a long-term prison sentence might make re-entry especially difficult for a prisoner with mental illness?

References

Alexander, M. (2010). *The new Jim Crow: Mass incarceration in the age of colorblindness.* New York, NY: The New Press.

American Psychiatric Association. (2012). *Position statement: Segregation of prisoners with mental illness.* Washington, D.C.: American Psychiatric Association.

Barry, L. C., Wakefield, D. B., Trestman, R. L., & Conwell, Y. (2016). Disability in prison activities of daily living and likelihood of depression and suicidal ideation in older prisoners. *International Journal of Geriatric Psychiatry.* doi: 10.1002/gps.4578.

Beck, A. J., Berzofsky, M., Caspar, R., & Krebs, C. (2013). *Sexual victimization in prisons and jails reported by inmates, 2011–12.* Washington, D.C.: U.S. Department of Justice, Bureau of Justice Statistics. Retrieved from https://www.bjs.gov/content/pub/pdf/svpjri1112.pdf.

Binelli, M. (2015, March 26). Inside America's toughest prison. *New York Times Magazine.* Retrieved from https://www.nytimes.com/2015/03/29/magazine/inside-americas-toughest-federal-prison.html.

Blitz, C. L., Wolff, N., & Shi, J. (2008). Physical victimization in prison: The role of mental illness. *International Journal of Law & Psychiatry, 31,* 385–393.

Brown v. Plata, 563 U.S. 493 (2011).

Coleman v. Brown, 912 F. Supp. 1282 E.D. Cal. (1995).

Collins, P. (2015). Intersectionality's definitional dilemmas. *Annual Review of Sociology, 41,* 1–20.

Courtney, D., & Maschi, T. (2012). Trauma and stress among older adults in prison: Breaking the cycle of silence. *Traumatology, 19,* 73–81.

Dudeck, M., Drenkhahn, K., Spitzer, C., Barnow, S., Kopp, D., & Duwert, P. (2011). Traumatization and mental distress in long-term prisoners in Europe. *Punishment & Society, 13,* 403–423.

Durose, M., & Langan, P. (2005). *State court sentencing of convicted felons, 2002: Statistical tables.* Washington, D.C.: U.S. Department of Justice. Retrieved from https://www.bjs.gov/content/pub/pdf/fssc00.pdf.

Dye, M., & Aday, R. (2013). "I just wanted to die": Preprison and current suicide ideation among women serving life sentences. *Criminal Justice and Behavior, 40,* 832–849.

Fazel, S., & Danesh, J. (2002). Serious mental disorder in 23,000 prisoners: A systematic review of 62 surveys. *The Lancet, 359,* 545–550.

Fellner, J. (2006). A corrections quandary: Mental illness and prison rules. *Harvard Civil Rights-Civil Liberties Law Review, 41,* 391–412.

Flanagan, T. (1980). The pains of long-term imprisonment: A comparison of British and American perspectives. *British Journal of Criminology, 20,* 148–156.

Frank, J. B., & Gill, E. A. (2015). The negotiated identities of long-term inmates: Breaking the chains of problematic integration. *Western Journal of Communication, 79*(5), 513–532.

Fries, B. E., Schmorrow, A., Lang, S. W., Margolis, P. M., Heany, J., Brown, G. P., ... Hirdes, J. P. (2013). Symptoms and treatment of mental illness among prisoners: A study of Michigan state prisons. *International Journal of Law and Psychiatry, 36,* 316–325.

Goff, A., Rose, E., Rose, S., & Purves, D. (2007). Does PTSD occur in sentenced prison populations? A systematic literature review. *Criminal Behaviour and Mental Health, 17,* 152–162.

Grounds, A. (2005). Understanding the effects of wrongful imprisonment. In M. Tonry (Ed.), *Crime and justice: A review of research* (Vol. 32, pp. 1–58). Chicago, IL: University of Chicago Press.

Hafemeister, T., & George, J. (2012). The ninth circle of hell: An Eighth Amendment analysis of imposing prolonged supermax solitary confinement on inmates with a mental illness. *Denver Law Review, 90,* 1–54.

Haney, C. (2003). Mental health issues in long-term solitary and "supermax" confinement. *Crime and Delinquency, 49*(1), 124–156.

Haney, C. (2017). "Madness" and penal confinement: Some observations on mental illness and prison pain. *Punishment & Society, 19,* 310–326.

Hankivsky, O., & Cormier, R. (2011). Intersectionality and public policy: Some lessons from existing models. *Political Research Quarterly, 64,* 217–229.

Heckman, C., Cropsey, K., & Olds-Davis, T. (2007). Traumatic stress disorder treatment in correctional settings: A brief review of the empirical literature and suggestions for future research. *Psychotherapy: Theory, Research, Practice, Training, 44,* 46–53.

Herman, J. (1992). Complex PTSD: A syndrome in survivors of prolonged and repeated trauma. *Journal of Traumatic Stress, 5,* 377–391.

Houser, K., & Belenko, S. (2015). Disciplinary responses to misconduct among female prison inmates with mental illness, substance use disorders, and co-occurring disorders. *Prison Rehabilitation Journal, 38*(1), 24–34.

James, D., & Glaze, L. (2006). *Mental health problems of prison and jail inmates.* Washington, D.C.: U.S. Department of Justice, Bureau of Justice Statistics. Retrieved from https://www.bjs.gov/content/pub/pdf/mhppji.pdf.

Johnston, E. L. (2013). Vulnerability and just desert: A theory of sentencing and mental illness. *Journal of Criminal Law and Criminology, 103,* 147–229.

Kazemian, L., & Travis, J. (2015). Forgotten prisoners: Imperative for inclusion of long termers and lifers in research and policy. *Criminology & Public Policy, 14,* 355–395.

Kupers, T. (1999). *Prison madness: The mental health crisis behind bars and what we must do about it.* New York, NY: Jossey Bass.

Lee, B., & Prabhu, M. (2015). A reflection on the madness in prisons. *Stanford Law & Policy Review, 26,* 253–268.

Leigey, M. E., & Reed, K. L. (2010). A woman's life before serving life: Examining the negative pre-incarceration life events of life-sentenced inmates. *Women & Criminal Justice, 20*(4), 302–322.

Liem, M. (2016). *After life imprisonment: Reentry in the era of mass incarceration.* New York, NY: New York University Press.

Liem, M., & Kunst, M. (2013). Is there a recognizable post-incarceration syndrome among released "lifers"? *International Journal of Law and Psychiatry, 36*(3–4), 333–337.

Luallen, J., & Cutler, C. (2015). The growth of older inmate population: How population aging explains rising age at admission. *Journals of Gerontology, Series B, Psychological Sciences and Social Sciences.* doi: https://doi.org/10.1093/geronb/gbv069.

Madrid v. Gomez, 889 F.Supp. 1146 N.D. Cal. (1995).

Maschi, T., Gibson, S., Zgoba, K. M., & Morgen, K. (2011). Trauma and life event stressors among young and older adult prisoners. *Journal of Correctional Health Care, 17*(2), 160–172.

Maschi, T., Viola, D., & Koskinen, L. (2015). Trauma, stress, and coping among older adults in prison: Towards a human rights and intergenerational family justice action agenda. *Traumatology, 21*(3), 188–200.

Metzner, J. L., & Fellner, J. (2010). Solitary confinement and mental illness in U.S. prisons: A challenge for medical ethics. *Journal of the American Academy of Psychiatry and Law, 38*(1), 104–108.

National Research Council. (2014). *The growth of incarceration in the United States: Exploring causes and consequences.* Washington, D.C.: The National Academies Press. Retrieved from https://www.nap.edu/read/18613/chapter/1.

Neal, T., & Clements, C. B. (2010). Prison rape and psychological sequelae: A call for research. *Psychology, Public Policy, and Law, 16*(1), 284–299.

Nellis, A. (2017). Still life: America's increasing use of life and long-term sentences. *The Sentencing Project.* Retrieved from http://www.sentencingproject.org/publications/still-life-americas-increasing-use-life-long-term-sentences/.

Noonan, M. (2015). *Prison and jail deaths in custody, 2000–2013 — Statistical tables.* Washington, D.C.: U.S. Department of Justice, Bureau of Justice Statistics. Retrieved from https://www.bjs.gov/content/pub/pdf/mljsp0013st.pdf.

Pew Center on the States. (2012). *Time served: The high cost, low return of longer prison terms.* Washington, D.C.: Pew Charitable Trusts. Retrieved from http://www.pewtrusts.org/~/media/legacy/uploadedfiles/wwwpewtrustsorg/reports/sentencing_ana_corrections/prisontimeservedpdf.pdf.

Price, J. M. (2015). *Prison and social death*. Piscataway, NJ: Rutgers University Press.

SpearIt. (2009). Mental illness in prison: Inmate rehabilitation & correctional officers in crisis. *Berkeley Journal of Criminal Law, 14*(1), 277–301.

Sullivan, H. (1971). The illusion of personal individuality. *Psychiatry, 12*, 317–332.

Toch, H., & Adams, K. (1986). Pathology and disruptiveness among prison inmates. *Journal of Research in Crime & Delinquency, 23*, 7–21.

Way, B. B., Kaufman, A. R., Knoll, J. L., & Chlebowski, S. M. (2013). Suicidal ideation among inmate patients in state prison: Prevalence, reluctance to report, and treatment preferences. *Behavioral Sciences & the Law, 31*, 230–238.

Williams, B., Stern, M., Mellow, J., Safer, M., & Greifinger, R. (2012). Aging in correctional custody: Setting a policy agenda for older prisoner health care. *American Journal of Public Health, 102*, 1475–1481.

Wolff, N., Blitz, C., & Shi, J. (2007). Rates of sexual victimization in prison for inmates with and without mental illness. *Psychiatric Services, 58*, 1087–1094.

Wolff, N., & Shi, J. (2009). Victimisation and feelings of safety among male and female inmates with behavioural health problems. *The Journal of Forensic Psychiatry & Psychology, 20*(1), 56–77.

Wolff, N., Shi, J., Blitz, C., & Siegel, J. (2007). Understanding sexual victimization inside prisons: Factors that predict risk. *Criminology & Public Policy, 6*, 535–564.

Wood, S. R. (2014). State prisoner misconduct: Contribution of dual psychiatric and substance use disorders. *International Journal of Forensic Mental Health, 13*, 279–294.

Wright, S., Crewe, B., & Hulley, S. (2017). Suppression, denial, sublimation: Defending against the initial pains of very long life sentences. *Theoretical Criminology, 21*(2), 225–246.

Yang, S., Kadoun, A., Revah-Levy, A., Mulvey, E. P., & Falissard, B. (2009). Doing time: A qualitative study of long-term incarceration and the impact of mental illness. *International Journal of Law and Psychiatry, 32*(5), 294–303.

Zamble, F. (1992). Behavior and adaptation in long-term prison inmates: Descriptive longitudinal results. *Criminal Justice and Behavior, 19*, 409–425.

Psychiatric Comorbidity and Reentry

Arthur J. Lurigio

Introduction

At year-end 2015, more than 2.2 million adults were incarcerated in U.S. jails and prisons (Kaeble & Glaze, 2016). Overall, the vast majority of these detainees and inmates, respectively, will return home after relatively short stays in confinement. In fact, 95 percent of all incarcerees eventually return to the community (Hughes & Wilson, 2002). The War on Drugs contributed greatly to the precipitous growth in the jail and prison population due to changes in policies that focused on drug-defined arrests and more serious penalties for drug-law violators. The habitual use of drugs can lead to addiction and a diagnosis of a substance use disorder, which is one of the 20 major categories of psychiatric disorders in the diagnostic nomenclature.

People with a substance use disorder are likely to be diagnosed with another type of psychiatric disorder. The presence of two or more psychiatric disorders in the same person at the same time is known as co-occurrence or comorbidity. People with co-occurring disorders (PWCDs) experience a wealth of clinical and social problems that often exacerbate one another. PWCDs have a more difficult time adjusting to life in a correctional institution and an even more difficult time adjusting to life in the community after a period of confinement.

Reentry programs have received considerable attention with the recognition that more than 600,000 formerly incarcerated men and women return annually from prisons, and they are ill-equipped to face the multifaceted demands of readjustment. PWCDs are disproportionately represented in jails and prisons. Their complex clinical conditions greatly complicate their ability to pursue productive and prosocial endeavors. Their practical needs are many (e.g., shelter, financial assistance, employment), and the services required to meet those needs are scanty. Consequently, they are more likely to recidivate after release than their counterparts with no psychiatric disorders or only one disorder or the other.

This chapter is divided into four major sections, which explore the nature and extent of co-occurring substance use and other psychiatric disorders among criminally involved people and the struggles they face when returning from jails and prisons. Section 1 briefly explains the basic neurochemistry of addiction, which changes the brain and locks users into the cycle of addiction, consisting of persistent and costly efforts to acquire and consume substances in order to enjoy the gratifying effects of drug use and to avoid the painful effects of drug withdrawal. Section 2 elucidates the relationship between drug use and crime, which is critical for understanding how people with co-occurring disorders (PWCDs) enter the criminal justice system and eventually leave confinement to confront the challenges of reentry into society. Section 3 discusses comorbidity between addiction and other mental disorders, the symptoms of which are complex, severe, and treatment-resistant. Section 4 describes reentry from jails and prisons and the primary obstacles that impede transitions from correctional institutions to communities as well as the particular difficulties faced by PWCDs coming home from carceral settings.

Nature of Addiction

Neural Chemicals and Circuitry

Addiction is easier to explain than to treat. People consume alcohol and drugs for three basic reasons: to feel good, to avoid feeling bad, or to enhance their athletic and cognitive performance. As manufactured chemicals, drugs flood the brain, producing states of euphoria, relaxation, and alertness at much greater levels than do the brain's natural chemicals (e.g., serotonin and dopamine). Drug use alters the brain's neural circuits, which fosters the addiction process (National Institute on Drug Abuse [NIDA], 2007).

Centrally involved in triggering addiction is the brain's mesolimbic dopaminergic circuit, consisting of the nucleus accumbens (reward center), the amygdala (emotional center), and the hippocampus (memory center). This circuit is responsible for the reinforcing sensations of substance use and for the memories and conditioned responses that impel drug-seeking behaviors (Volkow, Wang, Fowler, & Tomasi, 2012). During periods of addiction, the prefrontal cortex (rational thinking center) becomes unable to rein in uncontrolled drug use despite its damaging impact on users' lives. These and other areas of the brain constitute the neural network that is rewired as addiction progresses from use, intoxication, craving, and binging to withdrawal and relapse (Goldstein & Volkow, 2002).

Tolerance and Withdrawal

Drugs mimic natural chemicals (neurotransmitters) in the brain (drugs are neural agonists), or they block the reabsorption of these chemicals (drugs are neural antagonists) (NIDA, 2007). The first time a drug is introduced to the brain (use), its effects (intoxication) are more powerful than at any other time in a user's experience. Subsequent use elicits less intense pleasure and intensifies the desire for more drugs (craving). Habitual users increasingly seek and use drugs (binging) in an attempt to recapture their first high. Drug tolerance diminishes subsequent highs and thwarts users' efforts to re-experience their inaugural rush by raising the quantity and potency of the drugs or changing the mode of drug usage from ingestion to inhalation to injection (Volkow & Li, 2005).

The brain is supremely adaptive and favors a state of equilibrium. The influx of drugs starts to slow down the brain's production of its own drug-compatible neurotransmitters and to reduce the number and sensitivity of receptor sites that respond to those neurotransmitters. Thus, in a futile process of diminishing returns, subsequent drug use fails to spark the same peak sensations, involving greater use and dampened pleasure. With continued use, the brain expects elevated levels of drugs at primed receptor sites in its reward center (Goldstein & Volkow, 2002). As a result, during periods of decreased or no use, dependent users suffer from intense physical (e.g., tremors and gastrointestinal disturbances) or emotional (e.g., dysphoria, dysthymia, agitation, and irritability) withdrawal symptoms or both. Together, drug tolerance and withdrawal accelerate criminal and other risky behaviors aimed at obtaining more drugs. At some point, drug use is mostly a means to stave off withdrawal symptoms rather than to obtain pleasure (Kosten & George, 2002).

Addiction

The aforementioned drug-initiated changes in the brain lead to addiction: a chronic relapsing disease characterized by uncontrolled drug-seeking and -using behaviors that endure in the face of negative life-altering (and -ending) consequences (NIDA, 2007). People with addiction are obsessed with pursuing and consuming drugs in an iterative loop that is inimical to other aspects of their lives, resulting in loss of health, jobs, families, educational achievement, financial resources, and housing. Incessant drug-seeking and -using behaviors and their repercussions are among the criteria employed in diagnosing substance use disorders (American Psychiatric Association [APA], 2013; NIDA, 2007).

Polydrug Use

Users of both prescription and illegal drugs frequently consume more than one drug (i.e., they are polydrug users; Walker, Pratt, Schoenborn, & Druss, 2017). Polydrug users commonly select a preferred drug and supplement it with other drugs to modify or amplify the primary drug's effects. Users of every type of illegal drug are also likely to consume alcohol, nicotine, and marijuana (McKelvey, Ramo, Delucchi, & Rubinstein, 2017), which is now legal and widely accessible in many states (National Conference of State Legislators, 2016). Polydrug use in any combination greatly complicates and impedes recovery from addiction (Downey, Helmus, & Schuster, 2000).

Nexus between Drugs and Crime

Bidirectionality

Drug-defined crimes include possessing, using, manufacturing, distributing, or trafficking illegal drugs (Office of National Drug Control Policy, 2000). Offenders who break such laws also generally commit street crimes such as robbery, theft, burglary, and prostitution (Bureau of Justice Statistics, 1994). "Substance misuse and addiction are overwhelming factors in all types of crime, not just alcohol and drug law violations" (National Center on Addiction and Substance Abuse, 2010, p. 2). The connection between drug use and crime has been well established (Lurigio, 2000). However, the onset of drug use and criminal activity do not necessarily coincide. Both might be part of an overall predilection to engage in risky and illegal behaviors. Therefore, the relationship between drug use and criminal pursuits is more likely to be bidirectional and correlational rather than causal (Bean, 2004). Drug users become more active criminals when they are in the throes of addiction, which acts as a crime-intensifier. Drug consumption and criminal activity are positively associated; the rate of criminal activity (the number of crimes committed during discrete time intervals) rises and falls in tandem with the severity of drug use (the amount and frequency of drug use during discrete time intervals; Chandler, Fletcher, & Volkow, 2009).

The Cycle of Drug Use and Crime

The expense of illegal drugs can be considerable, and the compulsion to use drugs can be overwhelming. People with substance use disorders are less able or willing to work or may be unemployable (American Psychiatric Association, 2013). Hence, drug users' financial resources often fall short of the costs of illegal drugs, due to users' limited means and the expensive of their habits. Crimes can generate cash quickly, which is then spent even more quickly on drug purchases. These types of crimes are known as drug-related offenses (i.e., income-generating property, violent, and drug-selling crimes; Craddock, Collins, & Timrots, 1994). More crime garners more money to buy more drugs, leading to more severe addiction and more crime. In this cycle of behaviors, crime fuels drug use and drug use fuels crime. However, the cycle can be broken with participation in treatment and the attainment of sobriety (Lurigio, 2000).

Offenders who commit crimes when they are using drugs might continue violating the law when recovering from addiction, but they are typically less likely to do so (Lurigio, 2000). Also, people with substance use disorders involving illegal drugs might commit only drug-defined offenses, particularly if they have the sustained legal income to finance their habits, which obviates the need for criminal activities (Peele, Brodsky, & Arnold, 1992). In the past decade, an alarming number of individuals have been abusing prescription drugs, for example, OxyContin, Xanax, Adderall, Ambien, Vicodin, Percocet, and Ritalin. Police departments nationwide have reported spikes in crime attributable to the burgeoning use of opioid painkillers and prescription stimulants (e.g., Goodnough, 2010).

Social Networks and Systemic Violence

Addiction and criminality are potentiating in other ways. Abusers of illegal drugs, especially those living in criminogenic neighborhoods, could join social networks of other abusers who are also criminally active sellers of illegal drugs. Social contagion influences them to use more drugs, commit more crimes, and adopt a lifestyle that revolves around illegal drug markets and precludes legitimate economic and other prosocial endeavors (Office of National Drug Control Policy, 2000). Offenders who sell illegal drugs could commit violent crimes to protect drug markets by threatening or killing rival drug sellers. The crack wars of the late 1980s and early 1990s caused homicides and other violent crimes to reach unprecedented levels due to the systemic violence of the drug trade. By the mid-1990s, homicide rates began to plummet with the diminution of crack use and sales in major cities (Curtis, 1998).

Co-Occurring Substance Use and Other Psychiatric Disorders

As designated in the *Diagnostic and Statistical Manual of Mental Disorders, 5th Edition* (*DSM-5*), substance use disorders are one of 20 major categories of mental illness (APA, 2013). The general symptoms of psychiatric disorders are distress, impaired functioning, and disturbances in thoughts, feelings, and behaviors that are incongruous with cultural expectations (APA, 2013). Many diagnoses co-occur in the same people. For example, patients with anxiety disorders typically meet the diagnostic criteria for mood disorders such as major depression and vice versa. Substance use disorders are frequently found among people with other types of psychiatric disorders (Lurigio, 2011). In short, the boundaries between *DSM-5* diagnoses are sometimes blurry (Francis, 2013).

Explanations of Comorbidity

Similar Causes. Various models can explain comorbidity. As mentioned above, different mental illnesses could have a shared etiology, and within and between diagnostic categories, they often overlap in term of symptoms (what patients report) and signs (what diagnosticians observe) (Francis, 2013). Therefore, some psychiatric disorders are possibly the result of the same or similar causes that originate from mostly unspecified abnormalities in the brain. This model of comorbidity suggests that substance use and other psychiatric disorders emerge from underlying mutual pathologies, for example, deficits in the brain's reward-processing circuitry (Power et al., 2014). Genetic and environmental contributors to co-occurring disorders have been identified. Specifically, family and twin studies have found an inherited susceptibility to substance use and other psychiatric disorders. Moreover, stress or trauma can predispose people to both kinds of illnesses and their co-occurrences by affecting brain chemistry, structure, and function (NIDA, 2010).

People diagnosed with antisocial personality disorder and conduct disorder—its childhood precursor—are likely to be diagnosed with substance use or other psychiatric disorders and their co-occurrences (Compton, Conway,

Stinson, Colliver, & Grant, 2005). Among people with a substance use disorder, the presence of antisocial personality disorder (e.g., lack of empathy, impulsivity, criminal behavior, and disregard for others' rights) is related to the use of alcohol or drugs in early adolescence and the emergence of serious alcohol or drug use problems in adulthood (Mueser, Drake, & Wallach, 1998).

Hypersensitivities and Substance-Induced Disorders. Brain abnormalities associated with psychiatric disorders "may increase the vulnerability to abusing substances by enhancing their positive effects, reducing awareness of the negative effects, or alleviating the unpleasant effects associated with the mental disorder or the medication used to treat it" (NIDA, 2010, p. 5). People with substance use disorders appear to be hypersensitive to the effects of alcohol and drugs. For example, among individuals with substance use disorders, small amounts of alcohol and drugs impair cognitive and motor performance on a range of tasks (NIDA, 2010).

The use of even minor quantities of alcohol and drugs can increase the likelihood of substance use disorders and other medical problems among people with mental illness (Goodwin & Mayson, 1990; Mueser & Drake, 2007), "worsening symptoms, precipitating relapses, impairing functioning, and contributing to health problems in serious mental illness" (Mueser & Drake, 2007, p. 66). Cannabis use, for example, can produce the rank symptoms of schizophrenia, such as hallucinations (i.e., false perceptions) and delusions (i.e., false beliefs), among users predisposed to the disease (NIDA, 2010). Similarly, phencyclidine (PCP) can elicit psychotic symptoms, euphoria, and uncontrollable rage (Schmetzer, 2015). The *DSM-5* contains diagnostic entities reflecting the etiological role that drug use plays in mimicking or inducing the symptoms of mental illness. In addition, the *DSM-5* has provisions to rule out drug use before arriving at a definitive diagnosis for most serious mental disorders. Consequently, drug use can trigger the symptoms of mental disorders, as well as recurrent psychiatric episodes or relapses, particularly among people with a genetic predisposition toward such conditions.

Social Engagement. Comorbidities have a variety of causes and consequences. Complicated causal pathways and confluences of life experiences can lead to comorbidity, including "poverty, [lack of] education, deprivation, stress, unemployment, [impoverished] living conditions, and early trauma" (Mueser & Drake, 2007, p. 65). As a result, PWCDs might use illegal drugs to combat their marginalization, loneliness, and isolation. Accordingly, the effects of drugs can help PWCDs socialize more comfortably by reducing, for example, the negative symptoms of schizophrenia, which include an inability or unwillingness to interact with others. For them, purchasing and sharing illegal drugs is an interpersonal encounter, which gives PWCDs a purpose in life and occasions for social contact, motivating them to continue using drugs (Mueser, Noordsy, Drake, & Fox, 2003).

Self-Medication. PWCDs also might use illicit substances to relieve the symptoms of their conditions. In an attempt to self-medicate, they ingest illegal drugs to quell their anxiety (e.g., alcohol), elevate their mood (e.g., cocaine), or alleviate the sedating, disorienting, or numbing side effects of the psychiatric medications. Users report feeling more "normal" and better able to tune out the voices in their heads (i.e., auditory hallucinations) when they are intoxicated (Harris & Edlund, 2005).

PWCDs might self-medicate by selecting drugs with particular pharmacological properties. For example, people with depressive disorders might choose substances with stimulant effects, such as cocaine or amphetamines. Alternatively, individuals with anxiety disorders might choose substances with sedative effects, such as heroin or alcohol. Nonetheless, no studies have consistently found a precise match between drug choices and psychiatric symptoms (Mueser et al., 2003). Therefore, PWCDs rarely report that they use specific substances to palliate the symptoms of specific disorders. Instead, they use various substances to relieve the dysphoria that arises from boredom, loneliness, or the side effects of psychiatric medications. "Most offenders with co-occurring disorders use substances for the same reason that their non-mentally ill counterparts do — to be social, fight boredom, or achieve a 'high'" (Hills, 2000, p. 6).

Challenges of Reentry

Coming Home

As noted above, over two million adults are currently in U.S. jails and prisons, and nearly all will return to the community at some point. This statement is as true today as it was nearly 80 years ago when President Franklin D. Roosevelt noted that most prisoners are ultimately released from incarceration and need support in their efforts to readjust to community life. The president called for the establishment of parole as a vehicle for assisting releasees in the reentry process. In his exhortation, Roosevelt enumerated the major problems of the formerly incarcerated, which parallel many of the same formidable obstacles affecting releasees in 2017, such as estrangement from family and neighbors and a dearth of employment prospects (Jonson & Cullen, 2015).

By the twenty-first century, reentry had become a prominent issue in governmental and academic circles (Garland & Wodahl, 2014; Petersilia, 2009; Rhine & Thompson, 2011), with scholars referring to it as a "social movement" because of widespread bipartisan support for reentry initiatives from all levels of government, as well from as professional associations and faith-based organizations. "Academics have been particularly important in constructing reentry as a social problem, providing solutions, and calling for concerted efforts to transform the back-end of the correctional system" (e.g., Petersilia, 2003; Travis, 2005; Jonson & Cullen, 2015, p. 521).

The problem of reentry is an inexorable result of mass incarceration, which increased the prison population 500 percent from the early 1980s to date (Johson & Cullen, 2015). As both prison and jail populations exploded, so did the number of incarcerees released from correctional institutions—a seemingly unbidden eventuality of the imprisonment binge (Petersilia, 2009). For example, from 1978 to 2008, the number of inmates exiting state and federal prisons more than quintupled, from approximately 142,000 to 730,000. Since 1997, the number of released inmates has never been lower than 500,000, and from 2005 to 2010, that number was consistently higher than 700,000 (Carson & Golinelli, 2013; Sabol, West, & Cooper, 2009). In 2015, more than 600,000 state and federal inmates were released from prison (Carson & Anderson, 2016). Greatly surpassing the droves of released prisoners, more than nine million detainees exit local jails annually (Beck, 2006). Reentry challenges for PWCD (and others) returning from incarceration can be attributed to the behavioral health and other problems of the correctional population, the pernicious effects of the prison experience, the harmful corollaries of comorbidity, and the community's unpreparedness and unwillingness to accept those formerly incarcerated.

The Correctional Population

Drug Offenders. Beginning in the mid-1980s, the War on Drugs ushered in sentencing policies that substantially increased the rate of incarceration for drug-law violators (The Sentencing Project, 2017). Since the implementation of these policies, the number of inmates imprisoned for drug offenses has exploded from 40,900 in 1980 to 469,545 in 2015. Furthermore, harsh sentencing laws, such as mandatory minimums, have incarcerated drug-law violators for longer terms with fewer hopes for parole. For example, in 1986, federal drug offenders were incarcerated for an average of 22 months. By 2004, they were serving prison sentences nearly three times longer (62 months). Half of the federal prison population consists of inmates who were convicted of a drug crime. At the state level, the number of people imprisoned for drug offenses has risen tenfold since 1980 (Carson, 2014; Carson & Anderson, 2016). Most of these inmates were sentenced for lower-level drug offenses and had no record of violent crimes at intake (The Sentencing Project, 2017). Moreover, many received harsher penalties due to the passage of laws dictating more stringent penalties for drug crimes, especially mandatory prison sentences (Mauer, 2006).

Drug Use Problems and Comorbidity. Increases in inmates with drug convictions have led to corresponding increases in inmates with substance use disorders who are also likely to have co-occurring psychiatric disorders. For example, 80 percent of prison inmates report a history of illegal drug use (Mumola & Karberg, 2006), and high proportions of them meet the diagnostic criteria for a substance use disorder (Fazel, Bains, & Doll, 2006). Specifically, nearly two-thirds of inmates and detainees meet the diagnostic criteria for a substance use disorder, which is seven times greater than the prevalence of such disorders in the general population. Incarcerees with addiction are substantially more likely to re-offend after release from prison (National Center on Addiction and Substance Use, 2010). Similarly, people with chronic health conditions and infectious diseases—many of which are related to illegal and other drug use—are disproportionately represented in correctional populations (National Commission on Correctional Healthcare, 2002).

Nearly three-fourths of prison inmates and of jail detainees with mental illness reported substance use problems (drugs or alcohol or both). More than 40 percent of prison inmates and nearly 50 percent of jail detainees with serious mental illness reported the symptoms of substance use disorders, indicating the high prevalence of PWCDs in correctional institutions (James & Glaze, 2006). In addition, more than 550,000 prison and jail inmates in 2006 (24 percent of the correctional population) were assessed with a substance use and another co-occurring psychiatric disorder (National Center on Addiction and Substance Abuse, 2010). Nonetheless, only one-half of the prisons and one-third of the jails surveyed in 2007 reported any specialized programs to treat comorbidity (Friedmann, Taxman, & Henderson, 2007).

Mental Illness. People with mental illness are substantially over-represented within jail and prison populations. For example, in one national study, more than half of state prison inmates (56 percent) reported that they suffered from symptoms of a mental disorder; 24 percent reported symptoms of a major depressive disorder; 43 percent had symptoms of a manic disorder and 15 percent symptoms of a psychotic disorder. The percentages of these disorders were higher yet for jail detainees: 60 percent (overall), 30 percent (major depression), 55 percent (mania), and 24 percent (psychotic disorder; James & Glaze, 2006). Compared with the percentages of these mental illnesses in the general population, the percentages of prison inmates were three times greater for major depression, five times greater for psychotic disorders, and 21 times greater for mania (James & Glaze, 2006).

Prison inmates with mental illness were more likely than those without such illness to have an incarcerated family member (52 percent versus 41 percent, respectively), to have parents who abused alcohol or drugs (39 percent versus 25 percent, respectively), to have received public assistance (43 percent versus 31 percent, respectively), and to have experienced physical or sexual abuse (27 percent versus 11 percent, respectively). Incarcerated inmates with mental illness are more likely than those with no mental illness to be victimized by other inmates (Ditton, 1999). They are also more likely to be cited and punished for rule infractions. Such punishments include the highly deleterious and gratuitous use of solitary confinement as a disciplinary tool, which is especially harmful to people with mental illness (APA, 2012; Kaba et al., 2014; Olley, Nicholls, & Brink, 2009).[1]

A recent investigation found that nearly twice as many jail detainees (26 percent) than prison inmates (14 percent) reported suffering from serious psychological distress in the 30 days before entering the facility. Both groups reported much higher percentages of psychological distress than did respondents in the general population (5 percent). Among jail detainees, 44 percent stated that they had been diagnosed with a mental disorder; the percentage among prison inmates was 37 percent. The most common disorder within both groups was major depression: 31 percent among jail detainees and 24 percent among prison inmates (Bronson & Berzofsky, 2017).

Inmates with a psychiatric diagnosis were 70 percent more likely to return to prison than were those with no diagnosis (Baillargeon, Binswanger, Penn, Williams, & Murray, 2009). In general, prisoners with mental health problems are between 50 to 230 percent more likely to recidivate following release, irrespective of diagnosis (Gonzalez & Connell, 2014). Thus, although

> it remains unclear what strategies are needed to reduce, in the long term, the overrepresentation of the mentally ill in prison ... in the short-term, a greater percentage of ex-prisoners suffer from mental illnesses than is the case among the general populations and, accordingly, many merit greater attention (Mears & Cochran, 2012, p. 184).

Similarly, a major international review of studies of mental illness among inmates concluded "the risks of having serious psychiatric disorders are substantially higher in prisoners than in the general population ... and ... the burden of treatable serious mental disorder in prisoners is substantial" (Fazel & Danesh, 2002, p. 550). Hence, evidence of the disproportionate representation

---

1. For more on the deleterious effects of solitary confinement, see Chapter 10 in this reader.

of people with mental illness in jails and prisons is abundant, consistent, and incontrovertible. Behavioral health problems are a major service need that creates enormous challenges for returning detainees and inmates (Lurigio, 2011a, 2011b).

Poverty, Unemployment, and Homelessness. As discussed earlier, a comparatively large percentage of prison inmates suffer from behavioral health problems. They also reside in areas of remarkable disadvantage (Veysey & Bichler-Robertson, 2002), which contributes to a higher risk for mental illness, addiction, and criminality. Also related to their disadvantaged origins, they are undereducated and bereft of marketable job skills, which accounts in part for their high rates of unemployment and homelessness. Specifically, fewer than half of prison inmates have a high school degree or its equivalent (Harlow, 2003). Therefore, inmates and detainees enter correctional facilities with poor employment records and earning histories, which leaves them with even greater economic burdens and deficits (Holzler, Raphael, & Stoll, 2003). A five-year study of released prisoners showed that only half were able to secure employment upon release (Visher, Debus, & Yahner, 2008).

As expected in light of their impoverishment, jail detainees' homelessness rate was more than 10 times greater than the rate in the general population; among detainees with mental illness, the rate was 20 times greater (Greenberg & Rosenheck, 2008). Approximately 10 percent of prison inmates were homeless upon incarceration and for some period after release (Roman & Travis, 2006). More than three-quarters of inmates who were homeless and had severe mental illness at admission to prison also met the diagnostic criteria for a substance use disorder (McNiel, Binder, & Robinson, 2005). Moreover, homeless people with mental illness are more likely to engage in violent crime and less likely to participate in outpatient mental health programs or shelter-based services (Gelberg, Linn, & Leak, 1988; Martell, Rosner, & Harmon, 1995).

The Prison Experience

Prisonization. Prisons are total institutions that are highly structured in terms of physical layouts, schedules, and daily activities, all designed to exert the utmost control over inmates' movements and time utilization (Goffman, 1961). Inmates always significantly outnumber correctional officers. Hence, to protect the safety of officers and inmates and to prevent property destruction and disruptions of schedules and population movements, inmates' days are tightly regimented from lights on to lights out. A predictable environment is a safer and more orderly one. Inmates become accustomed to the predictability (i.e., the drudgery and monotony) of the setting and further routinize their stays through the adoption of habits and rituals to make the onerous and stultifying experience of imprisonment more tolerable (Montgomery, 2013). They also cluster in groups for protection and affiliative purposes along the lines of race, ethnicity, and gang membership—or some combination thereof (Johnson, 1996).

The socialization, or prisonization, of inmates inculcates a self-image that is difficult to readily undo when inmates depart from the prison setting to return to "normal life." They leave a state of total confinement, which robs them of agency and an individualized identity. And then they are expected to pivot to a life of freedom by adopting a new self-image as responsible, law-abiding, and productive citizens—roles for which they are ill-prepared (Lerman, 2009). Indeed, the prison experience itself undermines the ability of inmates to return to good citizenship (Latessa & Allen, 1999). Prison immerses inmates in a subculture of deviance, violence, criminality, and hyper-masculinity (Vedantam, 2013). Gang ties are solidified, and new opportunities for crime and criminal enterprises are learned and adopted (Bukstel & Kilmann, 1980).

Lack of Services. Numerous studies suggest that prisons fall short of meeting the service needs of inmates (Jonson & Cullen, 2015). Most important, prisons appear to have little effect on recidivism and therefore do not fulfill the fundamental goal of rehabilitation. Large-scale studies of cohorts of released inmates, published more than a decade apart, reached similar conclusions about the null or criminogenic effects of incarceration (Nagin, Cullen, & Jonson, 2009). In a sample of 300,000 inmates, investigators reported that within three years of release, more than two-thirds (68 percent) had been rearrested; 46 percent had been reconvicted, and 25 percent had been resentenced to prison. Failure was most pronounced during the first six months of leaving the institution (Langan & Levin, 2002).

In a different sample of 400,000 inmates released from prison in 30 states, from 2005 to 2010, researchers again found that 68 percent were arrested within three years of discharge. Within five years, 77 percent had been rearrested. Most at risk were young offenders (24 years old or younger), and they were most likely to fail between the first six months (37 percent) and the first year of coming home from prison (57 percent). More than 84 percent of the youngest releasees (24 years old or younger) were rearrested within five years of release (Durose, Cooper, Snyder, 2014). The absence of other kinds of prison services is also noteworthy (Jonson & Cullen, 2015). For example, only two percent of California inmates with serious substance use disorders ever received prison-based treatment for their conditions (Petersilia, 2008). Other researchers have reported that among prisoners awaiting release, only 13 percent participated in a prerelease program, 27 percent in a vocational program, and 35 percent in an educational program (Lynch & Sabol, 2001). Even when a range of treatment services is available, actual engagement in such programs is low. For example, 74 percent of prisons offer outpatient drug treatment programs, but only 13 percent of inmates partake in these services, leading to the conclusion that "access [to services] is an issue with correctional programs in that few inmates are involved with any program" (Taxman, Perdoni, & Harrison, 2007, p. 244).

Consequences of Comorbidity

Symptom Precipitation and Exacerbation. The corollaries of co-occurring substance use and other psychiatric disorders are generally worse than are those of one type of disorder or the other. As discussed earlier, the symptoms of one type of disorder can exacerbate the symptoms of another. For example, cocaine use can trigger or heighten the symptoms of mania, and marijuana can intensify the symptoms of schizophrenia, eliciting and worsening hallucinations and delusions, especially auditory hallucinations and paranoia. One study indicated that 42 percent of patients with schizophrenia have a comorbid cannabis use disorder, which significantly accelerates the progression of their psychotic symptoms (Fischer, Whitfield-Gabrieli, Roth, Brunette, & Green, 2014). Overall, PWCDs' symptoms are "more persistent, severe, and resistant to treatment compared with patients who have either disorder alone" (NIDA, 2010, p. 7).

Sequelae. PWCDs are susceptible to a much wider range of medical, legal, and social struggles than individuals who have only one type of disorder or the other (Mueser & Drake, 2007). For example, PWCDs have higher rates of violence, suicide, morbidity, mortality, psychoses, unemployment, homelessness, family problems, arrest, incarceration, and recurring episodes of substance use and other psychiatric disorders than do people with a single disorder only (Hills, 2004; Mueser et al., 2003; Mueser, Drake, & Noordsy, 1998). In addition, PWCDs are significantly more likely than those with no comorbidity to experience greater rates of infectious diseases (e.g., HIV and Hepatitis B and C) or premature death, to be hospitalized or use emergency rooms for psychiatric or other medical crises (Cournos & McKinnon, 1997; Woody, Metzger, Navaline, McLellan, & O'Brien, 1997), and to return to prison sooner after release (Messina, Burdon, Hagopian, & Prendergast, 2004).

Compared with offenders who have only a substance use or psychiatric disorder, those with co-occurring disorders are more likely to exhibit several cognitive, emotional, and behavioral impairments. These deficits include brief attention spans and a limited ability to concentrate, difficulty coping with stress-ful situations, a lack of social skills, poor judgment, and non-compliance with treatment directives and plans (e.g., non-adherence to medications). The cor-relates of comorbidity also include an inability to appreciate the ramifications of their behaviors (e.g., violations of parole or probation supervision), limitations in recognizing and incorporating the rules for participating in treat-ment and criminal justice programs, and low motivation to comply with treat-ment and case management regimens (Bellack, Bennett, & Gearon, 2007).

An Unwelcoming Community

The formerly incarcerated are often stigmatized, leading to stereotyping, discrimination, and marginalization in the general community (Link & Phelan, 2001). The label "ex-con" or "ex-offender" confers a master status that shapes how inmates are perceived by their families, neighbors, friends, and other members of the community (Lemert, 1974). The label also affects how they perceive themselves, becoming a core element of their self-image (Link & Phe-lan, 2001). The general public thinks negatively of "criminals, convicts, and felons" and attributes to them a variety of unfavorable personality traits (MacLin & Hererra, 2006), which are especially harmful to the formerly in-carcerated in the employment and housing arenas (Pogorzelski, Wolff, Pan, & Blitz, 2005).

Incarceration bankrupts the future of young offenders and robs them of years of emerging adulthood—a critical period for completing education, building a job resume, starting a family, and strengthening professional net-works (Manza & Uggen, 2006). Instead, inmates and detainees fall further and further behind on major life milestones with each episode of incarceration, experiencing diminished wage growth and marital instability. Stays in prison and jail can also culminate in lost jobs, housing, and interpersonal relationships (Schnittker & John, 2007). Many studies have found that employers are biased against people with felony and prison records and are disinclined to hire such individuals, all other factors being equal (Harris & Keller, 2005).

Laws and policies that preclude the formerly incarcerated from participating in society through the denial of certain types of employment, housing, and fi-nancial aid; voting rights; and licensure eligibility are expressions of structural stigma (Corrigan et al., 2005), which affect returning inmates by creating a multitude of barriers to successful reentry, "limit[ing] positive community op-portunities for ex-offenders and communicat[ing] that ex-offenders remain excluded from the law-abiding community-at-large" (Moore, Stuewig, & Tangney, 2016, p. 217). The formerly incarcerated who anticipate stigmatization are more likely to gravitate toward like-minded peers who populate antisocial groups, increasing the likelihood of recidivism and return to prison (Benson, Alarid, Burton, & Cullen, 2011). PWCDs with histories of incarceration are victims of multiple stigmatizations: mentally ill, drug addict, felon, prison convict, homeless, poor, and minority group member.[2]

The Uphill Climb of Reentry

The correctional population in the United States consists of the greatest concentrations of people with severe social and behavioral health problems. Detainees and inmates enter jail and prison facilities with remarkable deficiencies that stem from living in criminogenic and pathogenic environments. Intergenerational poverty and social inequality are correlated with criminality, addiction, mental illness, and comorbidity. Those conditions also contribute to crime. In addition, racial disparities lead to inequities in criminal justice processing, which keep poor people in jail and increase the likelihood that they will be sentenced to prison for drug-law violations. Large percentages of those sentenced for such crimes suffer from substance use and other psychiatric disorders and their comorbidities (Lurigio & Lyons, 2013).

The experience of incarceration is stultifying. Long prisons stays can alter an inmate's self-image and life trajectory. The socialization process renders inmates more capable of surviving inside prison but less capable of surviving outside prison. The coping skills and mindset that are instilled during incarceration can be antithetical to those needed to adjust successfully to life in the community. Inmates leave prisons with few resources and little preparation for community readjustment. They are burdened by a variety of stigmatizations that define their identities and push them out of the mainstream. Those with comorbidity have to climb steeper hills to meet any and every touchstone of successful reentry from incarceration.

Comorbidity interferes with effective transitions from jails and prisons in a multitude of ways. The cornerstones of reentry are education, work, housing, family reconciliation, and compliance with the rules of mandatory supervised release, which include refraining from illegal drug use and other criminal activity (Petersilia, 2003). These challenges are onerous for most formerly incarcerated people (Visher, DeBus-Sherrill, & Yahner, 2008). For PWCDs, the struggles become an order of magnitude greater and more com-

---

2. For more on the destructive effects of stigma, see that chapter in *The Criminalization of Mental Illness*, as well as Chapter 3 in this reader.

plex. Comorbidity also complicates transition plans. At the core of those plans is integrated treatment for co-occurring disorders, which fosters the symptom relief and stability needed in order to benefit from other treatment and service packages that relate directly to reintegration and assimilation into a more structured and prosocial life. For those returning from prisons and jails, the presence of mental illness or addiction alone is crippling to reentry efforts; the comorbidity of those types of disorders is devastating (Lurigio & Lyons, 2013).

Conclusion

In conclusion, the first order of business in helping PWCDs readjust to the community after a stint in jail or prison is to ensure that they are properly treated for their afflictions while incarcerated. This is currently not the case in either type of correctional facility. Only integrated treatment works for comorbidities, and only if it is continued seamlessly in the community after release from confinement. Interventions to achieve sobriety and mental health lie at the hub of reentry planning for PWCDs. The other services are the spokes that can extend from it but only with a measurable alleviation of psychiatric symptoms. The most promising reentry programs match participants' needs with evidence-based services. The better the identification of needs and closer the alignment of those needs with interventions, the lower the risk of recidivism (Gill & Wilson, 2017). Particularly useful are programs that focus on criminogenic needs, which are pronounced among PWCDs, and can include substance use disorders, mental health diagnoses, poor coping skills, and weak social support mechanisms (Epperson et al., 2011).[3] Finally, every path to reentry must involve stable housing and a network of prosocial support and encouragement.

Discussion Questions

1. In light of the scientific evidence that addiction is a brain disease, should drug possession be decriminalized?

2. How is drug use a moral, legal, social, and medical problem? How can those complexities be reconciled in the law?

---

3. For more on the criminogenic needs of people with mental illness, see Chapter 2 in this reader.

3. What have been the benefits and costs of the War on Drugs? Has one outweighed the other?

4. How can prisons and jails help inmates with comorbidity better prepare for their inevitable transitions back to the community?

5. Does "reentry" truly constitute a social movement?

6. How can communities change to become more open and hospitable to the formerly incarcerated with co-occurring disorders?

References

American Psychiatric Association. (2012). *Position statement on segregation of prisoners with mental illness.* Arlington, VA: Author.

American Psychiatric Association. (2013). *Diagnostic and statistical manual of mental disorders, fifth edition (DSM-5).* Arlington, VA: Author.

Baillargeon, J., Binswanger, I. A., Penn, J. V., Williams, B. A., & Murray, O. J. (2009). Psychiatric disorders and repeat incarcerations: The revolving prison door. *American Journal of Psychiatry, 166,* 103–109.

Bean, P. (2004). *Drugs and crime.* Cullompton, UK: Willan Publishing.

Beck, A. J. (2006). *The importance of successful reentry to jail population growth.* Paper presented at the Urban Institute's Jail Reentry Roundtable. Retrieved from https://urban.org/sites/default/files/beck.ppt.

Bellack, A. S., Bennett, M. E., & Gearon, J. S. (2007). *Behavioral treatment for substance abuse in people with serious and persistent mental illness: A handbook for mental health professionals.* New York, NY: Routledge Press.

Benson, M. L., Alarid, L. F., Burton, V. S., & Cullen, F. T. (2011). Reintegration or stigmatization? Offenders' expectations of community re-entry. *Journal of Criminal Justice, 39,* 385–393.

Bronson, J., & Berzofsky, M. (2017). *Indicators of mental health problems reported by prisoners and jail inmates, 2011–12.* Washington, D.C.: U.S. Department of Justice, Bureau of Justice Statistics.

Bukstel, L. H., & Kilmann, P. R. (1980). Psychological effects of imprisonment on confined individuals. *Psychological Bulletin, 88,* 469–493.

Bureau of Justice Statistics. (1994). *Fact sheet drug-related crime.* Washington, D.C.: U.S. Department of Justice, Office of Justice Programs.

Carson, E. A. (2014). *Prisoners in 2013.* Washington, D.C.: U.S. Department of Justice, Bureau of Justice Statistics.

Carson, E. A., & Anderson, E. (2016). *Prisoners in 2015.* Washington, D.C.: U.S. Department of Justice, Bureau of Justice Statistics. Retrieved from https://www.bjs.gov/content/pub/pdf/p15.pdf.

Carson, E. A., & Golinelli, D. (2013). *Prisoners in 2012: Trends in admissions and releases 1991–2012.* Washington, D.C.: U.S. Department of Justice, Bureau of Justice Statistics.

Chandler, R. K., Feltcher, B. W., & Volkow, N. D. (2009). Treating drug abuse and addiction in the criminal justice system: Improving public health and safety. *Journal of the American Medical Association, 301,* 183–190.

Compton, W. M., Conway, K. P., Stinson, F. S., Colliver, J. D., & Grant, B. F. (2005). Prevalence, correlates, and comorbidity of DSM-IV antisocial personality syndromes and alcohol and specific drug use disorders in the United States: Results from the National Epidemiological Survey on Alcohol and Related Conditions. *Journal of Clinical Psychiatry, 66,* 677–685.

Corrigan, P. W., Watson, A. C., Heyrman, M. L., Warpinski, A., Garcia, G., Slopen, N., & Hall, L. L. (2005). Structural stigma in state legislation. *Psychiatric Services, 56,* 557–563.

Cournos, F., & McKinnon, K. (1997). HIV seroprevalence among people with severe mental illness in the United States: A critical review. *Clinical Psychology Review, 17,* 259–269.

Craddock, A., Collins, J. J., & Timrots, A. D. (1994). *Fact sheet: Drug-related crime.* Washington, D.C.: U.S. Department of Justice, Bureau of Justice Statistics.

Curtis, R. (1998). The improbable transformation of inner-city neighborhoods: Crime violence, drugs, and youth in the 1990s. *Journal of Criminal Law and Criminology, 88,* 1233–1276.

Ditton, P. M. (1999). *Mental health and treatment of inmates and probationers.* Washington, D.C.: U.S. Department of Justice, Bureau of Justice Statistics.

Downey, K. K., Helmus, T. C., & Schuster, C.R. (2000). Treatment of heroin-dependent poly-drug abusers with contingency management and buprenorphine maintenance. *Experimental and Clinical Psychopharmacology, 8,* 176–184.

Durose, M. R., Cooper, A. D., & Snyder, H. N. (2014). *Recidivism of prisoners released in 30 states in 2005: Patterns from 2005 to 2010.* Washington, D.C.: U.S. Department of Justice, Bureau of Justice Statistics.

Epperson, M., Wolff, N., Morgan, R., Fisher, W., Frueh, B. C., & Huening, J. (2011). *The next generation of behavioral health and criminal justice interventions: Improving outcomes by improving interventions.* New Brunswick, NJ: Rutgers University Center for Behavioral Health Services and Criminal Justice Research.

Fazel, S., Bains, P., & Doll, H. (2006). Substance abuse and dependence in prisoners: A systematic review. *Addiction, 101*, 181–191.

Fazel, S., & Danesh, J. (2002). Serious mental disorder in 23,000 prisoners: A systematic review of 62 surveys. *The Lancet, 359*, 545–550.

Fischer A. S., Whitfield-Gabrieli, S., Roth, R. M., Brunette, M. F., & Green, A. I. (2014). Impaired functional connectivity of brain reward circuitry in patients with schizophrenia and cannabis use disorder: Effects of cannabis and THC. *Schizophrenia Research, 158*, 176–182.

Francis, A. (2013). *Essentials of psychiatric diagnosis.* New York: Guilford Press.

Friedmann, P. D., Taxman, F. S., & Henderson, C. E. (2007). Evidence-based treatment practices for drug-involved adults in the criminal justice system. *Journal of Substance Abuse Treatment, 32*, 267–277.

Garland, B., & Wodahl, E. (2014). Coming to a crossroads: A critical look at the sustainability of the prisoner reentry movement. In M. S. Crow & J. O. Smykla (Eds.), *Offender reentry: Rethinking criminology and criminal justice* (pp. 399–422). Burlington, MA: Jones & Bartlett Learning.

Gelberg, L., Linn, L. S., & Leak, B. D. (1988). Mental health, alcohol and drug use, and criminal history among homeless adults. *American Journal of Psychiatry, 145*, 191–196.

Goffman, E. (1961). *Asylums: Essays on the social situation of mental patients and other inmates.* New York: Anchor Books.

Goldstein, R., & Volkow, N. (2002). Drug addiction and its underlying neurobiological basis: Neuroimaging evidence for the involvement of the frontal cortex. *American Journal of Psychiatry, 159*, 1642–1645.

Goodnough, A. (2010, September 23). A wave of addiction and crime, with the medicine cabinet to blame. *The New York Times.* Retrieved from http://www.nytimes.com/2010/09/24/us/24drugs.html.

Goodwin, F. W., & Jamison, K. R. (1990). *Manic-depressive illness.* New York, NY: Oxford University Press.

Greenberg, G. A., & Rosenheck, R. A. (2008). Jail incarceration, homelessness, and mental health: A national study. *Psychiatric Services, 59*, 170–177.

Harlow, C. W. (2003). *Education and correctional populations.* Washington, D.C.: U.S. Department of Justice, Bureau of Justice Statistics. Retrieved from https://bjs.ojp.usdoj.gov/content/pub/pdf/ecp.pdf.

Harris, K. M., & Edlund, M. J. (2005). Use of mental health care and substance abuse treatment among adults with co-occurring disorders. *Psychiatric Services, 56*, 954–959.

Harris, P. M., & Keller, K. S. (2005). Ex-offenders need not apply. *Journal of Contemporary Criminal Justice, 21*, 6–30.

Hills, H. A. (2000). *Creating effective treatment programs for persons with co-occurring disorders in the justice system.* Delmar, NY: The National GAINS Center.

Hills, H. A. (2004). *The special needs of women with co-occurring disorders diverted from the criminal justice system.* Delmar, NY: The National GAINS Center.

Holzer, H. J., Raphael, S., & Stoll, M. A. (2003). Employment barriers facing ex-offenders. *Urban Institute Reentry Roundtable.* Retrieved from http://www.urban.org/sites/default/files/publication/59416/410855-Employment-Barriers-Facing-Ex-Offenders.PDF.

Hughes, T., & Wilson, D. J. (2002). *Reentry trends in the United States.* Washington, D.C.: U.S. Department of Justice, Bureau of Justice Statistics. Retrieved from https://bjs.ojp.usdoj.gov/content/pub/pdf/reentry.pdf.

James, D. J., & Glaze, L. E. (2006). *Mental health problems of prison and jail inmates.* Washington, D.C.: U.S. Department of Justice, Bureau of Justice Statistics.

Johnson, R. (1996). *Hard time: Understanding and reforming the prison.* Belmont, CA: Wadsworth.

Jonson, C. L., & Cullen, F. T. (2015). Prisoner reentry programs. In M. Tonry (Ed.), *Crime and justice: A review of research* (pp. 517–575). Chicago, IL: University of Chicago Press.

Kaba, F., Lewis, A., Glowa-Kollisch, S., Hadler, J., Lee, D., Alper, H., … Venters, H. (2014). Solitary confinement and risk of self-harm among jail inmates. *American Journal of Public Health, 104,* 442–447.

Kaeble, D., & Glaze, L. (2016) *Correctional populations in the United States, 2015.* Washington, D.C.: U.S. Department of Justice, Bureau of Justice Statistics. Retrieved from https://bjs.gov/content/pub/pdf/cpus15.pdf.

Kosten, T. R., & George, T. P. (2002). The neurobiology of opioid addiction: Implications for treatment. *NIDA Science and Practice Perspectives, 1,* 13–20.

Langan, P. A., & Levin, D. J. (2002). *Recidivism of prisoners released in 1994.* Washington, D.C.: U.S. Department of Justice, Bureau of Justice Statistics.

Latessa, E., & Allen, H. E. (1999). *Corrections in the community* (2nd ed.). Cincinnati, OH: Anderson Publishing Co.

Lemert, E. M. (1974). Beyond Mead: The societal reaction to deviance. *Social Problems, 21,* 457–468.

Lerman, A. E. (2009). The people prisons make: Effects of incarceration on criminal psychology. In S. Raphael & M. J. Stoll (Eds.), *Do prisons make us safer? Benefits and costs of the prison boom* (pp. 151–171). New York, NY: Russell Sage Foundation.

Link, B. G., & Phelan, J. C. (2001). Conceptualizing stigma. *Annual Review of Sociology*, *27*, 363–385.

Lurigio, A. J. (2000). Drug treatment availability and effectiveness: Studies of the general and criminal justice populations. *Criminal Justice and Behavior*, 27, 495–528.

Lurigio, A. J. (2011a). Co-occurring disorders: Mental health and drug misuse. In C. Leukefeld, T. P. Guilotta, & J. Gregrich (Eds.), *Handbook of evidence-based substance abuse treatment in criminal justice settings* (pp. 279–292). New York, NY: Springer.

Lurigio, A. J. (2011b). Examining prevailing beliefs about people with serious mental illness in the criminal justice system. *Federal Probation*, *75*, 37–45.

Lurigio, A. J., & Lyons, T. (2013). Criminality and co-occurring psychiatric and substance use disorders. In J. B. Helfgott (Ed.), *Criminal psychology* (pp. 321–340). Haverhill, MA: Praeger Press.

Lynch, J. P., & Sabol, W. J. (2001). *Prisoner reentry in perspective*. Washington, D.C.: Urban Institute.

MacLin, M. K., & Herrera, V. (2006). The criminal stereotype. *North American Journal of Psychology*, *8*, 197–208.

Manza, J., & Uggen, C. (2006). *Locked out: Felon disenfranchisement and American democracy*. New York, NY: Oxford University Press.

Martell, D., Rosner, R., & Harmon, R. (1997). Base-rate estimates of criminal behavior by homeless mentally ill persons in New York City. *Psychiatric Services*, *48*, 212–213.

Mauer, M. (2006). *Race to incarcerate*. New York, NY: The New Press.

McKelvey, K., Ramo, D., Delucchi, K., & Rubinstein, M. (2017). Polydrug use among a cohort of adolescent light smokers. *Drug and Alcohol Dependence*, *171*, e139.

McNiel, D. E., Binder, R. L., & Robinson, J. C. (2005). Incarceration associated with homelessness, mental disorder, and co-occurring substance use. *Psychiatric Services*, *56*, 840–846.

Mears, D. P., & Cochran, J. C. (2012). U.S. prisoner reentry health care policy in international perspective: Service gaps and the moral and public health implications. *The Prison Journal*, *92*, 175–202.

Messina, N., Burdon, W., Hagopian, G., & Prendergast, M. (2004). One year returns to custody rates among co-disordered offenders. *Behavioral Sciences and the Law*, *22*, 503–518.

Montgomery, L. (2013). *Inmate prison operations*. Baldwin, NY: Emerging Business Group.

Moore, K. E., Stuewig, J. B., & Tangney, J. P. (2016). The effect of stigma on criminal offenders' functioning: A longitudinal mediational model. *Deviant Behavior*, *37*, 196–218.

Mueser, K. T., & Drake, R. E. (2007). Comorbidity: What have we learned and where are we going? *Clinical Psychology; Science and Practice*, *14*, 64–69.

Mueser, K. T., Drake, R. E., & Noordsy, D. L. (1998). Integrated mental health and substance abuse treatment for severe psychiatric disorders. *Journal of Practical Psychiatry and Behavioral Health*, *8*, 129–139.

Mueser, K. T., Drake, R. E., & Wallach, M. A. (1998). Dual diagnosis: A review of etiological theories. *Addictive Behaviors*, *23*, 717–734.

Mueser, K. T., Noordsy, D. L., Drake, R. E., & Fox, L. (2003). *Integrated treatment for dual disorders: A guide to effective practice*. New York, NY: Guildford Press.

Mumola, C. J., & Karberg, J. C. (2006). *Drug use and dependence, state and federal prisoners, 2004*. Washington, D.C.: U.S. Department of Justice, Bureau of Justice Statistics.

Nagin, D. S., Cullen, F. T., & Jonson, C. L. (2009). Imprisonment and reoffending. In M. Tonry (Ed.), *Crime and justice: A review of research* (Vol. 38, pp. 115–200). Chicago, IL: University of Chicago.

National Center on Addiction and Substance Abuse. (2010). *Behind bars II: Substance abuse and America's prison population*. New York, NY: Author.

National Commission on Correctional Health Care. (2002). *The health status of soon-to-be-released inmates: A report to Congress*. Chicago, IL: Author.

National Conference of State Legislators (2016). *Marijuana overview*. Retrieved from http://www.ncsl.org/researc/cival and criminal justice/marijuana-overview.aspx.

National Institute on Drug Abuse. (2007). *Drugs, brains, and behavior: The science of addiction*. Washington, D.C.: Author.

National Institute on Drug Abuse. (2010). *Comorbidity: Addiction and other mental illnesses. Research report series*. Washington, D.C.: Author.

Office of National Drug Control Policy. (2000). *Drug-related crime*. Washington, D.C.: Executive Office of the President.

Olley, M. C., Nicholls, T. L., & Brink, J. (2009). Mentally ill individuals in limbo: Obstacles and opportunities for providing psychiatric serves to corrections inmates with mental illness. *Behavioral Science and the Law*, *27*, 811–831.

Peele, S., Brodsky, A., & Arnold, M. (1992). *The truth about addiction and recovery*. New York: Fireside.

Petersilia, J. (2003). *When prisoners come home: Parole and prisoner reentry*. New York, NY. Oxford University Press.

Petersilia, J. (2008). California's correctional paradox of excess and deprivation. In M. Tonry (Ed.), *Crime and justice: A review of research* (Vol. 37, pp. 207–278). Chicago, IL: University of Chicago.

Petersilia, J. (2009). *When prisoners come home: Parole and prisoner reentry.* New York, NY: Oxford University Press.

Pogorzelski, W., Wolff, N., Pan, K. Y., & Blitz, C. L. (2005). Behavioral health problems, ex-offender reentry policies, and the Second Chance Act. *American Journal of Public Health, 95,* 1718–1724.

Power R. A., Verweij, K. J., Zuhair, M., Montgomery, G. W., Henders, A. K., Heath, A. C., … Martin, M. G. (2014). Genetic predisposition to schizophrenia associated with increased use of cannabis. *Molecular Psychiatry, 19,* 1201–1204.

Rhine, E. E., & Thompson, A. C. (2011). The reentry movement in corrections: Resiliency, fragility, and prospects. *Criminal Law Bulletin, 47,* 177–209.

Roman, C. G., & Travis, J. (2006). Where will I sleep tomorrow? Housing, homelessness, and the returning prisoner. *Housing Policy Debate, 17,* 389–418.

Sabol, W. J., West, H. C., & Cooper, M. (2009). *Prison inmates, 2008.* Washington, D.C.: U.S. Department of Justice, Bureau of Justice Statistics.

Schmetzer, A. D. (2015). Phencyclidine (PCP)—related psychiatric disorders. *Medscape.* Retrieved from emedicine.medscape.com/article/29476-overview#95.

Schnittker, J., & John, A. (2007). Enduring stigma: The long-term effects of incarceration on health. *Journal of Health and Social Behavior, 48,* 115–130.

The Sentencing Project. (2017). Facts about prison and people in prison. Washington, D.C.: Author. Retrieved from www.sentencing.org/wp-content/uploads/2016/02/Facts-About-Prisons.pdf.

Swartz, J. A., & Lurigio, A. J. (2004). Psychiatric and substance use disorders and arrests among former recipients of supplemental security income for drug abuse and alcoholism. *Journal of Offender Rehabilitation, 39,* 19–38.

Taxman, F. S., Perdoni, M. L., & Harrison, L. D. (2007). Drug treatment services for adult offenders: The state of the state. *Journal of Substance Abuse Treatment, 32,* 239–54.

Travis, J. (2005). *But they all come back: Facing the challenges of prisoner reentry.* Washington, D.C.: Urban Institute.

Vedantam, S. (2013, February 1). When crime pays: Prison can teach some to be better criminals. *NPR.* Retrieved from http://npr.org/2013/02/01/169732840/when-crime-pays-prison-can-teach-some-to-be-better-criminals.

Veysey, B. M., & Bichler-Robertson, G. (2002). Prevalence estimates of psychiatric disorders in correctional settings. In *The health status of soon-to-*

be-released inmates: A report to Congress (Vol. 2, pp. 57–80). Chicago, IL: National Commission on Correctional Health Care. Retrieved from http://www.ncchc.org/filebin/Health_Status_vol_2.pdf.

Visher, C. A., Debus, S., & Yahner, J. (2008). *Employment after prison: A longitudinal study of releases in three states*. Washington, D.C.: Urban Institute.

Volkow, N. D., & Li, T. K. (2005). The neuroscience of addiction. *Nature Neuroscience, 11*, 1429–1430.

Volkow, N. D., Wang, G. J., Fowler, J. S., & Tomasi, D. (2012). Addiction circuitry in the human brain. *Annual Review of Pharmacology and Toxicology, 52*, 321–336.

Walker, E. R., Pratt, L. A., Schoenborn, C. A., & Druss, B. G. (2017). Excess mortality among people who report lifetime use of illegal drugs in the United States: A 20-year follow-up of a nationally representative survey. *Drug and Alcohol Dependence, 171*, 31–38.

Woody, G. E., Metzger, D., Navaline, H., McLellan, T., & O'Brien, C. P. (1997). Psychiatric symptoms, risky behavior, and HIV infection. In L. S. Onken, J. D. Blaine, S. Genser, & A. M. Horton (Eds.), *Treatment of drug-dependent individuals with comorbid mental disorders* (pp. 117–131). Washington, D.C.: U.S. Department of Health and Human Services.

12

Past and Current Perspectives on Offenders with Mental Illness

Arthur J. Lurigio

Introduction

Throughout U.S. history, people with serious mental illness (PWSMI) have been untreated, mistreated, misunderstood, maligned, abused, and marginalized. They have been shut away in one institution or another, from the asylum, to the state hospital, to the nursing home, to the state prison (Grob, 1991). Even with pharmacological and direct-to-consumer marketing campaigns designed to destigmatize mental disorders, most Americans are still frightened by people with mental illnesses (Lurigio & Harris, 2007). This fear stems largely from a steady barrage of media-fueled archetypes: the escaped lunatic, the ax murderer, and the demonic serial killer. The facts are rarely considered. Until the 1970s, PWSMI spent years, often decades, in hospitals; they "escaped" with the assistance of policy changes, medications, and legal interventions. They commit a small proportion of murders and rarely occupy the ranks of psychopathic serial killers or sexual predators (Lee, this volume). In instances of violence, PWSMI typically direct their attacks not against strangers, but family members, who bear the brunt of their care and the tremendous sting of their pain. PWSMI are more often the victims of violence than the perpetrators (Sporer, this volume).

Yet, as the chapters in this reader have underscored, PWSMI are seemingly being processed through the criminal justice system (CJS) in large numbers and with alarming regularity (Council of State Governments, 2002). This concluding chapter poses basic questions about PWSMI and their involvement in the CJS. The questions are aimed at clarifying essential notions that form the crux of continued debates about the problem of criminalization and strategies for improving the care of PWSMI who are often neglected or mislabeled. The interstices between the mental health system and the CJS, the paucity of community mental health care, and the continually shrinking social safety net have left PWSMI adrift and bereft of fundamental services (Lurigio, 2011). Who are PWSMI? Are they being criminalized in the strict definition of the term? Why are PWSMI disproportionately represented in the CJS? How can the criminalization of PWSMI be noticeably reduced and their care be significantly improved in the CJS?

Who Are People with Serious Mental Illnesses?

Mental Disorders in the Nomenclature

PWSMI are a heterogeneous group of individuals with complicated brain diseases that stem from biological, psychological, and social factors. The *Diagnostic and Statistical Manual of Mental Disorders* (*DSM 5*), published by the American Psychiatric Association, is the official nomenclature of psychiatric illnesses, containing 20 basic categories. The diagnostic entities within these categories share common features, and many of the illnesses within and between different categories have similar diagnostic criteria (e.g., mood disorders). The *DSM 5* describes more than 200 separate illnesses. Depending on how they are counted, the total is closer to 300 (American Psychiatric Association, 2013). Many mental illnesses are characterized by symptoms of anxiety and depression and, in general, are defined by levels of distress (i.e., psychological pain) and dysfunction (i.e., poor outcomes in school, at work, and in relationships) as well as feelings, thoughts, and behaviors that run athwart social expectations and conventions (Eckberg & Dexter, this volume). Notwithstanding these commonalities, the mental disorders in *DSM 5* diverge considerably regarding their symptoms (i.e., what patients report) and signs (i.e., what clinicians and others observe).

Just as PWSMI are heterogeneous with respect to their disorders, they also differ with respect to the nature of the crimes they commit, their reasons for committing those crimes, and the frequency of their criminal activity (Hiday,

1999). Furthermore, the association between their psychiatric symptoms and their illegal behaviors can also vary from one incident to another, depending on the waxing and waning of symptoms and criminal predilections and the availability of offending opportunities (Bonfine, this volume; Lee, this volume). In one of the few studies done on the types of crimes committed by PWSMI, a large number of newly released state hospital patients were tracked in the community for nearly two years. The investigation found that former patients could be divided into three groups concerning their contact with the police. The first group consisted of former patients who were criminalized (i.e., arrested for public displays of mental illness and associated disorderly conduct). These arrests could have been avoided with more enlightened policing tactics. The second group consisted of those who engaged in crimes for the sake of everyday survival. Their crimes were repeated and petty (e.g., shoplifting, drug selling, prostitution) and led to frequent stints in jail. The third group consisted of those who committed felonies, such as armed robberies, batteries, grand thefts, and burglaries, and had criminal histories of serious offenses and records of imprisonment (Lewis & Lurigio, 1994).

Socioeconomic Status, Mental Illness, and Criminalization

Mental disorders differ not only in kind but also in severity, duration, courses, and varieties of onset. These differences are known as specifiers that are employed to improve diagnostic precision and prognostication. PWSMI express symptoms in a particular time, place, and cultural context (Eckberg & Dexter, this volume). The manifestation of symptoms and others' reactions to and interpretations of those symptoms are also influenced by the person's socioeconomic status.

Whether PWSMI receive treatment, where they receive treatment, and the quality of that treatment depends largely on social class. Those with higher educational attainment and greater income are less likely to be stigmatized for their mental illness (Eckberg & Dexter, this volume). They are also more likely to afford treatment out of pocket or to have insurance coverage that contains parity in coverage for psychiatric problems, addictions, and other types of medical conditions. Most apropos to this chapter, ceteris paribus, the higher the social class of PWSMI and their families, the less likely PWSMI are to ever be arrested, jailed, or imprisoned as the result of their illness. PWSMI who belong to higher income families and communities have a much higher probability of obtaining care in private psychiatric facilities and hospital units than in correctional facilities. They can pay for legal representation that will argue for diversion from the CJS and alternatives to incarceration. Criminalization is best understood in terms of the aforementioned parameters (Erickson, Rosenheck, Trestment, Ford, & Desai, 2008).

Epidemiological studies of mental illness in the general population have consistently found a relationship between poverty and mental illness. PWSMI are overrepresented in areas of blight for several reasons. First, treatment is less available in poor communities, and poor people are less likely to seek treatment because of stigmatization and ignorance about the causes of mental illness and its remediation (Eckberg & Dexter, this volume; Shah, Tooley, & Corrigan, this volume; Sporer, this volume). Delayed treatment can exacerbate the symptoms of most mental illnesses and result in irreversible clinical deterioration, especially in cases of the most serious disorders, such as schizophrenia, bipolar disorder, and major depression.

The symptoms of mental disorders interfere with the ability to attend school or to secure gainful employment. Income and education are highly correlated and operationally define socioeconomic status. Many PWSMI are devastated by their illnesses and can "drift down" from financially secure positions to profound levels of poverty, which was an early explanation for the overrepresentation of PWSMI in low-income areas (Hurst, 2007). Recent studies suggest that being poor, in itself, is highly stressful and triggers mental illness among individuals with a genetic predisposition toward such diseases (World Health Organization, 2007). Perhaps greater concentrations of PWSMI in lower-class communities increase the chances of their offspring being at greater risk for mental disorders. Propinquity dictates the selection of partners within a common gene pool who have heritable psychiatric vulnerabilities, creating an intergenerational cycle of poverty and mental illness.

Poverty and social inequality spawn pathogenic and criminogenic environments. A multitude of studies have demonstrated the relationship between poverty and crime and the increased likelihood of arrest, prosecution, conviction, and incarceration among poor people of color, who are also more likely to receive care in public psychiatric institutions or no care at all (Eckberg & Dexter, this volume). In the late 1970s, growing percentages of psychiatric patients were poor, younger men of color with histories of arrest, which elevates the risk of future arrests, thereby establishing a pathway for PWSMI to enter the CJS in larger and larger numbers. Elevated risks for arrest are also explained by the increased police presence and aggressive policing tactics that are endemic to communities of color. Such tactics began escalating in the 1960s and were replaced by public order policing policies in the 1990s (e.g., arresting panhandlers, loiterers, and turnstile jumpers), which also ushered numerous PWSMI into the CJS. The intersection of the state hospital and CJS populations—both poor and disenfranchised—is attributable to shared and highly intercorrelated demographic characteristics (age, race, income, previous arrests) and environments (underclass neighborhoods) and not to an increased risk of criminality stemming directly from mental illness alone. When these demographic characteristics and environments are statistically controlled, the relationship between mental disorders and crime weakens or disappears (Lurigio, 2011).

Stigmatization

The lives of PWSMI are severely diminished by stigmatization (Shah, Tooley, & Corrigan, this volume). Through formal education and experiences, mental health professionals are mostly inoculated against stereotyping, prejudice, and discrimination directed at PWSMI; this is unlikely to be the case among CJS professionals (Eckberg & Dexter, this volume), who require special training on mental illnesses and their treatment. Such training is doubly important for police officers, the gatekeepers of the CJS and frontline caregivers during street encounters with PWSMI (Kerle, this volume).

CJS-involved PWSMI are highly susceptible to stigmatization. Mental illness is a primary source of public and self-stigma, especially within different cultural groups (Eckberg & Dexter, this volume; Shah, Tooley, & Corrigan, this volume). Records of hospitalization and imprisonment are additional sources of stigma. Many PWSMI also suffer from substance use disorders (Lurigio, this volume) and addiction is yet another source of stigmatization. Psychiatric disorders render individuals homeless, jobless, and socially isolated. The personal and structural stigmatization created by only one of these labels is difficult to overcome (Shah, Tooley, & Corrigan, this volume). Their cumulative effect is devastating. Media portrayals of PWSMI add to this stigmatization. Journalists have a responsibility to portray people with mental illness accurately, but in the rush to be the first to get a story in print or on the air, some unwittingly (or otherwise) end up perpetuating many of the pernicious stereotypes concerning the complicated relationship between mental illness and violent crime (Gray, this volume).

Prevalence Studies in the CJS

Studies of PWSMI in the CJS should consider the myriad differences among mental disorders. Common understandings of mental health problems affect how PWSMI are processed through the CJS, from their initial contact with the police, to their release from jails and prisons, to their struggles to reenter the community after periods of detention and imprisonment. Over the nearly 50 years during which scholars have described the criminalization of PWSMI, varying definitions of mental illness and diagnostic categories have complicated conceptualizations of criminalization and blurred research findings on the topic. For example, the only national studies of PWSMI in the CJS have been based on a handful of survey questions that were posed to jail detainees, prison inmates, and probationers (e.g., Ditton, 1999).

These studies were groundbreaking despite the crudeness and simplicity of the questions used to generate prevalence data. The studies kept widespread attention on the problem and produced rough estimates of the proportions of PWSMI in jails and prisons and on probation supervision. However, the short-comings of the surveys, which consisted of qualitative, self-report questions, compromised the validity of the estimates, which failed to meet the epidemiological standards of measurement necessary to capture the presence of diseases in large populations for the purpose of elucidating and projecting treatment needs (Lurigio, 2011; Skeem, Nicholson, & Kregg, 2008).

Specifying and Expanding the Inclusion of Disorders. In the most widely cited Bureau of Justice Statistics (BJS) study, offenders with self-reported histories of mental illness were counted as "mentally ill" (Ditton, 1999). However, histories can be gathered in different temporal intervals: 6 months, 12 months, or a lifetime. Future investigations should also incorporate point-prevalence estimates (i.e., present conditions). Moreover, debates about the criminalization of PWSMI must be clear about the specific diseases being considered in a study or disquisition.

If substance use disorders or antisocial personality disorder (ASPD) were included in estimates of psychiatric disorders among criminally involved PWSMI, nearly all the members of correctional populations would be deemed "mentally ill," as demonstrated repeatedly by the Arrestee Drug Abuse Monitoring (ADAM) Program and specified in the criteria of ASPD, which is defined by a history of criminal activities and conduct disorder. Intellectual development disorders (e.g., intellectual disability disorder) and attention deficit/hyperactivity disorders are rarely the subject of research or discussions regarding the criminalization of PWSMI, although evidence suggests that people with such diagnoses are numerous at every interception point in the criminal justice process (Swartz & Lurigio, 1999). Men and women with post-traumatic stress disorder (PTSD) are also disproportionately represented in the CJS but not registered in studies of criminalization (Ruzich, Reichert, & Lurigio, 2014).

Capturing Mental Illness. Neuroscience has made breakthroughs in understanding the biological correlates and sequelae of mental illness. Researchers can study the living brain and have documented differences in the structure and functioning of the brains of PWSMI and people without mental illnesses, especially among those with the most serious mental illnesses, including schizophrenia, dementia, and major depression (Bluhm et al., 2007). Nevertheless, these visualizations are rarely used for diagnostic purposes for several reasons, such as the expense of collecting the data and the challenge of interpreting the findings in terms that illuminate the clinical course and prognosis of any particular disorder or case.

In the face of substantial strides in diagnostic reliability, "mental illness" remains an elusive and elastic construct. Diagnoses of other diseases can be confirmed with objective testing. For example, plaque in arteries can be visualized, blood glucose levels can be measured, thyroid function is quantifiable, and cancer cells can be biopsied. Mental disorders generally defy reification. Similar to all chronic conditions, the symptoms of psychiatric illnesses can ebb and flow (Frances, 2013). PWSMI can be in remission and therefore considered asymptomatic. Nevertheless, for diagnostic purposes, the psychiatric record would indicate that an asymptomatic person still "has" the disorder with the specifier "in remission." Should they be counted in studies as a person with or without mental illness? What are the limits of inclusion with respect to the wide array of psychiatric conditions described in the *DSM 5*? Are broadly encompassing screenings and evaluations worth the time and effort if treatments for identified conditions are unavailable in correctional settings?

What Is Criminalization?

The increasing growth of PWSMI in the CJS has been presumed since the early 1970s. This presumption has never been rigorously tested, which would require several research conditions. Specifically, a baseline must be created (the starting point or first year of data collection), "mental illness" must be operationalized, sampling methodology must be consistent in each wave of data collection and designed to yield probabilistic and generalizable findings, and data collection protocols and instruments must be standardized in every wave of the study. Separate investigations of each criminal justice population (e.g., arrestees, detainees, prisoners, probationers) would be required. The expense of such an undertaking would be prodigious. In the BJS studies, questions about mental health histories were asked as part of larger studies of these populations and conducted as cross-sectional, not longitudinal, surveys.

Mental illness, Comorbidity, and Crime

Apart from the above discussion regarding shared environments, serious mental illness ipso facto rarely leads directly to criminal behavior (Bonfine, this volume). The formation of criminal intent and the exercise of volition to accomplish the steps needed to bring a crime to fruition are often beyond the capacity of those with major depression, schizophrenia, and other psychotic disorders. People with hypomania or in the manic phase of bipolar disorder often engage in reckless and high-risk behaviors, which are enumerated as diagnostic criteria and can include crimes. Bipolar disorder with psychotic features would likely result in the inability to form criminal intent and in such instances, culpability is dubious. At the very least, mental illness is a mitigating factor in the adjudicatory and punishment phases of the court process.

Among people with comorbid substance use and other psychiatric disorders, the addiction and not the other mental illness is typically the proximal or distal cause of the criminal act. Substance use is a crime accelerator. Addiction is often comorbid with a variety of other mental health problems, such as ASPD, that derail the recovery process for addiction and vice versa (Lurigio, this volume).

Criminalization Defined

The strictest definition of criminalization denotes that people are being processed through the CJS simply or mostly as a direct consequence of their mental illness and not their criminal activities. It is debatable whether PWSMI are actually being "criminalized" in large numbers. For example, being arrested, prosecuted, convicted, and sentenced for a felony offense is certainly not an instance of criminalization, as someone found guilty of a felony has ostensibly engaged in serious crimes that are harmful to others and a risk to public safety and social order. In terms of criminal blameworthiness, PWSMI fall into two legal categories: mentally ill and culpable or mentally ill and inculpable. The latter could be found unfit to stand trial, not guilty by reason of insanity, or guilty but mentally ill, and confined to a prison for the "criminally insane." These groups of PWSMI constitute a small percentage of those in the CJS and are rarely germane to discussions of criminalization. Furthermore, most mental illnesses are excluded from consideration in insanity defenses (e.g., any personality, anxiety, or substance use disorders) (Lurigio, 2011).

PWSMI and people without serious mental illnesses are at increased risk for criminal behavior as a consequence of the same set of factors, such as antisocial thinking, associates, attitudes, and behaviors (Wolff et al., 2013). Other criminogenic factors include drug use (Lurigio, this volume), poor employment records, family conflicts, and unstructured leisure time. As studies have shown, when ASPD and drug use are controlled statistically, the relationship between crime and mental disorders disappears (Swartz & Lurigio, 2007). Thus, programs for CJS-involved PWSMI, focusing only on mental disorders, are unlikely to reduce criminal tendencies or recidivism (Bonfine, this volume).

What Are the Drivers of Criminalization?

Police and PWSMI

Research suggests that a small percentage of PWSMI are being criminalized in the strictest definition of the term. Yet, county sheriffs, police chiefs, jail directors, journalists, and mental health advocates continue to perpetuate the notion that PWSMI are being criminalized widely and in large numbers. Most police departments, courts, and jails have instituted deflection mechanisms for people with apparent psychiatric symptoms (e.g., pretrial diversion programs and mental health courts [MHCs]) (Lurigio, this volume). Nonetheless, criminalization can result from interactions with the police gone awry and escalating (devolving) into an altercation and serious charges (e.g., resisting arrest or assaulting a police officer).

PWSMI can display symptoms that significantly alter the dynamics of interactions with police officers. Auditory hallucinations can distract subjects from listening to officers' directives. Some PWSMI also might have visual hallucinations, though much less common, that completely distort what they see and how they perceive and experience the street stop (Lurigio, Snowden, & Watson, 2006). PWSMI have a variety of cognitive deficits that impair their ability to clearly understand and comprehend the nature of the immediate interaction. Cultural and language differences can also lead to unnecessary arrests (Eckberg & Dexter, this volume).

Police officers who are unschooled about the signs and symptoms of mental illness might regard the behaviors of PWSMI as willful recalcitrance, aggression, or indicators of a dangerous and imminent threat. Officers are inclined to arrest when they are faced with uncooperative subjects. During psychotic episodes when delusions and hallucinations are active, PWSMI are typically frightened or paranoid and could be combative for self-protective purposes in response to imagined dangers from officers, who are often central characters in the fabric of many delusions.

Combativeness increases the risk of injuries and deaths for police officers and citizens alike. Poor outcomes are worsened when a person is under the influence of drugs and alcohol, which is a common occurrence. Police use of force ratchets up as the officer loses control of the situation, which can happen when people with mental illnesses become agitated and experience uncontrollable perceptions, feelings, and behaviors that are symptoms of their mental disorders. Tense interactions with PWSMI can be quietly defused and resolved when police officers are trained in recognizing the signs and symptoms of serious mental illness. Particularly critical is the adoption of proper de-escalation techniques (e.g., initiating a gradual approach, maintaining a quiet voice, giving a wide berth, deflecting, and refocusing). These techniques are the sine qua non of crisis intervention teams (CITs), which originated with the Memphis Police Department following the tragic death of a person with mental illness during a police incident. Such programs have been successfully implemented in several jurisdictions (Kerle, this volume).

CITs can lower the risk of injury to officers and PWSMI, lead to fewer arrests and detentions in local jails, and generate more referrals for mental health treatment in outpatient clinics and hospitals. Such strategies are most effective when police departments partner with jails and mental health facilities in an effort to create a seamless network of services and interventions aimed at closing the treatment gaps among the primary entities that serve PWSMI (i.e., jails, hospitals, prisons, and community mental health centers) (Kerle, this volume). Estimates suggest that roughly 4 percent of PWSMI enter the CJS through a process of criminalization (Peterson, Skeem, Hart, Keith, & Vidal, 2010). Indeed, the growth of CITs, MHCs, and jail diversion programs for PWSMI betokens a steady decline in criminalization, which has likely been the case over the past 20 years.

Lack of Services

The overrepresentation of PWSMI in the CJS was initially a nineteenth-century social crisis. Spurred by the unstinting crusades of Dorothea Dix and Louis Dwight, the country became outraged by the patently large numbers of PWSMI incarcerated in jails and prisons, where they were horrifically abused, neglected, and dehumanized. Although the term "criminalization" was absent from the public vocabulary at that time, it is certain that a large percentage of incarcerees with mental illnesses were confined wholly on the basis of their symptomatic behaviors, which were experienced by others as socially disruptive, disturbing, and unacceptable. During the 1960s and 1970s, the demise of the asylum era and release of sizable cohorts of psychotic patients into the community without adequate follow-up care created the same urban phenomenon: an influx of PWSMI wandering the streets, homeless, destitute, and disruptive (Grob, 1991).

History repeated itself a century after Dix's clarion calls for the unshackling of PWSMI. The critical path was similar: a decline in the population of an institution for the confinement of PWSMI (asylum or state hospital), the neglect of their needs for follow-up care in the community, the removal of PWSMI from the streets or homes in which their behaviors were deemed frightening and unpredictable, and the shunting of them to another total institution (prison or nursing home) in a hydraulic apparatus of trans- rather than de-institutionalization. As state budgets suffer, PWSMI, certainly including people with addictions, also suffer due to the dearth of services to treat their illnesses. Mental healthcare practitioners are often unable to ensure that PWSMI receive the ancillary services that are needed to complement the core of basic psychiatric care, which can improve the quality of their lives. The most critical among these services are stable housing and integrated treatment for comorbid substance use and other psychiatric disorders (Lurigio, this volume). Case management to combine and oversee the delivery of these services are crucial in reducing criminal recidivism and psychiatric readmission (Lurigio & Swartz, 2000).

More than 40 years of anecdotal and empirical evidence have demonstrated that PWSMI are being unnecessarily and deleteriously processed through the CJS when a mental health alternative would be preferable. In many instances, arrest is the only humane option, giving people with mental illnesses shelter, food, and behavioral healthcare programming. Police officers can sign a petition to initiate an emergency evaluation and treatment for people who are "dangerous" to themselves or others because of a mental illness. This is generally a time-consuming process with an uncertain outcome. Moreover, a lack of local services for people in dire need of psychiatric attention is common even in large jurisdictions. Therefore, an arrest might be the most practical, expeditious, and humane way to resolve an encounter with PWSMI, but it is certainly regrettable. A driving factor in the steady CJS processing of PWSMI has been the paucity of community-based psychiatric services and the continual closure of state psychiatric facilities for the indigent.

War on Drugs

The War on Drugs also was greatly responsible for the significant growth of PWSMI in the correctional population, including in jails and prisons, and on probation and parole. A large proportion of PWSMI with comorbidity entered the CJS for charges of drug possession or intent to sell. For decades, men and women arrested for drug-defined crimes have been among the fastest-growing subgroups in all correctional populations. PWSMI use drugs for a variety of reasons (Lurigio, this volume) and reside in communities where police officers engage in robust antidrug enforcement activities. PWSMI can be arrested for possession, sales, or public intoxication. Their addictions compel them to commit drug-related offenses (Lurigio, this volume). With criminal histories and without treatment, people with comorbid disorders cycle in and out of hospitals, but especially jails and prisons.

Are PWSMI Receiving Proper Care in the CJS?

Jails and prisons are now the largest mental health service providers in the United States. Psychologists play a wide range of roles in correctional facilities (e.g., as diagnosticians, therapists, and program evaluators), occupying a variety of positions as both in-house and brokered professionals and performing a number of essential behavioral health care functions. Nevertheless, more mental health and medical experts are sorely needed to meet the ever-growing demands of PWSMI in the CJS (Silva, Magaletta, & McLearen, this volume). The shortage of mental health services and the stress of confinement can take their toll on PWSMI, especially those who experience long-term confinement, which has become more common in the era of mass incarceration. Punitive isolation is particularly harmful to prisoners with mental illness, who enter the system with a history of trauma and are further traumatized by the everyday stressors of prison life and the severe psychological pain of solitary confinement (Haney, Conrey, & Davis, this volume).

In the best-case scenario, PWSMI would have unimpeded access to basic services. Clinicians would provide effective treatment that controls the symptoms of mental illness. Case managers would have low caseloads, linkages with law enforcement, and appropriate training to identify the precursors of potential criminal involvement. PWSMI's entanglements in the CJS that are related to their mental illness would be effectively eliminated. However, universal access to services remains elusive because of financial barriers, cultural obstacles, the stigmatization of people with mental illnesses, workforce issues, and geographic barriers. A lack of access to services, limited treatment effectiveness, and poor medication compliance mean that only a small proportion of PWSMI will have their symptoms controlled. Moreover, the lack of "wraparound" services, such as housing, employment, and life skills training, hamper the recovery process. Finally, promising case management models (e.g., assertive community treatment and the sequential intercept model) have been poorly funded or fall short of meeting the overall demand (Wolff et al., 2013).

Law Enforcement

Law enforcement personnel are frequently the frontline responders to PWSMI in diverse situations that range from self-harm, to public order offenses, to more serious nonviolent offenses (such as breaking and entering), to varying degrees of threatened or actual violence. Reflecting this diversity of situations, the roles that law enforcement officers play are also highly varied. Depending on the circumstances, police officers' responses to PWSMI can include the de-escalation of volatile interactions (sometimes in conjunction with mental health professionals), transportation to an emergency room or other clinical setting, or taking the person into custody.

The outcome of police encounters with PWSMI depends on the officer's level of mental health-related training, the implementation of effective policies on police-based mental health responses, and a mechanism that refers PWSMI to appropriate clinical services. With these resources and strategies, officers would be able to effectively and appropriately divert PWSMI away from the CJS and into the mental health system, limiting arrests to incidents that involve serious criminal activity (Lurigio, Snowden, & Watson, 2006).

The Courts

After PWSMI are arrested, they can appear before a judge to face criminal charges. At arraignment, the process can be profoundly complicated by psychotic symptoms, which are frequently exacerbated by the use of illicit substances. In these instances, judges, prosecutors, and defense attorneys must be able to understand the person's rendition of events, ascertain the facts of the case, and arrive at a temporary case disposition. As the legal process moves forward, these parties must confront issues, such as competency to stand trial, criminal responsibility, and dangerousness, and make complex determinations about treatment, sentencing, and release to the community (Epperson, Canada, & Lurigio, 2013).

In an ideal world, the courts and other components of the legal system would render decisions that preserve public safety and improve the quality of life for PWSMI. They would have foolproof methods for predicting dangerousness and apply those predictions in a legal framework. Judges and juries would have a solid understanding of how their sentencing decisions affect PWSMI, and the courts would have access to sufficient community services. Finally, the court system would operate in tandem with the mental health system in efforts to improve healing and recovery—a concept known as therapeutic jurisprudence, which is exemplified in the practices of the MHC, a popular problem-solving court that specializes in the care and supervision of PWSMI (Lurigio, this volume).

Institutional Corrections

Jails and prisons house nearly three times as many PWSMI as state psychiatric institutions do. Jails process nearly one million newly admitted detainees with serious mental illness each year. In many cases, jails are the final stop on the "institutional circuit" that includes homeless shelters, psychiatric institutions, and substance abuse residences (Bernstein & Seltzer, 2004).

The functions of jails and prisons in the mental health service delivery system are diverse and include initial screening and assessment, crisis intervention, long-term treatment, specialized housing, suicide prevention, and community linkages for reentry. Although practice standards have been developed in these areas, the quality and level of mental health services vary considerably in the nation's jails and prisons. Many jurisdictions modified their mental health case services only after litigation compelled them to do so (Lurigio & Rodriguez, 2004).

Ideally, newly admitted jail inmates would be screened for mental illness by a qualified professional within hours of admission. Detainees with serious disorders would be diverted to the mental health system. Treatment programs would be integrated with specialized housing, evidence-based medication regimens, and psychosocial rehabilitation services, which improve individual adjustment and facilitate recovery. Corrections-based mental health systems would coordinate with community-based mental health systems and share treatment protocols and reentry resources. Although these program practices have been adopted in many jurisdictions, they are far from uniformly implemented. Factors that can compromise care include funding limitations, mission conflicts, security considerations, insufficient physical capacity, and a host of treatment-related issues (Draine, Wilson, & Pogorzelski, 2007).

Community Corrections

For the general offender population without mental illness, community reintegration represents a major challenge—factors such as employment, housing, education, and social support are major issues for ex-offenders. Failure to address these fundamental issues places these individuals at considerable risk of future involvement with the CJS. For those with mental illness, the seriousness of these issues is greatly compounded (Lurigio, 2001). Beyond the barriers presented by their ex-offender status, they are faced with the considerable obstacles that are related to their psychiatric condition, including communication problems, lack of insight into illness, and disturbances of mood and perception. In light of these circumstances, PWSMI present particular challenges to the probation and parole officers charged with supervising them and facilitating the community reintegration process (Fisher, Silver, & Wolff, 2006).

In an ideal world, PWSMI under community supervision would receive supportive housing and related services. Specially trained probation and parole officers with mental health backgrounds would monitor specialized, reduced caseloads that permit intensive case management. Information systems and cross-agency collaboration would foster communication and integrated service planning with treatment providers and parole and probation personnel. These practices have been evaluated with promising results (Skeem & Manchak, 2010; Skeem, Manchak, Johnson, & Eno Louden, 2008), but they have been implemented on only a small scale.

In conclusion, the management of PWSMI, at every step in the CJS process, is fraught with complications, ignorance, and shortages of services and trained staff. The CJS was never designed or structured to treat those with behavioral health problems. Notwithstanding, most of the people involved in the system suffer from such conditions, which can often contribute to their initial and long-term pursuit of a criminal lifestyle. This contribution is particularly significant with respect to substance use disorders and crime. The CJS should continue to be prepared to respond to the needs of PWSMI, who are now a part of the permanent landscape of our nation's courts, jails, and prisons.

Discussion Questions

1. Describe the relationship between poverty and mental illness. What effect do you think ameliorating poverty would have on mental illness and why?

2. What are some of the challenges of measuring the prevalence of PWSMI in the CJS? What do you think are the consequences of inaccurate measurement?

3. Of the drivers of criminalization identified in this chapter, which do you think is most harmful to PWSMI and why?

4. What are the major barriers to putting into practice the ideal ways that CJS actors could manage PWSMI, as described in this chapter? What do you think is needed to overcome these barriers?

References

American Psychiatric Association. (2013). *Diagnostic and statistical manual of mental disorders: Fifth edition (DSM-5)*. New York, NY: Author.

Bluhm, R. L., Miller, J., Lanius, R. A., Osuch, E. A., Boksman, K., Neufeld, R. W., ... Williamson, P. (2007). Spontaneous low-frequency fluctuations in the BOLD signal in schizophrenic patients: Anomalies in the default network. *Schizophrenia Bulletin, 33*, 1004–1012.

Council of State Governments. (2002). *Criminal Justice-Mental Health Consensus Project report*. New York, NY: Council of State Governments. Retrieved from https://www.ncjrs.gov/pdffiles1/nij/grants/197103.pdf.

Ditton, P. (1999). *Mental health and treatment of inmates and probationers*. Washington, D.C.: Bureau of Justice Statistics. Retrieved from http://www.ojp.usdoj.go/bjs/abstract/mhtip.htm.

Draine, J., Wilson, A., & Pogorzelski, W. (2007). Limitations and potential in current research on services for people with mental illness in the criminal justice system. *Journal of Offender Rehabilitation, 45*, 159–177.

Epperson, M. W., Canada, K. E., & Lurigio, A. J. (2013). Mental health court: One approach for addressing the problems of persons with serious mental illnesses in the criminal justice system. In J. B. Helfgott (Ed.), *Criminal psychology* (pp. 367–392). Haverhill, MA: Praeger Press.

Erickson, S., Rosenheck, R., Trestment, R., Ford, J., & Desai, R. (2008). Risk of incarceration between cohorts of veterans with and without mental illness discharged from inpatient units. *Psychiatric Services, 59*, 178–183.

Frances, A. (2013). The past, present, and future of psychiatric diagnosis. *World Psychiatry, 12*, 111–112.

Grob, G. N. (1991). *From asylum to community: Mental health policy in modern America*. Princeton, NJ: Princeton University Press.

Hiday, V. A. (1999). Mental illness and the criminal justice system. In A. Horwitz & T. Scheid (Eds.), *The handbook for the study of mental health: Social contexts, theories, and systems* (pp. 508–525). Cambridge, MA: Cambridge University Press.

Hurst, C. E. (2007). *Social inequality: Forms, causes, and consequences* (6th ed.). Boston, MA: Pearson Education.

Lewis, D. A., & Lurigio, A. J. (1994). *The state mental patient and urban life: Moving in and out of the institution*. Springfield, IL: Charles C. Thomas.

Lurigio, A. J. (2001). Effective services for parolees with mental illnesses. *Crime and Delinquency, 47*, 446–461.

Lurigio, A. J. (2011, September). *Responding to the needs of people with mental illness in the criminal justice system: An area ripe for research and community partnerships.* Keynote address presented at the annual meeting of the Midwest Criminal Justice Association (Chicago, IL).

Lurigio, A. J., & Harris, A. (2007). The mentally ill in the criminal justice system: An overview of historical causes and suggested remedies. *Professional Issues in Criminal Justice, 2,* 145–169.

Lurigio, A. J., Snowden, J., & Watson, A. (2006). Police handling of the mentally ill: Historical and research perspectives. *Law Enforcement Executive Forum, 6,* 87–110.

Peterson, J., Skeem, J., Hart, E., Keith, F., & Vidal, S. (2010). Analyzing offense patterns as a function of mental illness to test the criminalization hypothesis. *Psychiatric Services, 61,* 1217–1222.

Ruzich, D., Reichert, J., & Lurigio, A. J. (2014). The prevalence of probable posttraumatic stress disorder and psychiatric problems in a sample of urban jail detainees. *International Journal of Law and Psychiatry, 37,* 455–463.

Skeem, J., & Manchak, S. (2010, October). Treatment as a condition of probation study. Paper presented at the meeting of the MacArthur Network on Mandated Community Treatment (Tucson, AZ).

Skeem, J., Manchak, S., Johnson, T., & Eno Louden, J. (2008, May). Exploring ''what works'' in probation and mental health. Paper presented at the meeting of the MacArthur Research Network on Mandated Community Treatment (Seattle, WA).

Skeem, J., Nicholson, E., & Kregg, C. (2008, March). Understanding barriers to re-entry for parolees with mental illness. *Mentally disordered offenders: A special population requiring special attention.* Symposium held at the Annual Meeting of the American Psychology-Law Society (Jacksonville, FL).

Swartz, J. A., & Lurigio, A. J. (1999). Psychiatric illness and comorbidity among adult male jail detainees in drug treatment. *Psychiatric Services, 50,* 1628–1630.

Swartz, J. A., & Lurigio, A. J. (2007). Serious mental illness and arrest: The generalized mediating effects of substance use. *Crime and Delinquency, 53,* 581–604.

Wolff, N., Frueh, B. C., Huening, J., Shi, J., Epperson, M. W., Morgan, R., & Fisher, W. (2013). Practice informs the next generation of behavioral health and criminal justice interventions. *International Journal of Law & Psychiatry, 36,* 1–10.

World Health Organization. (2007). *Breaking the vicious cycle between mental health and poverty.* Geneva, CH: Author.

Index